The Payroll Process

A Basic Guide to U.S. Payroll Procedures and Requirements

The Payroll Process

A Basic Guide to U.S. Payroll Procedures and Requirements

Gregory Mostyn
Mission College

W&J
Worthy & James
PUBLISHING

Worthy & James Publishing

Before you buy or use this book, you should understand . . .

Cataloging-in-Publication Data
Mostyn, Gregory R., author
Title: The payroll process: a basic guide to U.S. payroll procedures and requirements/Gregory Mostyn
Description: Milpitas, CA.: Worthy and James, 2018
Identifiers: ISBN 978-0-9914231-6-3 (pbk.) | ISBN 978-0-9914231-5-6 (ebook)
Subjects: LCSH: Payrolls. | Payroll tax—United States | Accounting | Labor
    laws and regulation—United States | Foreign workers—United States |
    United States Internal Revenue Service—Rules and practice |
    Compliance | BISAC: BUSINESS & ECONOMICS/Accounting/
    General. | BUSINESS & ECONOMICS/ Taxation/General.
Classification: LCC HF5681.W3 M67 2018 (print) | LCC HF56781.W3 (ebook) | DDC 657/.742—dc23

Library of Congress Control Number: 2018901226

Worthy and James Publishing
P.O. Box 362015
Milpitas, CA. 95036, USA
www.worthyjames.com

Suggestions, inquires: enquiries@worthyjames.com

To GZ

Contents

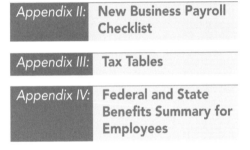

About the Author

Greg Mostyn is an accounting instructor at Mission College, Santa Clara, California. He is a member of the American Accounting Association and American Institute of Certified Public Accountants. He has served as accounting department chairman and has extensive experience in accounting curriculum design and course development. He has authored several books and published articles in the areas of learning theory and its application to accounting instruction, textbook use, and accounting education research.

Also by the author: Basic Accounting Concepts, Principles, and Procedures, Vol. 1, 2nd edition *(Worthy and James Publishing)*

Basic Accounting Concepts, Principles, and Procedures, Vol. 2, 2nd edition *(Worthy and James Publishing)*

Book orders: orders@btpubservices.com or 800-247-6553

Getting Started:
What You Should Know

This reference book is designed to be used in four ways:

- The book explains **the steps** needed to complete a proper payroll process. See the illustration on page 4 for an overview of the steps.
- The book acts as a concise, efficient, first reference that should be used as the **first source** for calculations, to meet compliance requirements and resolve payroll questions. In many business situations, this will be sufficient.
- The book functions as your guide to **more detailed reference** and advanced resources if more information is needed or more complex issues arise.
- **For new businesses:** See Appendix II for initial payroll procedures.

*What Else You
May Need to
Know*

*Combine the
Book With
Additional
Resources*

The table below is a suggested guide for initial steps:

Step	Procedure
1	Refer to the illustration on page 4. This is an overview of the process. Each section in the book explains the details of each of the five elements.
2	Because there are many deposit and filing deadlines, **you will need a tax calendar**. A comprehensive IRS calendar is available online as **Publication 509**. It contains three calendars: a general calendar, an employer calendar, and an excise tax calendar. Be sure to contact your state/local tax authorities.
3	Read the "Overview" of payroll on page 3. This provides a guideline for accessing additional resouces. It is important to know that especially the IRS provides many detailed resouces that are accessible on the Internet—for forms, use the form numbers from our discussion and then search for form instructions.

For more in-depth information, as you read by topic you often will see publication number references. These are IRS and/or Department of Labor publications, which are available online. Again, check state and local references; many are also available online by topic search. |

Common and Important Payroll Errors

When reviewing payroll operations one should understand that it is vital to remain aware of the most important and probable errors. These errors typically transform into needless and expensive penalties.

In 2017 the American Payroll Association reported that 54% of employees reported paycheck problems. The IRS alone reported that for 2016 it assessed over 5.8 million civil penalties related to payroll taxes. Worse yet, this statistic does not encompass state, local, and Department of Labor penalties. Be alert for:

- Misclassification between employee and independent contractor
- Misclassification between exempt and non-exempt
- Incorrect overtime calculation
- Violation of other Fair Labor Standards Act provisions
- Missed/delinquent payroll tax deposits
- Missed/delinquent form filing
- Errors in form preparation
- Hiring process violations
- Improper payroll record maintenance
- Incorrect exclusion of payments from wages

Overview of "Payroll"

Overview

The term "payroll" encompasses many activities that are critical to the successful operation of a business with employees. As well, practically all payroll activities are subject to numerous legal compliance requirements of federal, state, and local agencies, all of which will impose various penalties if requirements are violated. A business has no control over these requirements. A "payroll" consists of two broad knowledge domains: 1) The process within which payroll activities take place. These activities include human resources, management, and accounting functions. 2) The legal compliance requirements imposed on these activities, with which businesses must comply in order to prevent losses due to penalties. This book provides a basic reference to the essential elements of both of these knowledge areas, with compliance applications related primarily to federal requirements.

Finding Resources for Compliance Procedures and Questions

Although this book serves as a useful guide through many payroll topics, in practice there are times when more than one resource will have to be utilized; it is particularly wise to seek as much help as possible when dealing with compliance procedures and questions. Here are some suggestions for additional resources:

- **IRS Publications:** IRS publications are available online. In the context of our topics, the relevant payroll publications are referenced as part of discussions (also see index). The basic IRS employer publication is called Publication 15, also known as Circular E. Many Department of Labor publications and guidelines are also available online. All current IRS publications are available at irs.gov/forms/pubs/.
- **Other IRS Help:** The IRS has an online help center at IRS.gov/help or IRS.gov/letushelp for assistance. There is also an interactive assistance tool at IRS.gov/ita. The national call center is 800-829-4933.
- **State and Local Information:** Despite many similiarites to federal requirements, state and local rules vary. Therefore, this book focuses primarily on federal requirements. However, state and local information is often available online; for example, for state requirements you can: 1) Do an Internet search for "state (name of state) payroll taxes" 2) As of this writing some useful websites are www.taxsites.com and the American Payroll Association site. 3) Reference departments in local or school libraries may also provide help.
- **Professional Help:** If you are in business or going into business, it is prudent to obtain expert professional help, because requirements can change and at times can be complex to apply. Obtain client references and check with state licensing boards to find a competent CPA or attorney who has clients in the same type of business that you are in, and who is familiar with your type of business and payroll issues.

Overview of "Payroll", *continued*

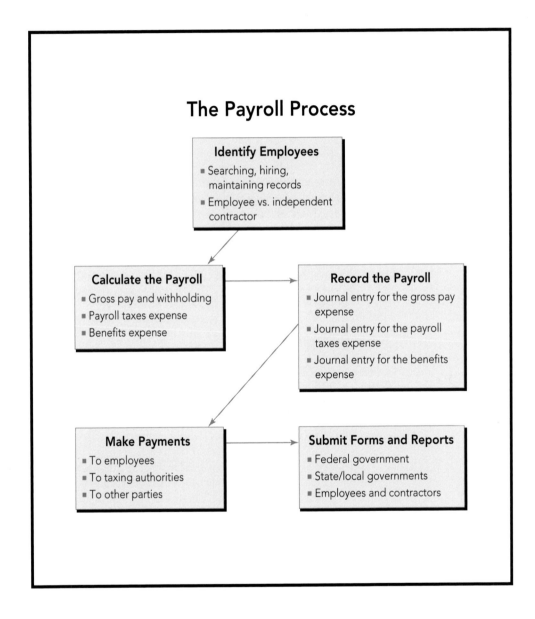

The Payroll Process

Identify Employees
- Searching, hiring, maintaining records
- Employee vs. independent contractor

Calculate the Payroll
- Gross pay and withholding
- Payroll taxes expense
- Benefits expense

Record the Payroll
- Journal entry for the gross pay expense
- Journal entry for the payroll taxes expense
- Journal entry for the benefits expense

Make Payments
- To employees
- To taxing authorities
- To other parties

Submit Forms and Reports
- Federal government
- State/local governments
- Employees and contractors

Section 1 Identify Employees

Introduction

Every payroll process begins with searching for, evaluating, and hiring employees, and continues a relationship with an employee until the employee leaves. The foundation of the process is the correct identification of a worker as an "employee".

Employees

Overview

Not all people who perform services for a business are employees. It is very important to accurately identify which workers qualify as employees because laws impose different requirements for workers who are employees and for those who are not. Not only is it necessary to comply with various laws, but correct identification also reduces potential fraud and waste.

"Employee" Defined

The general rule, called "common law" is that any person who performs services for another (the "employer"—see below) is an employee if the employer has the right to control:

- *what* will be done, *and*
- *how* it will be done

This definition must be applied to each individual. It makes no difference what job title or name is used, frequency or means of payment, or whether the work is full time or part time.

> *Note:* Form SS-8 can be submitted to the Internal Revenue Service (IRS) to determine employee status as employee or independent contractor. This form can be filed either by a business or a worker and can also be submitted online. Contact state employment offices for state rules.

Example of an Employee

Jane performs secretarial services for Smith Company and is given word-processing tasks that include preparing management reports. Jane is expected to be at the business location during certain hours and to allow her manager to review and make changes to her work at any time. She must use the business office and equipment and software used by the business. She also receives a regular paycheck from Smith Company. Jane is an employee primarily because Smith Company surpervises and controls not only what is done but also *how the work is done.*

continued ▶

Not an Employee   Mary also performs the same type of services for Smith Company. Mary is given a management report to complete, and she completes the job from her own office during her own work schedule. Mary uses her own equipment and software, and she completes the work during her own hours without review from Smith Company managers. Mary submits a bill to Smith Company for the work completed. Mary is not an employee primarily because Mary controls how the work is done.

Business Owners
- Proprietorship: A sole proprietor is never an employee of the business.
- Partnership: A partner performing duties as a partner is never an employee of a partnership.
- Corporation: Owners (shareholders) of a corporation who work in the business are employees of the corporation if they otherwise qualify under common law.

"Employer" Defined   The word "employer" is a general term. An employer is one who employs the services of another. In other words, under common law an employer is the party who employs the services of another and controls what work is done and how it is done.

Independent Contractors

Overview   It is important to identify independent contractors, because an independent contractor is not an employee, even though an independent contractor may do the same kind of work as an employee. The documentation and compliance rules that a business must follow for independent contractors are very different than for employees, so the distinction is significant. Only employees are considered to be part of a business "payroll". This is important because it means that employers do not withhold income tax, and do not withhold or pay social secutity taxes or unemployment taxes for independent contractors.

Definition   An "independent contractor" is the party who is in control of the manner in which services are performed. Therefore, independent contractors are not employees.

Independent Contractors, *continued*

Examples

- People who are in work for themselves such as doctors, lawyers, and construction contractors, are independent contractors.
- In the example above, Mary is an independent contractor.

Guidelines

In some circumstances following the above definition in order to determine exactly who is an independent contractor and who is an employee can be complicated, and an employer may need to seek professional help. The IRS, the Department of Labor, and individual states have their own guidelines in this matter. Here are some key (but not all) indicators of an independent contractor for various situations:

- The person doing the work determines how the work is to be done.
- The person doing the work also offers services to the public.
- The person doing the work operates as a buisness that makes a profit or loss.
- There is a contract for the services to be performed.
- Payment is not by paycheck, but rather when invoices for work are submitted.
- The person doing the work sets his/her own working hours and schedule.

IRS and DOL Guidelines

IRS Guidelines

The Internal Revenue Service (IRS) uses the following guidelines in the determination of worker status:

- **Behavioral Control:** Behavioral control refers to an employer's *right* to control how work is done (without necessarily needing to exercise that right). Behavioral control factors fall into these categories:

  - Type of instruction: 1) When and where work is to be done 2) Tools or equipment that are to be used. 3) The workers that are to be hired or that will help with the work 4) Where supplies or services are to be purchased 5) Specific individual assignments 6) Order or sequence of work activity
  - Degree of instruction: The greater the detail of instruction, the stronger the indication that the worker is an employee.
  - Evaluation: If an evaluation procedure or system is in place, then the greater the focus on details of how the work was done, the stronger the indication that the worker is an employee. Evaluation of only end results indicates an independent contractor.
  - Training: If the worker receives training by or on behalf of the employer on how to do a job, this is a good indication that the worker is an employee. Regular or ongoing training strenghthens this presumption.

continued ▶

■ **Financial Control:** The type of employer financial commitment or influence related to a worker is an indicator of status.

- Investment in equipment used: The greater an employer's investment in equipment used by a worker, the stronger the presumption of employee status.
- Expense reimbursement: Worker expense reimbursement by employer is an indicator of employee status.
- Profit or loss: The absence of an opportunity for an individual profit or loss is an indicator of employee status.
- Availability of services: A worker is not offering his or her services to the general public, which indicates employee status.
- Payment method: Wage payment (e.g. hourly or by other period of time or by commission), rather than being billed or invoiced is an indicator or employee status.

■ **Relationship:** The manner in which the parties perceive their relationship to each other is an indicator of a worker's status.

- Contract: A contract referencing the above factors can be an indicator. A statement of employee or independent contractor status in the contract is itself not determinative.
- Benefits: Items that are usually considered to be in the nature of fringe benefits (e.g. unemployment insurance, workers' compensation, health plan, retirement plan, vacation pay) indicate employee status.
- Permanency: An expectation that the work relationship is indefinite rather than for a specific task or tasks is an indication of employee status.

DOL Guidelines

The Department of Labor (DOL) uses its own guidelines for the purpose of determining employee or independent contractor status under the Fair Labor Standards Act (page 20.) There is no single determinative factor in this regard; rather, according to the Supreme Court the entirety or totality of the relationship must be considered when making a decision. Accordingly, the Department of Labor applies what it calls an "economic realities test", primarily emphasizing the following factors:

■ **Extent to which a worker's services are integral to employer:** This generally means the importance of a worker's services in completing an employer's product or service. The idea is that work that is a key part of the process means that the worker is likely to be financially dependent on the employer as an employee and less likely to be in business as an independent contractor.

■ **A worker's managerial or entrepeneurial skills:** The greater these skills, the greater a worker's opportunity for profit or loss as an independent contractor.

continued ▶

- **Relative investments in facilities and equipment:** Has a worker made a significant investment in tools and equipment necessary for completion of work? If a worker's investment is sufficient to bear a risk of loss with the employer, that is an indication of independent contractor status. However, a worker may also own tools in a capacity as an employee.
- **Worker skill and initiative:** Greater skills and judgment are considered to be associated with independent contractor status.
  - If a worker demonstrates skills sufficient to indicate independent business judgment, that may indicate independent contractor status.
  - If a worker offers services to the general public and is competing in an open market, that is an indicator of independent contractor status.
- **Permanency of relationship with employer:** Indefinite relationship with an employer is an indictor of employee status; however, lack of an indefinite relationship does not necessarily suggest independent contractor status.
- **Nature and degree of control of employer:** The greater the degree of employer control, the greater the likelihood of employee status. Examples of analysis of this element includes, but is not limited to, the following:
  - Who determines pay and working hours?
  - Who determines how the work is performed?
  - Is the worker free to hire others?

Generally immaterial factors in whether an employee or independent contractor relationship exists are: 1) The wording in a signed agreement relating to status, 2) Whether the worker is incorporated or licensed, 3) Financial method or timing of pay. The Department of Labor provides the following contacts for further information: www.wage/hour.dol.gov or 1-866-487-9243.

Important Applicable Federal Laws

Overview

Employers of individuals classified as employees are subject to the Fair Labor Standards Act (FLSA), which we discuss further in Section 2. Employment is an extremely important part of society and most people's lives, and is a major factor affecting quality of life. For that reason, there are also many other federal and state laws that affect most aspects of hiring and employment. Table 1.1 below provides an overview of many relevant federal laws and key compliance requirements that employers must consider. Except for tax laws, these are often referred to as "fair employment laws". At a minimum, an employer should carefully review the general requirements of relevant law or obtain professional guidance; lack of compliance results in penalties.

continued ▶

Important Applicable Federal Laws, *continued*

Table 1.1: Key Federal Working Condition Requirements

Key Employer Compliance Requirements	Name of Law
Check for required working conditions such as minimum wage, overtime calculations, and child labor prevention, according to guidelines. (See page 20)	Fair Labor Standards Act (FLSA)
Determine worker income tax status and apply income tax withholding, deposit, and record-keeping requirements when paying employees. (See pages 50,111.)	Federal Income Tax
Apply FICA tax withholding, employer matching, and deposit requirements when paying employees. (See pages 41–50 FICA discussion.)	Social Security: Federal Insurance Contribution Act (FICA)
Employers with health plans and 20 or more employees (counting part-time as fractional) on more than 50% of normal business days in prior year must allow workers/dependents to continue coverage for at least 18 (possibly 36) months if coverage is lost due to "qualifying events", such as death or loss of work."	Consolidated Omnibus Budget Reconciliation Act of 1985 (COBRA)
Apply employer FUTA tax and deposit requirements. (See pages 81–88 for FUTA discussion.)	Federal Unemployment Tax Act (FUTA)
In all aspects of hiring and employment, do not engage in various specified types of discrimination, according to guidelines, particularly discrimination based on race or national origin.	Title VII of the Civil Rights Act, also called "Equal Employment Opportunity" (EEO) and enforced by the Equal Employment Opportunity Commission (EEOC).
Prevent, identify, and correct unsafe working conditions, according to OSHA standards and guidelines.	Occupational Safety and Health Act (OSHA)
Offer employer-provided health insurance (See page 89)	Affordable Care Act (ACA)
Ensure that there are no compensation disparities based on gender, according to guidelines.	Equal Pay Act (amendment to FLSA)
Ensure that there is no age discrimination in hiring practices or employment, according to guidelines.	Age Discrimination in Employment Act (ADEA)
If an employer requires an investigative ("background check") or credit report for a job applicant or employee the employer must first notify that person in writing and receive written permission. The employer must provide advance notice that the report will be used and provide a copy of the report and the applicant's rights. If an adverse action is taken, the employer must notify the person that he/she was not hired in whole or in part because of information in the report.	Fair Credit Reporting Act (FCRA)

Important Applicable Federal Laws, *continued*

Table 1.1: Key Federal Working Condition Requirements *continued*

Key Employer Compliance Requirements	Name of Law
Ensure that there is no disability-related discrimination in hiring practices or employment, and maintain reasonable accommodations for disabled employees, according to guidelines. Applies to employers with 15 or more employees.	Americans with Disabilities Act (ADA). Enforced by the Equal Employment Opportunity Commission (EEOC).
Employers must report the name, address and social security number for each new employee to a designated state agency within 20 days of hire or sooner; see state requirements.	Welfare Reform Act - Federal Personal Responsibility and Work Opportunity Reconciliation Act (PRWORA)
All public agencies and private employers with 50 or more employees working within a 75 mile radius of a main office for at least 20 weeks in the current or preceding year, must grant qualified employees up to 12 weeks of unpaid leave (this does not restrict paid leave) for family or medical emergencies, according to guidelines. Note: Some states have enacted *paid* medical leave laws.	Family and Medical Leave Act (FMLA)
Employer must verify a person's eligibility to work in the United States upon offering employment, and comply with verification, reporting, and record-keeping requirements according to guidelines. (See page 154)	Immigration Reform and Control Act (IRCA) (Simpson-Mazzoli Act)
Employer must allow a leave of absence and reemploy with accrued seniority those employees required to perform active military service.	Uniformed Service and Reemployment Rights Act
Additionally, for employers with federal government contracts (minimum contract size in parentheses) the listed laws apply.	Davis-Bacon Act ($2,000), Walsh-Healy Act ($10,000), McNamara-O'Hara Service Contract Act ($2,500) also now called Service Labor Contract Standards (SCLS), Vocational Rehabilitation Act ($2,500), Vietnam Era Veterans Readjustment Act ($10,000), Federal Contractor Compliance Program ($25,000)
Some states combine daily overtime rules, such as hours worked in excess of 8 hours per day, with FLSA rules. Check state and local requirements.	Various—Daily Overtime Law

continued ▶

Important Applicable Federal Laws, *continued*

Record-Keeping See the Department of Labor fact sheet, Wage and Hour Division, for record-keeping guidelines *(https://www.dol.gov/whd/regs/compliance/whdfs21.htm)*.

In general, an employer can use any record-keeping method it wants for recording work hours and compensation, provided the employer can demonstrate that the method is complete and accurate. It is recommended that as a general rule for Department of Labor purposes, all records be kept for a minimum of three years following date of document.

Important Applicable State Laws

Table 1.2: Key State Working Condition Requirement Types

Key Employer Compliance Requirements	Name of Law
Procedures similar to federal: contact tax authority	State Income Tax (Some states)
Apply employer SUTA tax and deposit requirements. (See page 87.) SUTA is the similar state counterpart law to FUTA.	State Unemployment Tax Act (SUTA)
Make insurance payments for employee for work-related injury, disability, or death. (See page 91.)	Workers' Compensation
Some states have enacted laws that require a mandatory employee-paid insurance plan to provide income-replacement benefits for disabilities that are not work-related. The payments are made via employee withholding or employer funding for each payroll period. At this time the states are: California, Hawaii, New Jersey, New York, and Rhode Island, as well as the territory of Puerto Rico.	State Disability Insurance (SDI)
Many states have enacted their own minimum wage rates; additionally, local jurisdictions may enact their own minimum wage, often called "living wage" laws. Employer must pay the greater of FLSA, state, or living wage pay requirements.	Minimum Wage and "Living Wage" laws.
Most states have "Pay Day" laws that require a minimum frequency of paying employees, most often in the range of about every two weeks, sometimes depending on occupation. Access state employment laws using the URL on the right.	State "Pay Day" Laws https://www.dol.gov/whd/state/state.htm
Access state employment laws using the URL on the right.	https://www.dol.gov/whd/state/state.htm

Employee Identification and Classification

Overview

The term "internal control" means the policies and procedures that a business uses to safeguard its assets, particularly against theft and mismanagement, and to ensure required compliance. Internal control applies to many aspects of the payroll process, including employee identification. Some examples of potential losses related to improper employee identification are:

- Payments to fictitious ("ghost") employees and/or employees no longer working for the organization. There are various ways the payroll checks can be cashed, depending on the manner of payment and who receives the checks.
- Misclassification of employees as independent contractors: A worker who is really an employee but who is identified as an independent contractor can create large amounts of unpaid back payroll taxes and penalties for an organization. Moreover, owners, corporate officers, and even bookkeepers and accountants can be held personally responsible for these amounts.
- Employers can be subject to lawsuits for failure to pay gross pay, any overtime pay, and benefits that would have been payable to a worker that should have been classified as an employee.
- Failure to determine citizenship or residency status: An employer who fails to obtain, complete, and retain required citizenship verification form procedures (Form I-9) is subject to civil and possible criminal penalties.

The Human Resources (HR) Department

By ensuring correct employee identification, a human resources department acts an important internal control device to reduce potential fraud and error. However, a human resources department performs additional important functions. If a small business cannot afford a separate department, the owner(s) should perform most or all of the human resource functions. A checklist can be developed to ensure proper scope of action. An outside employee search firm or consultant can be used to assist the employer in the hiring process, but the owners still have related responsibilties.

What key functions does a human resource department fullfill? (Or, for a small business, what should the checklist contain?) Here is a basic summary:

TIP

Employees hired "at-will", can be fired at any time, without notice, for any reason or for no reason, except illegal, (e.g. discrimination, retaliation). At-will employment is the default condition unless a contract with no-fire provisions has been signed, the employer has written assurances of job security, or there are provable employer oral statements of job security.

continued ▶

New Employees:

- Search and hiring process complies with Department of Labor, state, and local regulations and internal guidelines such as job description, resume review, background checks, and interview process.
- Required forms are completed: I-9, W-4, and in some cases SS-5 or SS-8. Also, check for any documents that may be required for non-resident alien workers (I-129, I-140, and ETA-750), and possible state forms.
- Follow state reporting requirements under PRWORA. Private single-state employers contact and report a new hire or rehire to State Directory of New Hires in the state of business operations. Multi-state employers register with the federal Department of Health and Human Services.
- Create personnel file for all documentation, including work contract, if any.
- HR/manager communicates employee status such as pay rate and frequency, department, withholding allowances, benefits withholding, job title, etc. to the payroll department.
- Provide employee with policies and procedures manual, directory and location information, and required access items, such as passwords and badges.

Current Employees:

- Update personnel file with all employee status changes such as address, withholding, reviews, pay rate, and termination.
- Follow policy for conducting reviews.
- Communicate changes to payroll department.
- Verify continuing compliance with FLSA rules and other applicable employment laws.

Employee Termination

- Ensure that termination policy and procedures are followed, documented, and filed. Policy and procedures should be reviewed by employment law counsel. Check to see if a written termination notice is required under any agreements or state law. (Not required under FLSA, but suggested for best practices).
- Advise employee of rights and benefits following termination.
- Report a terminated employee with required child support withholding (garnishment) to the party that sent the mandatory withholding notice.
- Check for applicable state and local laws.
- Pay wages due and any accrued and vested benefits.

Employee Identification and Classification, *continued*

E-Verify

One comprehensive and potentially time-saving method to comply with employer worker eligibility requirements is *E-Verify*. E-Verify is an Internet-based system that is operated by the federal Department of Homeland Security.

An authorized employer who has obtained permission to access the system uses the system by inputting information obtained from Form I-9. This creates a "case". The system then compares information on Form I-9 with information contained in the Social Security Administration database, the Department of Homeland Security database, and the Department of State database. The system then provides a "case result" to determine an applicant's work eligibility.
The case results can be initial, interim, or final. Initial case results can be: 1) Employment authorized 2) Social Security Administration or Department of Homeland Security tentative nonconfirmation or Department of Homeland Secutiy verification in process. 3) Final nonconfirmation. Tentative nonconfirmation or verification in process case results require further action. The employee must be immediately notified and has the right to appeal the results within 10 days of notice. Interim case results require further information and final case results provide a final determination.

The E-Verify system requires that an employer create a case within three days after a new employee has started work. Eligibility verification occurs only once—employees are never re-verified.

Generally, use of E-Verify is voluntary. Exceptions are:

■ Federal contracts that require the use of E-Verify
■ States require the use of E-Verify.

How important is Form I-9? It's very important. By law, (Immigration and Control Reform Act of 1986) every employer must obtain a completed copy of Form I-9 for every person they hire and retain a copy for at least three years after date of hire or one year after termination, whichever is later. Furthermore, an employer must complete a key verification section within three days after an applicant is hired.

continued ▶

Employee Identification and Classification, *continued*

Illustration 1.1

Employment Eligibility Verification
Department of Homeland Security
U.S. Citizenship and Immigration Services

USCIS
Form I-9
OMB No. 1615-0047
Expires 08/31/2019

▶**START HERE:** Read instructions carefully before completing this form. The instructions must be available, either in paper or electronically, during completion of this form. Employers are liable for errors in the completion of this form.

ANTI-DISCRIMINATION NOTICE: It is illegal to discriminate against work-authorized individuals. Employers **CANNOT** specify which document(s) an employee may present to establish employment authorization and identity. The refusal to hire or continue to employ an individual because the documentation presented has a future expiration date may also constitute illegal discrimination.

Section 1. Employee Information and Attestation *(Employees must complete and sign Section 1 of Form I-9 no later than the **first day of employment**, but not before accepting a job offer.)*

Last Name *(Family Name)*	First Name *(Given Name)*	Middle Initial	Other Last Names Used *(if any)*

Address *(Street Number and Name)*	Apt. Number	City or Town	State	ZIP Code

Date of Birth *(mm/dd/yyyy)*	U.S. Social Security Number	Employee's E-mail Address	Employee's Telephone Number

I am aware that federal law provides for imprisonment and/or fines for false statements or use of false documents in connection with the completion of this form.

I attest, under penalty of perjury, that I am (check one of the following boxes):

☐ 1. A citizen of the United States

☐ 2. A noncitizen national of the United States *(See instructions)*

☐ 3. A lawful permanent resident   (Alien Registration Number/USCIS Number): _____

☐ 4. An alien authorized to work   until (expiration date, if applicable, mm/dd/yyyy): _____
Some aliens may write "N/A" in the expiration date field. *(See instructions)*

Aliens authorized to work must provide only one of the following document numbers to complete Form I-9:
An Alien Registration Number/USCIS Number OR Form I-94 Admission Number OR Foreign Passport Number.

1. Alien Registration Number/USCIS Number: _____
OR

2. Form I-94 Admission Number: _____
OR

3. Foreign Passport Number: _____
Country of Issuance: _____

QR Code - Section 1
Do Not Write In This Space

Signature of Employee	Today's Date *(mm/dd/yyyy)*

Preparer and/or Translator Certification (check one):

☐ I did not use a preparer or translator.   ☐ A preparer(s) and/or translator(s) assisted the employee in completing Section 1.
(Fields below must be completed and signed when preparers and/or translators assist an employee in completing Section 1.)

I attest, under penalty of perjury, that I have assisted in the completion of Section 1 of this form and that to the best of my knowledge the information is true and correct.

Signature of Preparer or Translator	Today's Date *(mm/dd/yyyy)*

Last Name *(Family Name)*	First Name *(Given Name)*

Address *(Street Number and Name)*	City or Town	State	ZIP Code

STOP   *Employer Completes Next Page*   STOP

Employee Identification and Classification, *continued*

Illustration 1.1, continued

Employment Eligibility Verification	**USCIS**
Department of Homeland Security	**Form I-9**
U.S. Citizenship and Immigration Services	OMB No. 1615-0047
	Expires 08/31/2019

Section 2. Employer or Authorized Representative Review and Verification

(Employers or their authorized representative must complete and sign Section 2 within 3 business days of the employee's first day of employment. You must physically examine one document from List A OR a combination of one document from List B and one document from List C as listed on the "Lists of Acceptable Documents.")

Employee Info from Section 1	Last Name *(Family Name)*	First Name *(Given Name)*	M.I.	Citizenship/Immigration Status

List A	OR	List B	AND	List C
Identity and Employment Authorization		Identity		Employment Authorization

Document Title	Document Title	Document Title
Issuing Authority	Issuing Authority	Issuing Authority
Document Number	Document Number	Document Number
Expiration Date *(if any)(mm/dd/yyyy)*	Expiration Date *(if any)(mm/dd/yyyy)*	Expiration Date *(if any)(mm/dd/yyyy)*

Document Title		
Issuing Authority	Additional Information	QR Code - Sections 2 & 3 Do Not Write In This Space
Document Number		
Expiration Date *(if any)(mm/dd/yyyy)*		
Document Title		
Issuing Authority		
Document Number		
Expiration Date *(if any)(mm/dd/yyyy)*		

Certification: I attest, under penalty of perjury, that (1) I have examined the document(s) presented by the above-named employee, (2) the above-listed document(s) appear to be genuine and to relate to the employee named, and (3) to the best of my knowledge the employee is authorized to work in the United States.

The employee's first day of employment *(mm/dd/yyyy)*: _____   *(See instructions for exemptions)*

Signature of Employer or Authorized Representative	Today's Date *(mm/dd/yyyy)*	Title of Employer or Authorized Representative	
Last Name of Employer or Authorized Representative	First Name of Employer or Authorized Representative	Employer's Business or Organization Name	
Employer's Business or Organization Address (Street Number and Name)	City or Town	State	ZIP Code

Section 3. Reverification and Rehires *(To be completed and signed by employer or authorized representative.)*

A. New Name *(if applicable)*			**B.** Date of Rehire *(if applicable)*
Last Name *(Family Name)*	First Name *(Given Name)*	Middle Initial	Date *(mm/dd/yyyy)*

C. If the employee's previous grant of employment authorization has expired, provide the information for the document or receipt that establishes continuing employment authorization in the space provided below.

Document Title	Document Number	Expiration Date *(if any) (mm/dd/yyyy)*

I attest, under penalty of perjury, that to the best of my knowledge, this employee is authorized to work in the United States, and if the employee presented document(s), the document(s) I have examined appear to be genuine and to relate to the individual.

Signature of Employer or Authorized Representative	Today's Date *(mm/dd/yyyy)*	Name of Employer or Authorized Representative

continued ▶

Employee Identification and Classification, *continued*

Illustration 1.1, continued

LISTS OF ACCEPTABLE DOCUMENTS
All documents must be UNEXPIRED

Employees may present one selection from List A
or a combination of one selection from List B and one selection from List C.

LIST A		LIST B		LIST C
Documents that Establish Both Identity and Employment Authorization	OR	Documents that Establish Identity	AND	Documents that Establish Employment Authorization
1. U.S. Passport or U.S. Passport Card		1. Driver's license or ID card issued by a State or outlying possession of the United States provided it contains a photograph or information such as name, date of birth, gender, height, eye color, and address		1. A Social Security Account Number card, unless the card includes one of the following restrictions: (1) NOT VALID FOR EMPLOYMENT (2) VALID FOR WORK ONLY WITH INS AUTHORIZATION (3) VALID FOR WORK ONLY WITH DHS AUTHORIZATION
2. Permanent Resident Card or Alien Registration Receipt Card (Form I-551)				
3. Foreign passport that contains a temporary I-551 stamp or temporary I-551 printed notation on a machine-readable immigrant visa		2. ID card issued by federal, state or local government agencies or entities, provided it contains a photograph or information such as name, date of birth, gender, height, eye color, and address		2. Certification of report of birth issued by the Department of State (Forms DS-1350, FS-545, FS-240)
4. Employment Authorization Document that contains a photograph (Form I-766)		3. School ID card with a photograph		3. Original or certified copy of birth certificate issued by a State, county, municipal authority, or territory of the United States bearing an official seal
5. For a nonimmigrant alien authorized to work for a specific employer because of his or her status: a. Foreign passport; and b. Form I-94 or Form I-94A that has the following: (1) The same name as the passport; and (2) An endorsement of the alien's nonimmigrant status as long as that period of endorsement has not yet expired and the proposed employment is not in conflict with any restrictions or limitations identified on the form.		4. Voter's registration card		4. Native American tribal document
		5. U.S. Military card or draft record		5. U.S. Citizen ID Card (Form I-197)
		6. Military dependent's ID card		6. Identification Card for Use of Resident Citizen in the United States (Form I-179)
		7. U.S. Coast Guard Merchant Mariner Card		7. Employment authorization document issued by the Department of Homeland Security
		8. Native American tribal document		
		9. Driver's license issued by a Canadian government authority		
		For persons under age 18 who are unable to present a document listed above:		
6. Passport from the Federated States of Micronesia (FSM) or the Republic of the Marshall Islands (RMI) with Form I-94 or Form I-94A indicating nonimmigrant admission under the Compact of Free Association Between the United States and the FSM or RMI		10. School record or report card		
		11. Clinic, doctor, or hospital record		
		12. Day-care or nursery school record		

Examples of many of these documents appear in Part 13 of the Handbook for Employers (M-274).

Refer to the instructions for more information about acceptable receipts.

Section 2 Calculate the Payroll

Introduction

A calculation of a payroll is at the heart of the payroll process. Depending on a number of factors, the calculation can be relatively straightforward or complex. Issues can involve both Department of Labor and tax authorities compliance. This section is subdivided into each of the key areas that play essential roles in the calculation procedure.

Part I: Gross Pay

Gross Pay Overview

Overview and Exampes

Gross pay is the total, called "gross" compensation earned by an employee. This usually is an amount shown on a paycheck before any deductions, but can also include other items such as various property and services. Typical examples of gross pay include:

- **Salary:** The term "salary" generally refers to a fixed amount per period that is not determined by hours worked. Salaries are usually earned by managers, administratiors, supervisors, and other professional staff.
- **Wage:** The term "wage" may be used generally to refer to compensation, but usually "wage" means an amount that is determined by hours worked or units of product completed. Typically wages are earned in skilled and un-skilled workers in manufacturing, manual labor, retail positions, and customer service positions.
- **Commission:** Commissions are usually earned based on a percentage of sales.
- **Bonus:** Bonus earnings are extra amounts usually given as a reward for some kind of achievement or meeting performance goals.
- **Tip:** A tip is an extra amount, also called a "gratuity", generally paid by a customer as a reward for good service.
- **In-kind:** Payment in some form of property or services (rather than money) is called "in-kind".
- **Part time/Temporary:** The FLSA applies to part time and temporary workers.

The Fair Labor Standards Act (FLSA) and Gross Pay

Overview

The FLSA significantly affects the amount and method of determining gross pay for employees. Employers must be aware of the numerous FLSA compliance requirements to avoid related penalties. The following pages discuss the major elements of this topic.

FLSA Compensation Overview

The *Fair Labor Standards Act (FLSA)* is a federal law that sets working condition requirements related to minimum wage, overtime, child labor, and record-keeping for employment in all states and the District of Columbia. The FLSA, as a result of both statute and broad case law interpretation, for practical purposes applies to most businesses, and cannot be waived by employee or employer. Key examples:

- Minimum wage: At this writing, the federal minimum wage is $7.25 per hour for nonexempt hourly workers. (Generally, the FLSA applies primarily to hourly workers; however, FLSA will also apply to "white-collar" salary employees who perform administrative, executive, or other specified duties, and who are not exempt because they do not receive the FLSA required minimum salary of $455 per week. *Note:* a proposed rate of $913 is now under judicial review.) In circumstances where state minimum wage rates exceed the federal rate, the higher state rate will apply.
- Workweek: The Department of Labor defines a standard workweek as fixed seven consecutive 24-hour periods (168 hours). An employee workweek is the number of hours worked during this period, and overtime rate requirements are referenced to this workweek.
- Working hours: The FLSA requires that employees be paid for all time worked. This includes fractions of hours. Employers are best served using a time clock and rounding time to the *nearest* 5 minutes or nearest 15 minutes at most, not consistently rounding down and not using some arbitrary rounding method.
- Overtime: All hours worked in excess of 40 hours per week must be paid at a rate 1.5 times the regular pay rate for nonexempt employees (See pages 22–40). For an employee who is paid by an hourly rate, overtime is simply calculated at the end of a workweek for hours in excess of 40 hours for that workweek at 1½ times the hourly, or "regular" rate. The FLSA does not limit the maximum number of hours per week for employees 16 and older. Caution: Check state laws.
- Absences: The FLSA specifies circumstances under which absences can result in pay deductions.
- Anti-discrimination and anti-retaliation rules, and child labor law are part of FLSA.
- Exemptions: If certain conditions are met, an employee can be exempt from the following FLSA standards: 1) minimum wage: 2) equal pay: (however, no

continued   ▶

The Fair Labor Standards Act (FLSA) and Gross Pay, *continued*

pay discrimination based on gender, color, race, religion, national origin) 3) overtime rate. Exemptions are discussed in the following pages.

For more information, the Department of Labor call center is 1-866-487-2365

What the FLSA Does Not Cover

Some employment issues are not covered by the FLSA. Following are some key items:

- Total hours worked per day or per week for persons 16 years of age or older
- Overtime pay based on weekend or holiday work
- Absences: There is no FLSA requirement for paid absences, such as for illness or personal emergency. Also time off absences do not count toward the 40 hours required for overtime to begin
- Requirement to give holidays off
- Requirement to give vacation time
- Requirement to grant sick leave
- Meals or rest periods
- Pay raises or fringe benefits

Employers Not Subject to the FLSA

An employer is exempt if it:

- Is a small farm (less than 500 equivalent employee days in any calendar quarter of the previous calendar year), or
- Does not have more than $500,000 of gross sales and does not engage in interstate commerce as part of business activity (Caution: "interstate commerce" is a very broad interpretation, such as any of the following examples: using mail, telephone, or email on an interstate basis or shipping or receiving products traveling interstate.). Additionally, any individual employee who engages in interstate commerce becomes a covered employee, who is not exempt.

Remember: State and local law may apply even if the FLSA does not.

More on Minimum Wage

Overview

As indicated above, an important objective of the FLSA is to ensure that workers receive a minimum wage. The FLSA requires that a minimum wage be paid to all employees for all hours worked (including work taken home and off-business site premises) unless employees are exempt. Exempt employees:

1) An employee who receives a salary of at least a designated amount (current amount is $455 weekly, however, this is currently under review.), and
2) The employee's primary duty is management, administration, professional, computer programs or systems, or outside sales activity.

continued ▶

Other specified exempt categories of workers include are: teachers and academic administrative personnel, employees in some seasonal operations, creative employees such as artists and writers, employees in fishing operations, some truck drivers (not agent-drivers) and mechanics, and farm workers on small farms.

Exemptions do not apply to police officers, firefighters, paramedics, nurses, and emergency medical staff. As well, manual laborers are not exempt, regardless of pay rate or duties description. Consult Department of Labor guidelines and state requirements; some have a higher exempt minimum.

Higher Minimum Wage Rates

In some cases a higher hourly minimum wage than $7.25 is required. This situation occurs with:

- States and localities that require a higher minimum than $7.25
- Employees of federal contracting companies ($10.10 hourly)

Reduced Minimum Wage Rates (Subminimum Wage)

In some cases, a lower hourly minimum wage rate than $7.25 is allowed. This rule applies to the following categories:

- Initial 90 days for new employees under 20 years old ($4.25/hr.)
- Student trainees in an a vocational training program at an accredited school ($5.44/hr.)
- Full-time students doing retail, service, or farm work ($6.17/hr.)
- College and university students working at the school at which they are enrolled ($6.17/hr.)
- Payment to employees who receive tips (See page 36)

Regular Hourly Wage and Overtime Calculations

Calculations Overview

In a discussion above, we referred to "overtime" as 1½ (1.5) times the regular rate. This is simply a useful shortcut calculation that combines the regular hourly rate plus an *overtime premium* of 50% of the regular hourly rate. For example, if the regular rate is $18 per hour, 50% of that is a $9 overtime premium that results in a combined total of $27 that is both regular rate plus the premium. This makes it easy to calculate both regular pay plus overtime premium when both are earned and paid together. It is important to understand this because there are some situations (we will see below) when the regular hourly rate and its overtime premium are calculated and paid separately. (In all cases, an employee always receives at least the regular rate for hours worked.)

Regular Hourly Wage and Overtime Calculations, *continued*

What is the Regular Hourly Rate?

The "regular (hourly) rate" as defined in the FLSA is a common point of reference in all overtime calculations, because overtime is calculated as a multiple of the regular rate. In the clearest situation, a base rate is given and this can be used as the regular hourly rate. Example: Bill earns $20 per hour and worked 46 hours this week. His regular hourly rate is $20 and his total pay is ($20 × 40) + ($20 × 1.5 × 6) = $980, or alternatively (using the .5 overtime premium): ($20 × 46) + ($10 × 6) = $980.

However, there are other circumstances in which a regular rate must be calculated. The table below shows regular hourly rate determination for various circumstances (but never less than minimum wage). The hours are on a weekly basis as defined by the Department of Labor.

	If	The "Regular Hourly Rate" Is
1	Base rate is given, and there is no other compensation	The base rate given
2	Base rate is given and there is other compensation (such as a bonus)	[(Total hours worked x base rate) + other compensation] / Total hours worked
3	Base compensation is a fixed amount (salary) for a fixed number of hours	Total compensation* / Fixed hours
4	Base compensation is a fixed amount (salary) for variable hours	Total compensation* / Total hours worked
5	Total compensation is variable (such as commission employee)	Total compensation* / Total hours worked

Overtime for Non-Exempt Salaried Employees*

Non-exempt employee salaries can create tricky calculation choices depending on how many weekly hours the employee and employer agree that the salary covers. 1) If a salary is for 40 hours of work: use regular rate up to 40 hours, then hours above 40 are a 1.5 overtime rate. 2) If a salary is intended to cover an amount above 40 hours - such as 50 hours - the pay rate would be: up to 40, regular rate; from 40-50: .5 premium rate (hours to 50 include regular rate); above 50: 1.5 overtime rate. 3) For less than 40 hours: use the regular rate up to 40 hours and above 40 use a 1.5 overtime rate. 4) For a salary that covers all hours worked, up to 40: regular rate, above 40: overtime is .5 premium. (All hours worked include regular rate)

* Although the regular rate is on a weekly basis, employees can be paid in other time periods such as biweekly, semi-monthly, or monthly. Because the FSLA requires that overtime also be determined weekly, compensation using other periods must be converted to a weekly basis as seen in the following examples. Other pay such as bonuses, shift differential, etc. must be included, except for excluded compensation (page 33).

continued   ▶

Regular Hourly Wage and Overtime Calculations, *continued*

Example:
Biweekly Pay
Period: Base Rate
Given, With Other
Compensation

Example: John Miller, an hourly non-exempt employee, earns $35 per hour and is paid biweekly. As well, the employer pays a $140 biweekly bonus for 100% non-absence, which John earned. John worked 90 hours in the biweekly period, 44 hours in the first week and 46 hours in the second week.

Step	Procedure
1	Determine the total regular weekly earnings.
2	Determine *regular hourly* pay rate (using total hours).
3	Determine *overtime hourly* pay rate: Multiply regular rate by 1.5.
4	Calculate overtime pay: Multiply overtime rate by overtime hours for the week.
5	Calculate total gross pay: Add regular weekly pay to overtime pay.

Step	Calculation
1	Week 1: [($35 × 44) + $140/2 = $1,610; Week 2: [($35 × 46) + $140/2 = $1,680
2	Week 1: $1,610/44 = $36.59; Week 2: $1,680/46 = $36.52
3	Week 1: $36.59 × 1.5 = $54.89; Week 2: $36.52 × 1.5 = $54.78
4	Week 1: 4 × $54.89 = $219.56; Week 2: 6 × $54.78 = $328.68
5	Biweekly: [($36.59 × 40) + $219.56] + [($36.59 × 40) + $328.68] = $3,475.44

Procedure:
Biweekly Period:
Fixed Pay, Fixed
Hours

Step	Action
1	Determine the total weekly base pay. Divide biweekly pay by 2.
2	Determine *regular hourly* pay rate (using fixed hours).
3	Determine *overtime hourly* pay rate: Multiply regular rate by 1.5.
4	Calculate overtime pay: Multiply overtime rate by overtime hours for the period.
5	Calculate total gross pay: Add regular weekly pay to overtime pay.

continued ▶

Regular Hourly Wage and Overtime Calculations, *continued*

Example: Conversion From a Biweekly Pay Period: Fixed Pay, Fixed Hours

Example: Maxie Doing, a non-exempt employee, worked 90 hours during the biweekly period, with 4 hours of overtime in the first week and 6 hours of overtime in the second. This employee earns a $3,000 salary every two weeks **for 40-hour weeks**. What is the total pay for the biweekly period?

Step	Action
1	$3,000/2 = $1,500 per week regular weekly earnings.
2	$1,500/40 = $37.50 per hour regular rate
3	$37.50 x 1.5 = $56.25 per hour overtime rate
4	$56.25 x 10 = $562.50
5	$3,000 + $562.50 = $3,562.50 total pay

Note: There are 26 biweekly periods per calendar year.

Conversion From a Semi-Monthly Pay Period: Fixed Pay for Variable Hours

A semi-monthly pay period means that pay is earned over two periods per month, and that employees are paid twice per month, such as on the 15th and last day of a month. However, the FLSA requires that: 1) A company must use a fixed 7- consecutive day workweek; 2) Overtime is calculated at the end of a workweek for hours in excess of 40 hours for that workweek.

Semi-monthly periods add complexity to overtime calculations because usually there are not an exact number of full workweeks that begin and end within a semi-monthly period. The result is that a workweek may begin during the last days of one semi-monthly period and end during the first days of the next semi-monthly period. The overtime resulting from the part of a workweek that begins in the last days of a semi-monthly period will be included and paid in the following semi-monthly period.

Also it is important to note that employees always receive their regular pay for hours worked even if overtime pay premium is delayed because of the above overlapping effect. Therefore, when those regular hours are used as part of total hours in a workweek ending in a later pay period only to calculate overtime hours, only the overtime premium is paid.

continued ▶

Regular Hourly Wage and Overtime Calculations, *continued*

Procedure:
Conversion From
a Semi-Monthly
Pay Period: Fixed
Pay, Variable
Hours

Step	Action: Calculate Regular and Overtime Hours
1	First workweek ending in the current period: ■ Determine total hours worked. ■ Calculate overtime hours for this week.
2	Second workweek ending in the current period: ■ Determine total hours worked. ■ Calculate overtime hours this week.
3	Third workweek beginning in the current period (if any): ■ Determine total hours worked. ■ Calculate overtime hours this week.
Step	**Action: Calculate Pay Rates and Gross Pay**
1	Convert base semi-monthly pay into base weekly pay: Multiply by 24 and divide by 52.
2	Calculate regular rate for each week ending in the pay period: Divide base pay by hours worked.
3	Determine overtime for each week ending in the pay period: Apply overtime premium to hours above 40.
4	Calculate gross pay: Add overtime pay for the period to base pay for the period.
Note: Semi-monthly employees are paid 24 times per year.	

Example:
Conversion From
a Semi-Monthly
Pay Period

John Evans, an non-exempt employee, earns a $2,600 salary semi-monthly as his base pay **for all hours worked**. He is paid on the 15th and last day of a month. The workweek is Sunday-Saturday. The illustration below shows John's hours worked from March 28 to April 17. What is John's gross pay for his April 15th paycheck?

continued   ▶

Regular Hourly Wage and Overtime Calculations, *continued*

Sunday	Monday	Tuesday	Wednesday	Thursday	Friday	Saturday
MARCH				APRIL		
28	29	30	31	1	2	3
0	8	9	8	10	8	2
4	5	6	7	8	9	10
0	9	8	8	8	7	0
11	12	13	14	15	16	17
0	11	8	8	8	8	3

Example: Conversion From a Semi-Monthly Pay Period: Fixed Pay, Variable Hours

Step	Action: Calculate Regular and Overtime Hours
1	First workweek ending in the current period: ■ Total hours: $(8 + 9 + 8 + 10 + 8 + 2) = 45$ (Base pay for last week in March was already paid.) ■ Overtime hours: 45 total hours − 40 = 5 (Carried over and paid in April.)
2	Second workweek ending in the current period: ■ Total hours: $(9 + 8 + 8 + 8 + 7) = 40$ ■ Overtime hours: 40 total hours − 40 = 0
3	Third workweek beginning in the current period (if any): ■ Regular pay hours: $(11 + 8 + 8 + 8 + 8 + 3) = 46$ ■ Overtime hours: 46 − 40 = 6 (Payable next pay period)

Step	Action: Calculate Pay Rates and Gross Pay
1	$2,600 × 24/52 = $1,200 weekly base pay
2	■ First workweek: $1,200/45 = $26.67 regular rate (rounded) ■ Second workweek: $1,200/40 = $30.00 regular rate ■ Third workweek: $1,200/46 = $26.09 regular rate (rounded) (Hours are not fixed, so divide by hours worked. If hours were fixed, divide by fixed hours.)
3	■ First workweek: $26.67 × .5 × 5 = $66.68 ■ Second workweek: $0 (no overtime hours) ■ Third workweek: $26.09 × .5 × 6 = $78.27 (paid next period)
4	$66.68 + $2,600 = $2,666.68
	Note: 6 hours of overtime in week three will be paid in the following pay period of April 16 – April 30.

continued ▶

Regular Hourly Wage and Overtime Calculations, *continued*

Overview: Conversion From a Monthly Pay Period

Although most monthly pay periods probably apply to exempt salaried employees, there could be cases in which monthly pay periods apply to nonexempt salaried employees or hourly employees. Therefore, overtime calculations may be needed. This is illustrated below.

A monthly pay period means that pay is earned over a full month, and payment is made once per month. However, the FLSA requires that: 1) A company must use a fixed 7-consecutive day workweek; 2) For an employee who is paid by an hourly rate, overtime is calculated at the end of a workweek for hours in excess of 40 hours for that workweek.

Usually there are not an exact number of full workweeks that begin and end within a monthly period. The result is that a workweek may begin during the last days of one monthly period and end during the first days of the next monthly period. The overtime resulting from the part of a workweek that begins in the last days of a monthly period will be included and paid in the following monthly period.

Procedure: Conversion From a Monthly Pay Period: Fixed Pay, Variable Hours

Step	Action: Calculate Regular and Overtime Hours
1	First workweek ending in the current period: ■ Determine total hours worked. ■ Calculate overtime hours for this week.
2	Second, third, and fourth workweeks ending in the current period: ■ Determine total hours worked. ■ Calculate overtime hours this week.
3	Fifth workweek beginning in the current period (if any): ■ Determine total hours worked. ■ Calculate overtime hours this week.
Step	**Action: Calculate Pay Rates and Gross Pay**
1	Convert base monthly pay into base weekly pay: Multiply by 12 and divide by 52.
2	Calculate regular rate for each week ending in the pay period: Divide base pay by hours worked.
3	Determine overtime for each week ending in the pay period: Apply overtime premium to hours above 40.
4	Calculate gross pay: Add overtime pay for the period to base pay for the period.
Note: Monthly employees are paid 12 times per year.	

Regular Hourly Wage and Overtime Calculations, *continued*

TIP

Other overtime calculations: Some states: require overtime to be calculated on a daily basis instead of weekly as required by the FLSA. The following states and territories require overtime to be paid for hours worked in excess of 8 per day: Alaska, California, Nevada, Puerto Rico, and Virgin Islands. Colorado requires overtime in excess of 12 hours per day. Also check local requirements. In all cases the highest overtime amount is what must be paid.

Example:
Conversion From
a Monthly Pay
Period: Fixed Pay,
Variable Hours

Melanie Jones, a non-exempt employee, earns $5,700 monthly as base gross pay for all hours worked. She is paid on the last day of a month, and there is a Sunday – Saturday workweek. The illustration below shows Melanie's hours worked from March 28 to May 1. What is Melanie's gross pay for her April 30 paycheck?

Sunday	Monday	Tuesday	Wednesday	Thursday	Friday	Saturday
MARCH				APRIL		
28	29	30	31	1	2	3
4	8	8	8	11	8	4
4	5	6	7	8	9	10
0	8	8	8	8	8	4
11	12	13	14	15	16	17
0	8	8	10	8	8	3
18	19	20	21	22	23	24
0	8	8	8	8	8	0
						MAY
25	26	27	28	29	30	1
4	8	8	10	8	8	4

continued ▶

Regular Hourly Wage and Overtime Calculations, *continued*

Example
Continued:
Conversion From
a Monthly Pay
Period: Fixed Pay,
Variable Hours

Step	Action: Calculate Regular and Overtime Hours
1	First workweek ending in the current period: ■ Total hours: (4 + 8 + 8 + 8 + 11 + 8 + 4) = 51 ■ Overtime hours: 51 total hours − 40 = 11
2	Second – fourth workweeks ending in the current period: ■ Total hours: (8 + 8 + 8 + 8 + 8 + 4) = 44 ■ Overtime hours: 44 total hours − 40 = 4 Third workweek beginning in the current period ■ Total hours: (8 + 8 + 10 + 8 + 8 + 3) = 45 ■ Overtime hours: 45 − 40 = 5 Fourth workweek beginning in the current period (if any): ■ Total hours: (8 + 8 + 8 + 8 + 8) = 40 ■ Overtime hours: 40 − 40 = 0
3	Fifth workweek beginning in the current period (if any): ■ Total hours: (4 + 8 + 8 + 10 + 8 + 8 + 4) = 50 ■ Overtime hours: 50 − 40 = 10 (Payable next pay period)

Step	Action: Calculate Pay Rates and Gross Pay
1	$5,700 × 12/52 = $1,315.39 weekly base pay
2	■ First workweek: $1,315.39/51 = $25.79 regular rate ■ Second workweek: $1,315.39/44 = $29.90 regular rate ■ Third workweek: $1,315.39/45 = $29.23 regular rate ■ Fourth workweek: No overtime hours ■ Fifth workweek: $1,315.39/50 = $26.31 regular rate (Amounts Rounded)
3	■ First workweek: $25.79 × .5 × 11 = $141.85 ■ Second workweek: $29.90 × .5 × 4 = $59.80 ■ Third workweek: $29.23 × .5 × 5 = $73.08 ■ Fourth workweek: No overtime hours ■ Fifth workweek: $26.31 × .5 × 10 = $131.55 (Amounts Rounded)
4	$141.85 + $59.80 + $73.08 + $131.55 + $5,700 = $6,106.28
	Note: 10 hours of overtime in week five will be paid in the next Monthly pay period (May).

Recalculating
Overtime
From Delayed
Information

Example: Suppose that a $3,000 non-discretionary efficiency bonus cannot be determined until the end of a six-month period (52 × 6/12 = 26 weeks). If the employee worked overtime during any of the 26 weeks, that overtime must also be recalculated when the bonus is paid because the regular rate will increase by $3,000/ 26 = $115.39 /week.

continued ▶

Regular Hourly Wage and Overtime Calculations, *continued*

Fixed Pay, Fixed Hours Less Than 40: Paid Weekly

Most salaried employees are exempt from overtime, but some are not (See page 21). If a salaried employee is not exempt from overtime requirements and the employee works for a fixed salary for a fixed number of hours per week, then the "regular" hourly rate is the weekly salary divided by the fixed hours. (Note: an employer can always begin overtime at a lower number of hours.) Example: Walter Smith, a nonexempt employee, agrees to receive a salary of $1,150 per week, to work 38 hours per week, and is paid weekly. This week Walter worked 47 hours.

- $1,150/38 = $30.26 regular hourly rate.
- $30.26 × 1.5 = $45.39 overtime hourly rate
- Overtime hours: 47 − 40 = 7 hours.
- Total pay: $1,150 + (40–38) × $30.26 + (7 × $45.39) = $1,528.25

Fixed Pay, Variable Hours, With Alternative Method: Paid Weekly

As shown on previous pages, if a fixed amount (a salary) is paid for all hours worked, the regular rate is calculated by dividing the fixed amount by the weekly hours worked. This is acceptable when both employee and employer agree that hours will fluctuate above and below 40. Be sure to also check state law. In the example above, assume that Walter receives the same fixed amount for a variable number of hours and worked 47 hours in the current week.

- $1,150/47 = $24.47 regular hourly rate for the week
- $24.47 × .5 = $12.24 overtime hourly premium for the week
- Overtime pay: $12.24 premium × 7 overtime hours = $85.68
- Total pay: $1,150 (47 hours regular pay) + $85.68 = $1,235.68

Alternative: The following method can be used with fluctuating hours, with a fixed amount for all hours worked, according to the Department of Labor:

- $1,150/40 = $28.75 fixed regular hourly rate (based on a 40-hour week)
- $28.75 × .5 = $14.38 fixed overtime hourly premium
- Total pay: $1,150 + (7 × $14.38) = $1,250.66

TIP

Did you know..? Employers are legally required to display posters that inform employees of their rights under various labor laws. These may be federal, state, or local laws. The U.S. Department of Labor has website that an employer can check for federal poster requirements. There is a federal poster advisor at the Department of Labor 'elaws' Internet website.

Selecting a Payroll Cycle

Payroll Cycle
Considerations

What is the best payroll period ("payroll cycle") to use? Aside from minimum period legal requirements, there is no one best answer. Some considerations are:

- Monthly: Financial reports and benefits are typically prepared on a monthly basis, so this correlates easily with monthly payroll costs and minimizes accruals. Overtime calculations are difficult.
- Semi-monthly: This also easily correlates with financial and benefits preparation. Overtime calculations are also difficult with semi-monthly periods.
- Bi-weekly: Overtime is easier to calculate with bi-weekly periods, and hourly employees may prefer to be paid more frequently. However, more frequent payrolls involve greater cost, and also more accruals occur.
- Weekly: Overtime is easiest to calculate with a weekly payroll. As with bi-weekly payroll, employees may prefer to be paid more frequently; however, weekly payrolls involve the greater cost, and also more accruals occur.
- Consider likely cash flow. If cash flow will generally follow a pattern, an employer will want to have sufficient cash available to meet payroll requirements. Frequent payments may result in smoother cash flow.
- Time considerations: Are some times of a month or year predictably busy? More frequent payrolls also create greater time demands.
- It may be convenient to maintain two cycles. For example: biweekly for non-exempt employees and monthly for exempt employees.

Other Types of Regular Pay and Overtime Calculations

Overview

In addition to hourly wages and salaries, "regular pay" includes other compensation. Common examples are:

- Commissions
- Tips
- Piecework
- Non-discretionary bonus
- Longevity pay
- Shift differential or other differential

These are discussed in the following pages.

Other Types of Regular Pay and Overtime Calculations, *continued*

Not Part of Regular Pay

"Regular pay" does not include all compensation. In general, fringe benefits are excluded from the definition of "regular pay". As well, other items are also excluded. Examples:

- Gifts unrelated to work or output
- Payments made for periods when no work is performed (vacation, holiday, illness, insufficient work)
- Travel expense reimbursements
- Discretionary bonuses
- Insurance premiums paid by employer on behalf of employee
- Stock rights and grants in a qualified stock purchase plan as defined by the FLSA (§778.200)
- Overtime premium

Commission Employees: Examples

Commissions are earnings that are typically calculated as a percentage of sales revenue. Also, commissions can be calculated in various ways—examples:

- As only a percentage commission: Arthur is a nonexempt inside salesman for a manufacturing company and earns a 10% commission on all sales from his customers, which for the 40-hour week are $22,000. Gross pay: $22,000 × .10 = $2,200.
- As a combination of hourly wages plus commission: Jane is a nonexempt employee summer camp employee and worked 40 hours during the week at $18 per hour, plus she receives a 10% commission on total customer billings. For the current week these billings are $12,000. Jane's gross pay is: $720 of hourly earnings + ($12,000 × .10) = $1,920.
- As a combination of salary plus commission: Susan is a nonexempt employee and earns a weekly salary of $1,500 plus 5% commission on all sales in a specific territory, for which she is responsible. She is compensated based on 40-hour workweeks. For the week these sales are $28,000. Jane's gross pay is: $1,500 + ($28,000 × .05) = $2,900.
- Other examples: As incentive, certain types of products may offer higher commission percentages; employees may receive a percentage of company profits; commissions are paid on sales that result from development of innovative products.

Overview: Minimum Wage and Overtime on Commissions

In general, FLSA minimum wage and overtime requirements apply to compensation by commission, except for outside sales employees (who make sales away from the employer's physical place of business) and some retail employees—check FLSA definitions and guidelines.

continued ▶

Other Types of Regular Pay and Overtime Calculations, *continued*

A commission employee must receive minimum wage for all hours worked whether the amount comes from commissions, commissions plus wage or salary, or some other combination. This can be no lower than minimum wage requirements under the FLSA, including overtime on minimum wage.

Minimum Wage Examples for Commission Employees

- A full-time non-exempt commission sales person makes no sales during a week. That person should receive minimum wage for a 40-hour week.
- A nonexempt sales person earns $400 of commissions during a week in which 45 hours were worked. Therefore the regular hourly compensation for that week is $400/45 = $8.89, which exceeds the FLSA minimum wage of $7.25. In this example, overtime is $8.89 × .5 × (45 − 40) = $22.23. (Remember to check state and local minimum wage and overtime requirements.)
- The same commission sales person earns $200 of commissions during the next week in which 40 hours were worked. The regular hourly compensation for that week is $200/40 = $5.00, which does not meet the hourly FLSA minimum wage of $7.25 per hour. The employer must pay an additional ($7.25 − $5.00) × 40 = $90.
- A nonexempt sales person worked 45 hours in a week. He earned $150 base weekly salary plus $120 commissions. Therefore, the regular rate of pay is ($150 +$120)/45 = $6.00. The employer must increase regular pay to minimum wage plus pay overtime based on the minimum wage rate. The total wages would be: $270 + [($7.25 − $6.00) × 45] + ($7.25 × 5 × .5) = $344.38.

TIP

How expensive can worker misclassification be? Sometimes pretty expensive. In a famous Microsoft case, workers that were classified as independent contractors were determined to be employees by the IRS. This required Microsoft to pay substantial back payroll taxes and penalties. Microsoft was then required to pay the workers overtime for the misclassification period as required by the Department of Labor. Upon the reclassification, employees then sued Microsoft for full benefits including 401(k) and stock purchase plan rights, for the period of misclassification. The appeals court decided in favor of the employees. In another case, FedEx paid almost $230 million to settle a case in which delivery drivers had been classified as independent contractors. Moral? Correct worker classification really does matter.

Other Types of Regular Pay and Overtime Calculations, *continued*

Commission Employee: More Overtime Examples

As we know, the FLSA requires overtime pay for hours worked in excess of 40 hours per week for nonexempt employees. This includes commission employees. However, an exemption is available for outside sales employees (majority of time is spent away from the office) and for retail sales commission employees with a regular weekly rate greater than 1½ times the applicable minimum wage and commissions that are more than 50% of compensation in a pay period. Check FLSA guidelines for details and state guidelines for additional requirements.) For workers such as commission employees who are not paid by an hourly rate, the "regular rate" is the dollar amount of compensation divided by the actual hours worked. Overtime is still calculated for hours in excess of 40 hours per week.

- As only a percentage commission with overtime: In the example on page 33, assume that Arthur actually worked 45 hour during the week. Therefore Arthur's regular rate becomes $2,200/45 = $48.89. Overtime *premium* (Arthur already received $2,200 regular pay for his 45 hours): $48.89 × .5 = $24.45. Gross pay: $2,200 + 5 hours overtime × $24.45 = $2,322.25.
- Commission with hourly wages plus overtime: In the second example above, assume that Jane works 50 hours during the week instead of 40 hours. Jane now earns $18 × 50 = $900 + $1,200 = $2,100. Regular rate: $2,100/50 = $42. Overtime *premium* (Jane already received $2,100 regular pay for her 50 hours): $42 × .5 = $21. Gross pay: $2,100 + (10 hours overtime × $21) = $2,310.
- Commission plus salary with overtime—salary is intended to cover up to 40 hours per week: In the third example above, Susan and her employer have agreed that her compensation is for 40 hours per week of work. Assume that Susan worked 55 hours in the current week. Susan's regular rate is $2,900/40 = $72.50. Overtime rate: $72.50 × 1.5 = $108.75. Gross pay: $2,900 (for 40 hours) + (108.75 × 15) = $4,531.25.
- Commission plus salary with overtime—salary is intended to cover more than 40 hours per week: In the third example above, assume that Susan and her employer have agreed that her compensation is for 50 hours per week of work. Susan worked 55 hours. Susan's regular rate is $2,900/50 = $58. Gross pay: $2,900 + ($58 × .5 × 10) + ($58 × 1.5 × 5) = $3,625

Commission Employee Other Pay Periods

All of our examples above are based on weekly pay periods. It would not be unusual for an employee to be compensated by commission and paid on a different basis, such as biweekly, semi-monthly or monthly as we discussed earlier. An acceptable method is to convert a commission to an equal weekly amount. For example suppose that John, a nonexempt employee, earns $3,200 commissions in a semi-monthly pay period. During a workweek within this pay period he worked 46 hours. This week would be allocated a commission of: ($3,200 × 24)/52 = $1,476.92. The overtime allocation would

continued ▶

Other Types of Regular Pay and Overtime Calculations, *continued*

be $1,476.92/46 = $32.11 regular rate. Overtime: $32.11 × .5 × 6 = $96.33. This method can be used for other forms of nonexempt employee compensation such as salary and piecework.

Tips and Minimum Wage

In general, employers must pay a required minimum base wage of at least $2.13 per hour to employees who earn at least $30 per month in tips. However, if the combination of tips plus the base does not equal at least $7.25 per hour (the current hourly minimum wage), the base minimum wage must be increased until the hourly total is $7.25. Therefore, the maximum differential is $5.12 per hour; in other words, the maximum credit the employer takes when calculating a regular hourly wage rate. (Some states do not allow tip credits. This means the employer pays the $7.25 minimum wage regardless of total tips received.)

Tips and Overtime

An employee who receives tips must be paid overtime for working hours that exceed 40 hours per week. The overtime rate is 1½ times the regular hourly pay.

Tipped Employees Example

A restaurant employee works a standard 40-hour week. The employer pays the minimum amount of $2.13 per hour as the regular hourly rate, with the employee tips accounting for the difference to reach the minimum hourly wage of $7.25. During the week, the employee worked 44 hours, which resulted in 4 hours of overtime.

Step	Action
1	Determine regular hourly rate.
2	Calculate overtime rate at 1½ times regular hourly rate.
3	Subtract tip credit from standard overtime rate.
4	Multiply tip overtime rate times overtime hours.

Calculation:

Step	Action
1	Given as $7.25 per hour (minimum wage)
2	1½ × $7.25 per hour = $10.88 per hour
3	$10.88 per hour − $5.12 = $5.76 per hour
4	4 × $5.76 per hour = $23.04 overtime pay.

Other Types of Regular Pay and Overtime Calculations, *continued*

Total pay: (40 regular hours × $2.13) + $23.04 = $108.24
Check:
($7.25 × 40) + (4 × $5.76 overtime) – ($5.12 × 40 offset) = $108.24

Employee Reporting Tips to the Employer

The Internal Revenue Service (IRS) requires an employee to report all net cash tips, received directly or indirectly, to the employer if the tips exceed $20 per month.

Tip income (which is subject to both income tax and social security/Medicare withholding) must be reported to the employer no later than the 10th day of month following the month in which the tips were received. Employees use Form 4070 or equivalent for reporting. (See page 56 for tip reporting by employers.) Form 4070A can be used for daily record keeping by employees. Note: Tips paid by credit card can be reduced by the percentage transaction fee, but must be paid to employees by the next payroll period regardless of when the employee receives wage payment.

Piecework

Piecework is compensation paid to an employee based on the number of units the employee produces or completes using a rate per piece..

Piecework and Minimum Wage

Piecework employees must be paid at least the required minimum wage. The regular hourly rate is the total earned by piecework plus other compensation divided by hours worked. If compensated by both hourly rate and piecework, each must meet the minimum wage.

Piecework and Overtime

An employer must keep a detailed record of the number of units of output for each employee compensated by piecework. Overtime requirements apply to piecework employees. There are two alternative methods that can be used:

- The employer must pay an overtime premium of one-half the regular hourly rate for hours worked in excess of 40 hours. The regular rate of pay is the total amount earned in a workweek from the piecework, divided by hours worked.
- Employees and employer agree—prior to doing the work—that the employees will be paid at 1½ times the standard piecework rate for all piecework done for work in excess of 40 hours per week.

Hospital and Medical Work

Hospitals and residential care organizations may utilize a fixed work period of fourteen consecutive days instead of a 40-hour workweek for the purpose of

continued ▶

Other Types of Regular Pay and Overtime Calculations, *continued*

computing overtime. To use this exception, an employer must have a prior agreement or understanding with affected employees before the work is performed. An "eight and eighty" (8 and 80) exception allows employers to pay time and one-half the regular rate for all hours worked over eight in any workday and eighty hours in a fourteen-day period. An employer can use both the standard 40-hour overtime system and the 8 and 80 overtime system for different employees in the same workplace, but they cannot use both for a single individual employee.

An employer's work period in this system must be a fixed and regularly recurring 14-day period. It may be changed if the change is designated to be permanent and not to evade the overtime requirements. If an employer changes the pay period permanently, it must calculate wages on both the old pay period as well as the new pay period and pay the amount that is more advantageous to each employee for the pay period when the change was made.

The overtime premium pay for the daily overtime calculation may be credited by the employer towards the overtime compensation due employees for their hours worked in excess of 80 for the 14-day period.

Bonus, Differentials, and Longevity

All of the following are included in regular pay:

- Non-discretionary bonus: A non-discretionary bonus is an amount that is in addition to regular compensation and that is paid according to a predetermined plan. In other words, the method for calculating the amount of the bonus has been fixed and disclosed in advance. (A discretionary bonus is not disclosed in advance.) Examples of a non-discretionary bonus are bonuses for meeting productivity goals, attendance, hiring, and work quality.
- Shift or other differential: A shift differential is a higher pay rate received by working outside of what are considered to be normal working hours—typically 8 am to 5 pm. Other differential pay examples: hazard pay, on-call pay, and differential between civilian and military pay while on active duty.
- Longevity pay: Compensation or wage adjustment received as a result of seniority is also regular pay.

Other Activities

The following circumstances affect hours worked and are included as part of regular hours. These are often referred to as part of employee "principal activities":

- Waiting time: If an employee is on the job and idle, but ready to work and waiting for work, this is part of regular hours.
- An employee who must remain on call, available to work, at the employer's premises or nearby is considered to be working, if the time cannot be used effectively for the employee's own purposes.

Other Types of Regular Pay and Overtime Calculations, *continued*

- Travel time: Travel time spent as part of employee duties qualifies as regular hours. Time spent commuting to and from work in most cases is not regular time, but there may be limited exceptions.
- Training time: Required training directly related to an employee's work during work hours is part of principal activities.
- Rest periods: short rest periods (5–20 minutes) are counted as work time.
- Medical assistance: Receiving or waiting for medical assistance at the place of work is part of principal activities.
- Unauthorized and permitted: If an employer knows that an employee is performing work on his/her own time, even if not specifically authorized, that time is counted as work time.

Salaried Employees and Overtime

The FLSA provides an executive exemption from overtime pay. The general requirements are:

1) The employee receives a salary of at least a designated amount (Under current rules this is $455 per week. A proposed amount of $913 weekly is now under judicial review), and
2) The employee's primary duty is management, administration, professional, computer programs or systems.

Therefore, if either or both of these requirements are not met, an employee is not exempt and must be compensated for overtime in the same manner as an hourly employee, based on hours worked in excess of 40 hours per week at a rate of 1½ times their regular hourly rate.

Other Job Types and Overtime Exemption

Some examples of other job categories that are fully exempt from FLSA overtime requirements are:

- Teachers, school administrators
- Baby sitters
- Taxicab drivers
- Live-in domestic employees
- Many airline employees (see DOL guidelines).
- Small-agency (less than 5) police and fire.

- Companions for elderly
- Agricultural workers
- Movie theater employees
- Recreational activity employees
- Some truck drivers
- Creative arts employees

The Department of Labor at dol.gov can provide more information on exempt job categories for overtime, minimum wage, and equal pay.

continued   ▶

Other Types of Regular Pay and Overtime Calculations, *continued*

Overview of "Comp Time": FLSA Rule for Compensatory Time in Lieu of Overtime

"Comp time" is an abbreviated expression for "compensatory time" off from work. This means that instead of receiving pay, an employee receives time off from work. Typically, employees will accumulate or "bank" time off to be used at a later date.

For nonexempt employees, the FLSA does not allow the use of compensatory time as a substitute for overtime pay, with a limited specific exception.

The limited exception applies to state and local government agencies, which, with prior agreement with employees, may allow employees to accumulate compensatory time off. Time off must be at the rate of 1½ hours for each overtime hour worked. If an employee's employment is terminated prior to using all accumulated comp time, the unused time must be paid in cash at the overtime rate.

There are limits to the amount of comp time that can be accumulated. Public safety, emergency, and seasonal employees can accumulate up to 320 hours of overtime work (which results in 480 hours of comp time). Employees working in other areas can accumulate up to 160 hours of overtime (which results in 240 hours of comp time). These limits do not have to be reached in order for an employee to use accumulated comp time, and the time must be allowed on the date requested unless it creates undue hardship for the employer.

For exempt employees, the FLSA does not require the use of overtime pay. Therefore an employer may offer comp time as a form of overtime pay to exempt employees at the employer's discretion.

Partial Pay Periods

Partial pay period issues typically arise in the following circumstances:

- New employees
- Payroll period-end payroll accruals
- Terminating employees

In general, all previously discussed pay requirements and procedures apply to partial payroll periods. Typical issues that arise are: 1) For new and terminating employees, verify starting and ending compensation dates, including all benefits. 2) Payroll period-end accruals are an accounting issue (See Section 3) that requires unpaid payroll liabilities to be recorded.

Rate Change or Two Different Rates in a Period

If an employee's hourly rate changes within a payroll period, calculate total pay as old rate multiplied by hours worked at that rate plus new rate multiplied by hours at that rate. Divide the total by hours worked to determine a regular rate (or just pay higher rate). This method also applies to employees who work jobs at different rates in the period.

Part II: FICA Withholding

Overview

What is Payroll Withholding?

Payroll withholding means that an employer withholds (deducts) amounts from an employee's gross pay. These amounts are then paid by the employer to taxing authorities and other third parties. The amounts withheld from an employee's pay are called "payroll deductions". The remaining amount of gross pay that an employee actually receives is called "net pay". Payroll deductions are not a tax on the employer; the employer is simply acting as a collection agent. The two categories of payroll deductions are:

- Deductions required by law
- Voluntary deductions by agreement

Deductions Required by Law

The following items are imposed upon individuals classified as employees and must be withheld (deducted) by the employer from employee gross pay:

- Employee social security (FICA) tax, discussed in this part.
- Employee income taxes
- State and local income and employment taxes
- Other deductions imposed by law such as wage garnishment*

In some circumstances, withholding may also be required for individuals who are not employees. See "backup withholding", pages 64, 65.

* "Wage garnishment" or "garnishment" typically means that either someone has obtained a court order to collect an unpaid debt, there is required child support or an unpaid student loan, or that the Internal Revenue Service or state tax collection agencies have imposed levies for unpaid taxes. A garnishment will take part of a worker's gross pay to make regular required payments. An employer is directed to withhold a certain amount and remit the amount withheld to a designated third party. At the same time, there are limits to garnishment, depending on type of creditor, set by the Consumer Credit Protection Act, and administered by the Department of Labor.

Voluntary Deductions by Agreement

Optional deductions can consist of many different items. Some examples are:

- Savings and stock purchase plan contributions
- Union dues
- Charitable contributions

Employee and Employer Social Security (FICA)

Overview

The "social security tax" is a general term and is a result of a very dramatic and difficult time in American history. This period began in 1929 with the onset of a stock market crash and the "great depression". In 1935, the United States Congress enacted the Federal Insurance Contribution Act (*FICA*). This act imposed a tax on employees that is matched by employers (see page 81) to provide employees with a guaranteed minimum amount of old age, survivor, and disability insurance benefits (*OASDI*).

FICA was expanded in 1965 to provide limited medical benefits for people without medical insurance (*Medicare*), generally at age 65 and who otherwise qualify for OASDI; **therefore, "FICA" really consists of two parts: OASDI and Medicare.** An employer is required to determine the amount of an employee's FICA tax each payroll period, withhold the tax, and forward the amount withheld to the Internal Revenue Service (IRS).

The definitions of "employer" and "employee" for FICA purposes are the same as discussed on pages 5–6. For FICA purposes most workers are considered employees based on common law; however, FICA both expands the definition of employee for some workers who would otherwise be considered as independent contractors ("statutory" employees) and exempts other workers, as explained below. Keep in mind that these designations are for FICA purposes.

Statutory Employee Categories

In some cases a worker does not qualify as an employee under common law, but that person will still be classified as a "statutory employee" as follows:

- An agent or commission driver. Duties are to deliver food, beverages (other than milk), laundry, or dry cleaning for the provider of these items.
- A full-time life insurance salesperson who sells insurance primarily for one company.
- A worker who works at home according to the specifications of the person for whom the work is done, using materials furnished by that person with product and materials returned to that person or their agent (e.g. a "homeworker"). Note: there are some cases in which homeworkers are not deemed to be statutory employees.
- A traveling salesperson who works full time for one firm or person, taking orders for merchandise for resale or supplies for use in the customer's business. Additional incidental part-time work does change the worker's status.

Exception: If the workers either have a substantial interest in the facilities used to perform their services or the services are from a single transaction not part of a continuing relationship they are not covered by FICA.

Employee and Employer Social Security (FICA), *continued*

Statutory Non-Employees	Persons who perform the following activities are considered to be independent contractors for both income tax and employment tax purposes. This means that they are not subject to FICA withholding or income tax withholding. (They must make quarterly estimated tax payments for income tax and self-employment tax.)

- Direct sellers
- Licensed real estate agents
- Certain companion sitters (e.g. baby sitters, caretakers, nannies, cooks), are generally considered as self-employed for federal tax purposes.

FICA Wages	For FICA, "wages" is a general term that includes all compensation unless that which is exempt by law.

Payments Exempt From FICA	Social Security, or FICA, (referring to both OASDI and Medicare) exempts specific payment categories. The table below shows common employment categories and types of payments that are exempt from FICA.

Table 2.1: Payments Exempt From FICA Tax

Exempt Item	Description
Achievement Awards	Exempt up to $1,600 for qualified awards and $400 for non-qualified awards.
Agricultural Labor	Non-cash payments are exempt. For each worker, annual cash payments of less than $150 are exempt. If total annual expenses for all workers are less than $2,500, FICA withholding is not required. Foreign agricultural workers temporarily admitted with H-2A visas and doing H-2A related-work are exempt from FICA.
Business Expense Reimbursements	Exempt if under an accountable plan
Deceased Worker	Exempt for wages paid to estate after calendar year of worker's death

continued ▶

Table 2.1: Payments Exempt From FICA Tax *continued*

Exempt Item	Description
Dependent Care	Employer payments to employees or by third parties for dependent care under a qualified dependent care assistance program and/or the value of employer-maintained dependent care facilities use to a maximum of $5,000 ($2,500 married filing separately) are exempt.
Disabled Worker's Wages	For wages paid after year in which worker became entitled to disability insurance benefits under FICA are exempt if worker did not perform any services for the employer during this period.
Education	Annual payments up to $5,250 made by an employer under an education assistance plan to maintain or improve employee job skills are exempt to both active and prior employees. Undergraduate and graduate tuition reduction by an educational institution is also generally exempt.
Emergency Workers	Exempt if hired on a temporary basis for major emergencies such as flood, fire, or earthquake
Employee Discounts	Subject to certain limitations, employer discounts on property other than real estate, stocks, and bonds purchased by employees are exempt.
Family Employee	1) Child employed by parent: exempt under age 18 for all services in a sole proprietorship trade or business or in a partnership in which each partner is a parent; exempt until 21 if not in parent's trade or business. 2) Parent employed by child: Exempt if services are *not* in the child's trade or business; however, may be subject to tax for certain domestic services (See Publication 15). 3) Spouse employed by spouse: exempt if services are *not* part of the employer spouse's trade or business.
Foreign Affiliates	Foreign affiliates of American employers.

Employee and Employer Social Security (FICA), *continued*

Table 2.1: Payments Exempt From FICA Tax *continued*

Exempt Item	Description
Government Employee	Federal employees hired before 1984 pay into the Civil Service Retirement System and Medicare. If hired in 1984 or later, employees pay into the Federal Employees Retirement System and pay FICA. In general, for state and local government employees use the following table. (Note: Other factors may also apply.) In most cases, FICA is mandatory for current employees who are not members in a qualified state retirement system. **Category / FICA / Medicare** 1) For services before March 31, 1986* — No / No 2) For employees hired before April 1, 1986 with continuous employment since that date, and with membership in a qualified state employee retirement system* — No / No 3) For employees hired or rehired after March 31, 1986, with membership in a qualified state retirement system* — No / Yes 4) For services after July 1, 1991 and not a member in a qualified state retirement system — Yes / Yes * Not employed in a state with a federal-state §218 coverage agreement.
Health Savings Accounts	Employer payments under qualified plans exempt up to contribution limits.
Homeworker	Exempt if paid *less* than $100 per year in cash and is a statutory employee
Household employee	▪ Domestic service in private homes: exempt if paid less than $2,100 annually (this amount is subject to annual changes). Also exempt if services performed by a spouse, parent (subject to exceptions), person under age 18 at any time during the year and these services are not a principal occupation, or employer's child who is under 21. ▪ Domestic service in college clubs, fraternities, and sororities: exempt if payment is to a regular student; also exempt if the employee is paid less than $100 per year by a tax-exempt employer. Note that a household employee is not someone who works in an employer's trade or business or is a home worker, or who is an independent contractor with their own business. See Publication 926.
Insurance	Employee accident and health insurance premiums are exempt. Life insurance is also exempt except for portion required to be included in taxable income.
Meals and Lodging	The value of meals and lodging provided for the convenience of the employer are exempt if furnished on employer's business premises. Lodging must be a condition of employment. Occasional light meals (coffee, snacks, etc.) are exempt.

continued ▶

Employee and Employer Social Security (FICA), *continued*

Table 2.1: Payments Exempt From FICA Tax *continued*

Exempt Item	Description
Military Service Differential Pay	The amount paid by an employer for the difference between military pay for activation to active service exceeding 30 days and regular employee compensation is exempt. (This applies to FICA, and not income tax.)
Newspaper Carriers And Vendors	Exempt based on same rules as for income tax withholding
No-Additional Cost Services	Employer services provided to employees when no substantial additional cost will be incurred because of excess capacity are exempt.
Railroad Retirement Act	Exempt for employees subject to this act (See Publication 915)
Religious Exemption	Services performed in connection with duties of an ordained ministry, a religious order, or Christian Science practitioner, including the fair value of housing, are exempt from FICA but are subject to self-employment tax under **SECA** (Self-Employment Contributions Act) with the following exempt from both: 1) Membership in an order that takes a vow of poverty unless FICA coverage elected or non-required work outside the order, 2) The IRS approves an exemption request (see Forms 4361 and 4029), 3) A person who is subject only to the social security laws of a foreign country by treaty. Earnings separate from the above are generally subject to FICA or SECA. Otherwise exempt religious orders may request to be covered by filing SS-16. See also Publication 517.
Retirement Planning Services	Exempt
Retirement Plans	1) Exempt for employer contributions to a qualified plan (except for amounts contributed under a SEP salary reduction agreement) 2) Exempt for distributions from qualified retirement plans and 403(b) annuities Note: Employee wages (gross pay) is subject to FICA at the time they are earned, even though some is tax- deferred for income tax purposes because of contributions.
Sick Pay	Payments made by or on behalf of an employer to an employee for sickness or personal injury after the first six continuous calendar months following the last month of employment are exempt. Payments must be according to a plan between employee and employer.
Statutory Non-Employees	Exempt

Table 2.1: Payments Exempt From FICA Tax *continued*

Exempt Item	Description
Students Enrolled And Regularly Attending Classes	1) Exempt for domestic services in college clubs, fraternities, or sororities while working as a regular student; also exempt if paid less than $100 per year by income tax-exempt school. 2) Generally exempt when performing services for a school, college, or university not for academic credit—some exceptions may apply. 3) Student nurses performing part-time services at hospitals for nominal charge as part of training.
Tips	Tips of less than $20 per month are exempt. See pages 55 and 56 for required employee and employer tip reporting.
Workers' Compensation	Employer payments for workers' compensation insurance, either into state funds or by private insurance contract, are exempt. Workers' compensation benefit payments are also exempt.
Working Condition Benefits	Working condition benefits are services or property provided to an employee by an employer so that the employee is able to perform his or her duties. Examples are company-provided car, cell phone, computers, and training.

FICA Calculation

FICA is calculated using a tax rate that is applied to a wage base. A **wage base** is a maximum *calendar year* amount of gross pay that is subject to payroll tax. Gross pay that exceeds the annual base is not subject to OASDI tax. **The OASDI wage base usually increases each year.**

The Social Security Tax Bases and Rates (OASDI and Medicare)

There is a separate wage base and tax rate for each part of the social security plan (OASDI and Medicare). Here are the components of FICA:

- The current wage base for the OASDI part is $128,400. The tax rate is 6.2%. This means that during a calendar year, the first $128,400 of gross pay of each employee is subject to a 6.2% OASDI tax.
- The wage base for Medicare is unlimited. This means that all gross pay is subject to Medicare tax. The tax rate is 1.45%. (A .9% surtax applies to high-income, which is annual gross wages subject to Medicare exceeding: $250,000 married, $125,000 filing separately, $200,000 single and other. Individuals see Form 8959.)
- For wages not exceeding $128,400 (i.e. the OASDI wage base), the combined FICA rate (OASDI and Medicare) is 7.65%.

continued ▶

Employee and Employer Social Security (FICA), *continued*

Procedure with Examples

The table below illustrates the FICA tax calculation procedure. Suppose that a business has two employees, Adam and Amy. The business needs to calculate the individual and total social security tax for the monthly payroll period ending November 30. During the current year prior to this period, Adam had gross pay of $77,500 and Amy had $127,200. Adam's November gross pay is $5,900, and Amy's November gross pay is $7,500. Assume a $130,000 wage base.

Step 1
Subtract the cumulative gross pay from the wage base.
If the result is zero or positive, cumulative pay is still below the OASDI limit, so all of the current gross pay is taxable. Go to Step 3. **If** the result is negative, cumulative pay has exceeded the limit, and this excess is not taxable for OASDI. Some or all of the current gross pay is excluded from the OASDI tax. Go to Step 2.

Examples:

Adam		Amy	
Wage base	$130,000	Wage base	$130,000
Cumulative gross pay	83,400	Cumulative gross pay	$134,700
Go to Step 3	$46,600	Go to Step 2	($4,700)

Step 2
Offset the negative amount (the amount excluded) against the current gross pay to find the OASDI taxable portion of the current gross pay (but not less than zero). Then go to Step 3.

Examples:

Adam		Amy	
Not applicable—all current gross pay is fully taxable for FICA		Current gross pay	$7,500
		Excluded portion	(4,700)
		Taxable portion	$2,800

continued ▶

Employee and Employer Social Security (FICA), *continued*

Step 3
IF all the current gross pay is taxable, multiply the current gross pay by the 7.65% combined rate.
IF some of the current gross pay is excluded from OASDI:

- Multiply the taxable portion of current gross pay by 6.2% (OASDI tax).
- Multiply all the current gross pay by 1.45% (Medicare tax).
- Add the results.

Examples:

Adam	Amy
$5,900 × .0765 = $451.35	$2,800 × .062 = $173.60 (OASDI)
	$7,500 × .0145 = $108.75 (Medicare)
	Total $282.35

Employer and Employee Identification Numbers

EIN

Every employer with one or more employees (including household employees) must have an employer identification number (EIN). An EIN is required on many forms and in employer correspondence with the Social Security Administration and employment-related matters with the Internal Revenue Service. An EIN can be found online at https://www.irs.gov/pub/irs-pdf/fss4.pdf.

Employee Identification (SSN)

Every employee and self-employed person must obtain a social security number (SSN). Application Form SS-5 is available from the Internal Revenue Service and the Social Security Administration and is filed with the Social Security Administration local office. The form is available online at www.ssa.gov/forms/ss-5.

Employer note: An ITIN Individual Tax Identification Number cannot be used as a substitute for a SSN for Form W-4. ITINs are used only for federal income tax reporting by foreign nationals and others who do not qualify for a SSN.

Employer FICA
Reporting

- An employer annually reports Social Security wages and withholding as part of Form W-2 with copies to employees, IRS, and state taxing authorities. (See page 125.).
- An employer also files quarterly reports to the IRS on either Forms 941 or 943 or annually on Form 944 for Social Security and Medicare wages, withholding, deposit obligation, and deposits made. (See pages 119, 139–141).
- An employer is also required to make timely deposits of withheld income tax and social security taxes. We discuss deposit requirements on pages 112–115, and 139.

Employer Over-
Withholding FICA

If an employer withholds excessive FICA from an employee, the employee can take the following actions:

1) Ask the employer for a refund of the excessive amount, as well as a corrected Form W-2, if there is a single employer.
2) If the employer does not provide the refund and corrected W-2, an employee can file Form 843, *Claim for Refund and Request for Abatement*. Calculate individually for joint return filers. (Non-resident aliens should also include Form 8316, *Information Regarding Request for Refund of Social Security Tax Erroneously Withheld on Wages Received by a Nonresident Alien on an F, J, or M Type Visa*.)
3) If the over-withholding is the result of having multiple employers during a year, the employee can claim a credit against tax on an individual tax return.

When a single employer becomes aware of the over-withholding, a refund should be provided to the employee that is over-withheld. As well, Form W-2c is used for corrected employee information reporting and Form 941-X is used for corrected quarterly payroll tax reporting.

Part III: Income Tax Withholding

Employee Income Tax

Overview

As we discussed on pages 5–9, it is very important for an organization to correctly determine the distinction between an employee and an independent contractor. This is true not only for FLSA purposes, but also for income tax withholding purposes. For workers who qualify as employees based

Employee Income Tax, *continued*

on common law, for income tax withholding purposes each pay period an employer must:

- Correctly determine each employee's taxable compensation
- Estimate each employee's income tax for the period
- Withhold the income tax from the gross amount earned by an employee, thereby reducing the amount paid to the employee
- Regularly forward the withheld amounts to taxing authorities according to a required payment procedure.

If an employer fails to correctly identify an employee or fails to properly follow the above requirements, significant penalties will be imposed by federal, state, and local taxing authorities, as applicable.

The following discussion in this section addresses each of the above points.

General Rule: Taxable Compensation

The federal income tax code refers to taxable gross income as "from whatever source derived" (code §61). Simply stated, what this means is that all income (even illegal income) is taxable unless it is otherwise excluded by law from taxation. State and local taxing authorities follow this same general procedure, using the federal approach as reference. Therefore, it follows that all employee compensation is taxable, unless a specified form of compensation is otherwise excluded by law by a particular taxing authority. IRS Publications 525, 515, 15, 15-A, 15-B can provide detailed guidance.

Employer Payments Exempt From Federal Income Tax Withholding

Overview

The table below shows a list of common payments to or on behalf of employees that are exempt from employee federal income tax (sometimes abbreviated "FIT") withholding. Most of the exempt categories below are for non-taxable payments or benefits. In some cases such as qualified retirement plans, the benefits are generally taxable to the beneficiary at a later date. These are called "tax-deferred plans". For all items, some state rules may vary from federal rules. Also see Publication 15-B related to fringe benefits.

continued ▶

Employer Payments Exempt From Federal Income Tax Withholding, *continued*

Table 2.2: Payments Exempt From Income Tax Withholding

Exempt Item	Description
Achievement Awards	Exempt up to $1,600 for qualified awards and $400 for non-qualified awards.
Adoption Expenses	If certain requirements are met, employer-paid adoption child adoption expenses are exempt, to a designated limit.
Advances to Employees (Also see reimbursements below)	Business-related expenses incurred by an employee under an accountable plan that includes reimbursements and repayments of excess
Accident Insurance	Employer-paid accident insurance premiums are not taxable to employees.
Combat Zone Pay	Pay received while serving in a designated combat is exempt.
Compensatory Damages	Compensatory damages from personal injury are exempt.
Deceased Employee	Wages, salaries, vacation pay and other compensation due an employee paid to the estate are exempt. (However, social security reporting and withholding is required for payments in year of death.)
Dependent Care	Employer payments to employees or third parties for dependent care under a qualified dependent care assistance program and/or the value of employer-maintained dependent care facilities use to a maximum of $5,000 ($2,500 married filing separately) are exempt.
Disability Benefits	Disability insurance benefits resulting from the portion of premium payments made by the recipient are exempt.
Disability Insurance	Disability insurance premiums paid by employer are exempt.
Employee Discounts	Subject to certain limitations, employer discounts on property other than real estate, stocks, and bonds purchased by employees are exempt.
Education and Tuition Payments	Annual payments up to $5,250 made by an employer under an education assistance plan to maintain or improve employee job skills are exempt for both active and former employees. Undergraduate and graduate tuition reduction by an educational institution is also generally exempt.

Employer Payments Exempt From Federal Income Tax Withholding, *continued*

Table 2.2: Payments Exempt From Income Tax Withholding *continued*

Exempt Item	Description
Family Member Employment	Child employed by parent: Exempt if for domestic work in a parent's home, or work is for payments other than in a trade or business and less than $50 per quarter, or the child is not regularly employed in such work.
Foreign Employment	Wages of a U.S. citizen or resident alien performing services for a foreign employer are exempt to the extent subject to income tax withholding by the foreign employer. Also exempt to the extent of the foreign earned income and housing exclusion under Internal Revenue Code §911.
Gifts	Small or minimal (called "de minimis") gifts and prizes, not including cash (except occasional local transportation fare), are excludable from employee gross wages and therefore exempt from withholding. Examples are small holiday gifts and food, occasional local transportation, snacks, and small parties.
Group-Term Life Insurance	Employer-paid group-term life insurance premium payments for a maximum $50,000 individual employee death benefit are exempt.
Health/Medical Insurance	Employer-paid health insurance premium payments for employees and their families are exempt, except for employees who own more than 2% of an S corporation making the payments.
Health Reimbursement Plans	Employer-paid contributions used to reimburse employee medical expenses are exempt. (Caution: in legal review)
Health Savings Accounts	Employer-paid contributions are exempt for qualified plans up to specified limits. Non-discrimination rules apply.
Homeworker	Exempt if a statutory employee.
Household Employees	Compensation is exempt from federal income tax withholding. (Note: Be sure to verify both household and employee status. Included are babysitters, caretakers, house cleaners and various other domestic workers who are not independent contractors. See IRS Publication 926.)
Long-Term Care Insurance	Employer-paid contributions as part of an accident or health plan are exempt from employee withholding.

continued ▶

Table 2.2: Payments Exempt From Income Tax Withholding *continued*

Exempt Item	Description
Meals and/or Lodging	The value of meals and/or lodging are not taxable to an employee if provided primarily for the benefit of the employer and are on the employment premises, and the lodging is a condition of employment. Occasional light meals (coffee, snacks, etc.) are exempt.
Ministerial Services	Ordained clergy, members of religious orders, and Christian Science practitioners are exempt from withholding for salary related to their ministerial services.
Newspaper Carriers/Vendors	Exempt if under 18; also, vendors buying at fixed prices and retaining receipts from retail sales to customers.
No-Additional Cost Services	Employer services provided to employees when no substantial additional cost will be incurred because of excess capacity are exempt.
Reimbursement of Business Expenses	Documented expenses incurred as part of employment (excluding commuting expense) by an employee and reimbursed according to a written plan are exempt.
Reimbursement of Moving Expenses	Employer-paid moving expense reimbursements are exempt if they would otherwise be deductible, according to moving expense deduction rules, if the employee had paid them.
Retirement Planning Services	Employer-paid retirement planning services are exempt when an employer maintains a qualified retirement plan.
Retirement Plans	Employer contributions to retirement plans are exempt according to plan rules (plans such as 401(k), 403(b), and 457(b) See following descriptions below.).
Transportation Benefits	Employee transportation benefits paid by an employer under a qualified written plan are exempt to designated monthly dollar limits. This includes commuter highway vehicles, parking, transit passes, and a qualified bicycle commuting agreement.
Incentive Stock Option Plans	Employers do not withhold income tax upon the exercise of qualified incentive stock options; however, the timely payment for any potential tax as the result of an alternative minimum tax effect is the responsibility of the employee.
Workers' Compensation	Employer payments for workers' compensation insurance, either into state funds or by private insurance contract, are exempt. Workers' compensation benefits are also generally not taxable unless received simultaneously with supplemental social security benefits.

Employer Payments Exempt From Federal Income Tax Withholding, *continued*

Table 2.2: Payments Exempt From Income Tax Withholding *continued*

Exempt Item	Description
Working Condition Benefits	Working condition benefits are services or property provided to an employee by an employer so that the employee is able to perform his or her duties. Examples are company-provided car, cell phone, computers, and training.
Exemption based on prior year tax liability	Employee is exempt from withholding if: ■ For the prior tax year there was a right to a full refund because there was no tax liability for that year, and ■ The employee expects the same condition to apply in the current tax year. The exemption is valid for one year. See IRS Publication 505 for further details.

Statutory Non-Employees

Persons who perform the following activities are considered to be independent contractors for both income tax and FICA employment tax purposes. This means that they are not subject to withholding for income tax or for FICA. (However, they must make quarterly estimated tax payments for income tax and self-employment tax.)

■ Direct sellers
■ Real estate agents
■ Household workers (e.g. baby sitters, caretakers, nannies, cooks), subject to specific requirements.

Review: Recall that specifically for FLSA employee designation purposes there are also certain exempt categories of activities. (See page 21–22)

Tip Income

Withholding on Tip Income

Employee tip income received either directly or indirectly (such as tip sharing or pooling) is includable as employee taxable income.

Employees are required to report tip income to the employer for any month in which tips exceed $20. Employees can use Form 4070-A or an equivalent daily written account for record keeping. Employees then report total monthly tips to the employer by the 10th day of the month following the month that is being reported, by using Form 4070. Fixed and required service charges added to bills and that are later distributed to employees are treated as wage income rather than tips.

continued ▶

Large food and beverage employers (normally more than 10 total employees on an average business day during the preceding year) must allocate tips to directly tipped employees. *The amount to be allocated* is the difference between 8% (or IRS approved lower rate) of gross receipts and total reported tips, when reported tips are less than 8% of the gross receipts. The allocation procedure is discussed below.

Allocated Tip Income

A large employer annually reports tip allocation to the IRS on Form 8027 for each individual establishment no later than February 28 following the year being reported (March 31 for electronic filing). See Form 8027 instructions for definitions, detailed calculation examples, and protocol for application for an IRS approved lower rate. An employer will select one of three methods to allocate tip income:

1) Hours-Worked Method: Businesses with less than 25 full-time equivalent employees may use this method. (Fewer than 200 employee hours worked per day meets this test.) Each employee's share is calculated using the following ratio: the hours worked by a tipped employee divided by the hours worked by all tipped employees. Note: a drawback to this method is that the amount of tips may be different for different shifts and that hours will not measure tips received.

2) Gross Receipts Method:

Step	Action
1	Calculate total direct tips as 8%(or a lower IRS-approved percentage) of gross receipts and subtract the amount of indirect tips.
2	Calculate each directly tipped employee's share of the Step 1 amount. For each directly tipped employee, multiply the Step 1 amount by the ratio (the fraction) of the gross receipts attributable to the employee to the gross receipts attributable to all employees.
3	For each directly tipped employee, determine if there is any reporting shortfall. Subtract the employee's reported tips from the amount in Step 2.
4	Calculate total shortfall based on the 8% allocation. From the amount in Step 1, subtract all reported tips by both directly and indirectly tipped employees.
5	For any employee who had a shortfall from Step 3, allocate his/her share of the total shortfall. Multiply the amount in Step 4 by the ratio of the employee's shortfall to the total of all employees with a shortfall.

continued ▶

3) Good-Faith Agreement: An allocation of the difference between 8% of gross receipts (no reduction for indirect tips) and total reported tips can be based on a written agreement between the employer and at least two-thirds of employees who receive tips.

Allocated tips are also reported on Form W-2, box 8 by January 31 and are part of total compensation on forms 941, 943, and 944 as applicable.

Overview of Tax-Deferred Retirement and Health Plans

General Description of Tax-Deferred Retirement Plans

These plans permit employees to reduce their gross income by making a contribution into a plan, typically with each paycheck for a designated dollar amount, that the employee instructs the employer to withhold. At the same time, the employer can also make a contribution on behalf on the employee subject to the same rules, if that is part of the arrangement.

In the current period, the employee contribution reduces the employee's pretax income (i.e. the amount is not taxed). As well, an employer's contribution is not taxed to the employee. In turn, the contributed amounts are invested according to choices available to the employee within a particular plan. While the contributions remain in the plan, gains and income are not taxed. The accumulated amount is later taxed when the employee retires or removes the amount from the plan, according to various rules. These plans usually have annual contribution and income limits that are often adjusted annually. Review plan details and limitations carefully.

Summary of Tax-Deferred Retirement Plans

In the summary of plans below, employee and employer contributions are tax-deferred, and an employer can take a deduction for the amount of contribution made. Because these plan rules are often quite detailed and because they change, further details are omitted here. IRS Publications 560, 571, 4460 and Department of Labor Publications 3998, 4222 and others provide additional details.

- 401(k): This qualified plan applies generally to for-profit employers to offer to their employees. This type of plan can also be set up by a sole proprietor. The current contribution limit is $18,500 and for age 50 and older is $24,500.
- 403(b): This qualified plan applies to tax-exempt organizations such as schools or hospitals to offer to employees. Features are similar to 401(k) plans

continued ▶

with lower administrative fees. The current contribution limit is $18,500 and for age 50 and older is $24,500.

- 457(b): This plan can be offered by state and local governments and other tax-exempt organizations, except churches. It has a number of different features and rules from 401(k) and 403(b) plans. It can be used simultaneously with a 403(b) plan. The current contribution limit is lesser of 100% of compensation or $18,500 and for age 50 and older is same income limit or $24,500.
- SEP-IRA: ("Simplified Employee Pension-Individual Retirement Account"). This is probably lowest-cost employer option, but lacks some features available in a 401(k) plan. The plan is generally used by smaller businesses, including sole proprietors. Contributions are made by the employer both for the employer and employees. The current contribution limit is lesser of 25% of compensation or $55,000 per employee and must be proportional.
- SIMPLE IRA: ("Savings Incentive Match Plan for Employees") This plan is for businesses with 100 employees or less, including sole proprietors, and has different rules than a SEP-IRA. The employer makes both employer and employee contributions, but employees make the majority of the contributions, which are exempt from withholding. The current contribution limit is $12,500 and for age 50 and older is $15,500 per employee.

Note: the identifying numerical designations shown above are simply references to sections of Internal Revenue Code that describe the plans.

Individual Retirement Accounts

Individuals can also set up their own retirement plans, subject to contribution limits. If an individual is also a participant in an employer plan, rules reduce the amount of allowed tax-deferred contributions.

- IRA ("Individual Retirement Account"): This is often called a "traditional" IRA. Individuals must have earned income as an employee in order to make tax-deferred contributions. Gains and income within the plan are tax-free, but are taxed upon distribution. The current contribution limit is $5,500 and for age 50 and older is $6,500.
- Roth IRA: Contributions to this type of IRA are after-tax; in other words, there is no tax-deferral for the contributions. However, all gains and income are non-taxable within the plan, and distributions are also tax-free. The current contribution limit is $5,500 and for age 50 and older is $6,500.

ERISA

ERISA (Employee Retirement Income Security of 1974) is a federal law that sets the minimum standards for most non-governmental, non-church, employee retirement and health plans. ERISA also does not apply to non-U.S. plans that are primarily for the benefit of non-resident aliens. ERISA was created to ensure

continued ▶

Overview of Tax-Deferred Retirement and Health Plans, *continued*

that workers who are retirement plan participants would receive the proper amount of benefits in accordance with their years of service and particular plan features. The key ERSIA requirements are:

- Plan information: Particpants must receive plan information that explains the features of the plan, minimum standards for participation, how the plan will be funded, information on plan assets and investment results, how benefits accrue, how the plan will be managed and the responibilities of managing the plan, and greivance and appeals procedures.

Plans can be "defined benefit" or "defined contribution". A defined benefit plan is designed to provide a fixed amount of retirement payments. This plan may require changes (usually increases) in contributions depending on investment results, but provides a predictable source of retirement income. A defined contribution plan is designed to maintain a fixed amount of contribution, and the ultimate amount of retirement payments depend on investment results and cannot be determined in advance. Because the Pension Protection Act of 2006 required that pension providers fully fund defined benefit plans, most companies have been shifting to defined contribution plans.

- Regulation of funds: ERISA regulates how funds can be obtained and how funds can be disbursed.
- Vesting: "Vesting" means the right of an employee to receive payment if they terminate employment prior to retirement. Vesting is based on years of service required in order to receive full or partial payment. Upon full vesting, an employee has the right to full retirement benefits, regardless of whether the employee is working for the same or a different employer.
- Termination of a defined benefit plan: If a defined benefit plan is terminated, ERISA guarantees designated benefit payments thourgh the Pension Benefit Guaranty Corporation (below) created by ERISA.
- Reporting: The plan administratior must file either Form 5500 or 5500-SF depending on the number of participants in a plan. The due date is the last day of the seventh following the end of a plan year. Note: one-participant and foreign plans not subject to ERISA file form 5500-EZ.
- Document Retention: Documents described should be retained for at least six years from date of document.

Pension Benefit Guarantee Corporation

The Pension Benefit Guarantee Corporation (PBGC) is an independent federal agency created by ERISA for the primary purpose of guaranteeing that workers receive at least basic pension benefits for defined benefit pension plans that have been terminated without sufficient funds to pay promised benefits ("distress" termination). The amount that a worker receives depends upon age or service and other factors. The current annual maximum benefit amount for a

continued ▶

worker at age 65 is approximately $60,000, and lower for younger workers or with fewer years of service. The PBGC additionally attempts to recover funds from employers terminating plans. The PBGC also supervises payouts of financially sound funds that terminate ("standard" termination) by lump sum or annuity.

The PBGC is funded by insurance premiums paid by employers with defined benefit pension plans. The amount of the premium depends on the number participants in a plan. Because companies have been shifting to defined contribution plans, there is substantially less insurance premium funding, and in the future the PBGC may require taxpayer funds to continue operating.

Overview of Health-Related Plans

The plans below are specifically intended for the payment of medical and health-related expenses. Plan limits and requirements differ. See Publication 969 for further details.

- *Flexible spending account (FSA):* An FSA allows employees to contribute pre-tax amounts to pay for eligible medical expenses for themselves, spouses, and dependents. The employer initially funds a savings account that is used to pay medical expenses and is reimbursed as employees make payments. Generally employee contributions must be used within the plan year or they a forfeited, subject to a possible grace period, to the employer for any plan losses and administrative costs. The current contribution limit is $2,650.
- *Health savings account (HSA):* This plan is set up by individuals with high health insurance deductibles. Contributions are deductible by an individual without needing to itemize (but are not pre-tax contributions). Employer contributions are deductible for the employer and not included in employee income. Interest earnings accumulate tax deferred; payments for medical expenses are tax-free. Account balances are carried to the next year. The current contribution limits are $3,450 for singles and $6,900 for families. For age 50 and older limits are $4,450 and $7,900.
- *Health reimbursement arrangement (HRA):* This is a plan set up and entirely funded by an employer for the purpose of reimbursing employees and former employees tax-free for eligible medical expenses. Employer contributions are unlimited and are not included in employee income. HRA's can be used in combination with other health plans. Account balances are carried to the next year. These plans generally result in more personalized benefits. For small businesses (less than 50 employees) a qualified small business employee health reimbursement arrangement is available (QSEHRA) with annual contribution limits of $5,050 for singles and $10,250 for families.

Withholding Allowances and How They Are Determined

What Is a Withholding Allowance?

The underlying idea of income tax withholding is to make, during the course of a year, a prepayment that roughly approximates the total income tax that will be due at year-end. A withholding allowance reduces the amount withheld; in effect, each allowance is an estimate of a reduction in taxable income. For example, in 2018 each allowance equates to a $4,150 reduction in taxable income. The following discussion explains the allowances in greater detail.

Additional Allowances

Keep in mind that the idea of withholding is to approximate the amount of tax due at year-end. In certain cases taxpayers may have various other deductions, investment or business losses, or credits that will reduce the tax. To reduce the potential for tax overpayment, i.e., over-withholding, additional allowances are permitted. Therefore, the number of "allowances" are simply for the purpose of withholding and do not actually appear as a deduction on an individual income tax return. The Internal Revenue Service provides a worksheet that an employee can use to calculate the correct number of withholding allowances, which are then entered on Form W-4, described below.

Form W-4

- Form W-4, called *Employee's Withholding Allowance Certificate*, is used by an employer to calculate an employee's withholding each pay period. An employee completes a W-4 when beginning employment. If the employee status changes, the employee can prepare an amended W-4. The new withholding then becomes effective not later than the beginning of the first payroll period ending on or after 30 days from the date the employer received the new form.
- An employer must retain the W-4 form on file for all employees until 4 years following employee departure. An employer does not file any W-4 forms with the IRS unless requested to do so by an IRS written notice. If a W-4 is not prepared, the employer must withhold as if the employee were single with no allowances.
- Employers can make online W-4 filing available, but must make paper copies available to any employee who does not want to use the electronic system.
- If an employee does not have a social security number, he or she should apply for one by completing and mailing in Form SS-5, which is available online. The form can also be taken to a local Social Security office. A list of these offices are available at https://secure.ssa.gov/apps6z/FOLO/fo001.jsp

Withholding Allowances and How They Are Determined, *continued*

TIP

You can find current W-4 information by going to the IRS website at www.irs.gov/w4. Individuals should also see Publication 505.

Illustration 2.1: Form W-4

Form **W-4** Department of the Treasury Internal Revenue Service	**Employee's Withholding Allowance Certificate** ▶ Whether you're entitled to claim a certain number of allowances or exemption from withholding is subject to review by the IRS. Your employer may be required to send a copy of this form to the IRS.	OMB No. 1545-0074 20**18**

1 Your first name and middle initial	Last name	2 Your social security number

Home address (number and street or rural route)	3 ☐ Single ☐ Married ☐ Married, but withhold at higher Single rate. **Note:** If married filing separately, check "Married, but withhold at higher Single rate."
City or town, state, and ZIP code	4 If your last name differs from that shown on your social security card, check here. You must call 800-772-1213 for a replacement card. ▶ ☐

5	Total number of allowances you're claiming (from the applicable worksheet on the following pages) . . .	5	
6	Additional amount, if any, you want withheld from each paycheck	6	$
7	I claim exemption from withholding for 2018, and I certify that I meet **both** of the following conditions for exemption.		
	• Last year I had a right to a refund of **all** federal income tax withheld because I had **no** tax liability, **and**		
	• This year I expect a refund of **all** federal income tax withheld because I expect to have **no** tax liability.		
	If you meet both conditions, write "Exempt" here . . . . ▶	7	

Under penalties of perjury, I declare that I have examined this certificate and, to the best of my knowledge and belief, it is true, correct, and complete.

Employee's signature
(This form is not valid unless you sign it.) ▶   Date ▶

8 Employer's name and address (**Employer:** Complete boxes 8 and 10 if sending to IRS and complete boxes 8, 9, and 10 if sending to State Directory of New Hires.)	9 First date of employment	10 Employer identification number (EIN)

For Privacy Act and Paperwork Reduction Act Notice, see page 4.   Cat. No. 10220Q   Form **W-4** (2018)

Source: Internal Revenue Service

Exemption From Withholding

In some circumstances an employee can be exempt from withholding. An employee is qualified for exempt status if:

- For the prior tax year there was a right to a full refund because there was no tax liability for that year, and
- The employee expects the same condition to apply in the current tax year.

In some cases the employer and employee may receive a follow-up notice from the Internal Revenue Service limiting the number of allowances until additional information is provided by the employee to the IRS.

The exemption is valid for one year; therefore, a new W-4 must be completed each year. Employees may not claim exemption from withholding if they are

continued ▶

claimed on another's tax return, and their employee income exceeds $1,050 per year with unearned income (not wage income) of more than $350, or less than $350 of unearned income but more than $6,300 total income.

Additional Withholding

Employees with other sources of income and/or insufficient withholding may wish to amend Form W-4 and increase their withholding, so that they do not incur penalties for underpayment of tax when they file their tax returns. Examples of when this can occur are:

- Significant amount of interest, dividends, or asset sales
- Two-wage earner married couples
- Domestic workers in a private residence
- Members of the clergy

Estimated Tax Payments

Employees with other income that does not involve employer withholding can also make estimated tax payments. This is usually needed for individuals with other sources of income that are substantially more significant than their wages. These payments increase tax payments, but are not in lieu of withholding. Estimated tax payments are made by completing Form 1040-ES worksheet and vouchers with payment. States have similar forms.

Non-Resident Alien Withholding

Exclusive of tax treaties, nonresident aliens will incur a 30% federal tax rate for most types of income. Employee withholding is required at the time a person realizes income whether or not cash or property is received, as long as the payment is made for the person's benefit.

Federal withholding is generally required at a 30% rate unless exceptions apply. As well, employers are required to add an amount to wages only for the purpose of determining the withholding. Refer to Publication 15, Chapter 9, for table and instructions, and pages 158–159 in Section 6.

In completing Form W-4, a nonresident alien (See Section 6) individual should note the following:

- Check "single" on line 3 regardless of marital status
- Claim only one withholding allowance unless a resident of Canada, Mexico, or South Korea, or a U.S. national.
- Write "Nonresident Alien" or "NRA" above the dotted line on line 6.

continued ▶

Determination by the IRS	In some cases, an employer may receive a written notice called a *lock-in letter* from the IRS to increase the income tax withholding on a particular employee; the letter will specify the maximum number of allowances. A copy of this should be provided to the employee. An employee may submit additional information to the IRS to revise the number of allowances; however, an employer cannot change the number of allowances until approval from the IRS is received. An employer must wait at least 45 days from the letter date before implementing the lock-in letter allowance limit. If the person is no longer an employee, no further action is required. An employer who does not implement the maximum becomes liable for paying the additional amount of tax that should have been withheld.
Backup Withholding: Miscellaneous Income	Federal backup withholding is required at a 24% rate on certain types of miscellaneous income payments if a taxpayer identification number is not provided and the payments are $600 or more. Payment types subject to backup withholding are: interest, dividends, rents, royalties, payments to independent contractors, payments from brokers for stock and bond transactions, and payments from fishing boat operators. Payment is reported at year-end on Form 1099 series, depending on the type of payment. (See page 135)
State Requirements	Different states may have different withholding requirements. Be sure to check with your individual state for guidelines.
Withholding on Tips	Employers are required to withhold both income tax and FICA taxes on employees' net cash tips, received directly or indirectly, reported by employees on Form 4070 or equivalent, as well as on their wages. If an employee reports tips and also earns wages, the amounts are combined for income tax withholding calculation. Withholding on allocated tips is not required.
	Wages for tipped employees are often minimal As a result, when an employee receives a paycheck for wages, the withholding will be calculated on both reported tips plus wages; however, because the wages are a small amount, they may not be sufficient to cover the required withholding. In this case, the withholding shortfall carries over to subsequent payroll periods. The employer is required to apply withholding in the following order: 1) Social Security and Medicare tax on wages 2) federal income tax on wages 3) state and local income tax on wages 4) Social Security and Medicare tax on tips 5) federal income tax on tips 6) state and local income tax on tips

Withholding Allowances and How They Are Determined, *continued*

If this situation occurs, the employer should notify the employee that to avoid year-end underpayment of tax penalties he or she can: 1) Give the employer cash in order to make the additional withholding payments, or 2) Make his or her own estimated tax payments using Form 1040-ES.

Other Income Automatic Withholding for Employees	For employees, withholding applies to more than just salary and wages. It also applies to any taxable income related to employees: pensions, annuities, stock bonus plans, profit sharing, and deferred compensation income. All of these payments are treated as the equivalent of wages for tax withholding purposes. Withholding will automatically be made based on a filing status of married with three allowances UNLESS the recipient elects to change withholding by completing Form W-4P. A W-4P remains in effect until the recipient revokes or changes it. Finally, if an employee fails to submit a correct W-4, withholding status is single, with no allowances.

How does a business obtain a taxpayer identification number as an alternative to 24% backup withholding? The business requests that a Form W-9 be completed by the party being paid by the business. A W-9 request is a valid request only for non-employee income, as explained above. For non-resident aliens or foreign businesses, use a Form W-8 (various types depending on entity). Note: for persons ineligible for a social security number, use Form W-7 to obtain an ITIN: Individual Tax Identification Number.

Small business tax guide: In addition to the payroll publications available such as Publications 15, 15-A, 15-B and others, the IRS also provides a publication specifically for small businesses: Publication 334.

continued

Withholding Allowances and How They Are Determined, *continued*

Illustration 2.2

Form **W-9** (Rev. November 2017) Department of the Treasury Internal Revenue Service	**Request for Taxpayer** **Identification Number and Certification** ▶ Go to *www.irs.gov/FormW9* for instructions and the latest information.	**Give Form to the requester. Do not send to the IRS.**

Print or type.
See Specific Instructions on page 3.

1 Name (as shown on your income tax return). Name is required on this line; do not leave this line blank.

2 Business name/disregarded entity name, if different from above

3 Check appropriate box for federal tax classification of the person whose name is entered on line 1. Check only **one** of the following seven boxes.

☐ Individual/sole proprietor or single-member LLC   ☐ C Corporation   ☐ S Corporation   ☐ Partnership   ☐ Trust/estate

☐ Limited liability company. Enter the tax classification (C=C corporation, S=S corporation, P=Partnership) ▶ _____

Note: Check the appropriate box in the line above for the tax classification of the single-member owner. Do not check LLC if the LLC is classified as a single-member LLC that is disregarded from the owner unless the owner of the LLC is another LLC that is **not** disregarded from the owner for U.S. federal tax purposes. Otherwise, a single-member LLC that is disregarded from the owner should check the appropriate box for the tax classification of its owner.

☐ Other (see instructions) ▶

4 Exemptions (codes apply only to certain entities, not individuals; see instructions on page 3):

Exempt payee code (if any) _____

Exemption from FATCA reporting code (if any) _____

(Applies to accounts maintained outside the U.S.)

5 Address (number, street, and apt. or suite no.) See instructions.

Requester's name and address (optional)

6 City, state, and ZIP code

7 List account number(s) here (optional)

Part I   Taxpayer Identification Number (TIN)

Enter your TIN in the appropriate box. The TIN provided must match the name given on line 1 to avoid backup withholding. For individuals, this is generally your social security number (SSN). However, for a resident alien, sole proprietor, or disregarded entity, see the instructions for Part I, later. For other entities, it is your employer identification number (EIN). If you do not have a number, see *How to get a TIN*, later.

Note: If the account is in more than one name, see the instructions for line 1. Also see *What Name and Number To Give the Requester* for guidelines on whose number to enter.

Social security number

☐☐☐ – ☐☐ – ☐☐☐☐

or

Employer identification number

☐☐ – ☐☐☐☐☐☐☐

Part II   Certification

Under penalties of perjury, I certify that:

1. The number shown on this form is my correct taxpayer identification number (or I am waiting for a number to be issued to me); and

2. I am not subject to backup withholding because: (a) I am exempt from backup withholding, or (b) I have not been notified by the Internal Revenue Service (IRS) that I am subject to backup withholding as a result of a failure to report all interest or dividends, or (c) the IRS has notified me that I am no longer subject to backup withholding; and

3. I am a U.S. citizen or other U.S. person (defined below); and

4. The FATCA code(s) entered on this form (if any) indicating that I am exempt from FATCA reporting is correct.

Certification instructions. You must cross out item 2 above if you have been notified by the IRS that you are currently subject to backup withholding because you have failed to report all interest and dividends on your tax return. For real estate transactions, item 2 does not apply. For mortgage interest paid, acquisition or abandonment of secured property, cancellation of debt, contributions to an individual retirement arrangement (IRA), and generally, payments other than interest and dividends, you are not required to sign the certification, but you must provide your correct TIN. See the instructions for Part II, later.

Sign Here   Signature of U.S. person ▶   Date ▶

General Instructions

Section references are to the Internal Revenue Code unless otherwise noted.

Future developments. For the latest information about developments related to Form W-9 and its instructions, such as legislation enacted after they were published, go to *www.irs.gov/FormW9*.

Purpose of Form

An individual or entity (Form W-9 requester) who is required to file an information return with the IRS must obtain your correct taxpayer identification number (TIN) which may be your social security number (SSN), individual taxpayer identification number (ITIN), adoption taxpayer identification number (ATIN), or employer identification number (EIN), to report on an information return the amount paid to you, or other amount reportable on an information return. Examples of information returns include, but are not limited to, the following.

• Form 1099-INT (interest earned or paid)

• Form 1099-DIV (dividends, including those from stocks or mutual funds)

• Form 1099-MISC (various types of income, prizes, awards, or gross proceeds)

• Form 1099-B (stock or mutual fund sales and certain other transactions by brokers)

• Form 1099-S (proceeds from real estate transactions)

• Form 1099-K (merchant card and third party network transactions)

• Form 1098 (home mortgage interest), 1098-E (student loan interest), 1098-T (tuition)

• Form 1099-C (canceled debt)

• Form 1099-A (acquisition or abandonment of secured property)

Use Form W-9 only if you are a U.S. person (including a resident alien), to provide your correct TIN.

If you do not return Form W-9 to the requester with a TIN, you might be subject to backup withholding. See What is backup withholding, later.

Cat. No. 10231X   Form **W-9** (Rev. 11-2017)

Source: Internal Revenue Service

Calculating Income Tax Withholding

Overview

At this point, we have discussed what compensation is subject to income tax withholding, what allowances are and their effect on withholding, and the W-4 form that is used to determine the proper number of allowances.

In this discussion we review how to calculate income tax withholding. For manual calculation, either the *percentage method* or the *wage-bracket* method is most often used. To use these methods we refer to the tables illustrated below. As previously mentioned, the purpose of tax withholding is to make prepayments that will as accurately as possible approximate the tax due at year-end. In order to do this, several factors must be incorporated into the tables. As you look at the tables below, note the following factors:

1) Number of allowances: allowances account for deductions against income resulting from additional deductible expenses and losses.
2) Filing status: (single, married, or head of household) filing status affects both the tax rate and the basic *standard deduction* allowed all taxpayers according to filing status (instead of using itemized deductions), which is built into the tables. Note: an additional standard amount of deduction is added to the basic standard deduction when a tax return is prepared at year-end for taxpayers and dependents 65 or older and/or blind.
3) Gross wages: As gross wages increase or decrease both the amount and percentage rate of tax increases or decreases.
4) Pay period: A portion of the total tax is allocated equally into each pay period during the year.

**Example 1:
Percentage
Method**

The percentage method is often used by employers with automated payroll systems. The following example shows a manual calculation. Assume that Wilson Smith is married and claims three withholding allowances. He is paid monthly and this month earned gross wages of $5,420. (Refer to Table 2.3 below.)

continued

Calculating Income Tax Withholding, *continued*

Step	Action	Example
1	Determine the gross wages	Given as $5,420 for the month.
2	Identify the value of one withholding allowance	From Table 2.3: For monthly pay period: $345.80
3	Multiply the number of allowances by step 2 value.	3 × $345.80 = $1,037.40
4	Subtract the step 3 amount from gross pay to find "excess".	$5,420. – $1,037.40 = $4,382.60
5	Determine withholding amount by reference to correct percentage method tax table for filing status and period (Illustration 2.3).	Gross wage range for "married", "monthly" table: $2,550 to $7,413 Calculation: .12 × ($4,382.60 – $2,550) + $158.70 = $378.61 monthly withholding

Table 2.3: Percentage Method (2018 Allowance Values) One Withholding Allowance

Payroll Period	One Withholding Allowance
Weekly	$ 79.80
Biweekly	159.60
Semimonthly	172.90
Monthly	345.80
Quarterly	1,037.50
Semiannually	2,075.00
Annually	4,150.00
Daily or Miscellaneous per Day	16.00

Calculating Income Tax Withholding, *continued*

Example 2:
Percentage
Method

Sandra Smith is single and claims two withholding allowances. Her gross pay is $2,618, paid semimonthly. (Refer to Table 2.3 above.)

Step	Action	Example
1	Determine the gross wages	Given as $2,618 for the semimonthly pay period.
2	Identify the value of one withholding allowance	From Table 2.3: For a semimonthly pay period: $172.90
3	Multiply the number of allowances by step 2 value.	2 × $172.90 = $345.80
4	Subtract the step 3 amount from gross pay to find "excess".	$2,618. – $345.80 = $2,272.20
5	Determine withholding amount by reference to correct percentage method table for filing status and pay period (Illustration 2.3).	Gross wage range for "single", "semimonthly" table: $1,767 to $3,592 Calculation: .22 × ($2,272.20 – $1,767) + $185.62 = $296.76 semimonthly withholding

continued

Calculating Income Tax Withholding, *continued*

Illustration 2.3

Percentage Method Tables for Income Tax Withholding

(For Wages Paid in 2018)

TABLE 1—WEEKLY Payroll Period

(a) SINGLE person (including head of household)—				(b) MARRIED person—			
If the amount of wages (after subtracting withholding allowances) is:		The amount of income tax to withhold is:		If the amount of wages (after subtracting withholding allowances) is:		The amount of income tax to withhold is:	
Not over $71		$0		Not over $222		$0	
Over—	But not over—		of excess over—	Over—	But not over—		of excess over—
$71	—$254 . .	$0.00 plus 10%	—$71	$222	—$588 . .	$0.00 plus 10%	—$222
$254	—$815 . .	$18.30 plus 12%	—$254	$588	—$1,711 . .	$36.60 plus 12%	—$588
$815	—$1,658 . .	$85.62 plus 22%	—$815	$1,711	—$3,395 . .	$171.36 plus 22%	—$1,711
$1,658	—$3,100 . .	$271.08 plus 24%	—$1,658	$3,395	—$6,280 . .	$541.84 plus 24%	—$3,395
$3,100	—$3,917 . .	$617.16 plus 32%	—$3,100	$6,280	—$7,914 . .	$1,234.24 plus 32%	—$6,280
$3,917	—$9,687 . .	$878.60 plus 35%	—$3,917	$7,914	—$11,761 . .	$1,757.12 plus 35%	—$7,914
$9,687	. . . .	$2,898.10 plus 37%	—$9,687	$11,761	. . . .	$3,103.57 plus 37%	—$11,761

TABLE 2—BIWEEKLY Payroll Period

(a) SINGLE person (including head of household)—				(b) MARRIED person—			
If the amount of wages (after subtracting withholding allowances) is:		The amount of income tax to withhold is:		If the amount of wages (after subtracting withholding allowances) is:		The amount of income tax to withhold is:	
Not over $142		$0		Not over $444		$0	
Over—	But not over—		of excess over—	Over—	But not over—		of excess over—
$142	—$509 . .	$0.00 plus 10%	—$142	$444	—$1,177 . .	$0.00 plus 10%	—$444
$509	—$1,631 . .	$36.70 plus 12%	—$509	$1,177	—$3,421 . .	$73.30 plus 12%	—$1,177
$1,631	—$3,315 . .	$171.34 plus 22%	—$1,631	$3,421	—$6,790 . .	$342.58 plus 22%	—$3,421
$3,315	—$6,200 . .	$541.82 plus 24%	—$3,315	$6,790	—$12,560 . .	$1,083.76 plus 24%	—$6,790
$6,200	—$7,835 . .	$1,234.22 plus 32%	—$6,200	$12,560	—$15,829 . .	$2,468.56 plus 32%	—$12,560
$7,835	—$19,373 . .	$1,757.42 plus 35%	—$7,835	$15,829	—$23,521 . .	$3,514.64 plus 35%	—$15,829
$19,373	. . . .	$5,795.72 plus 37%	—$19,373	$23,521	. . . .	$6,206.84 plus 37%	—$23,521

TABLE 3—SEMIMONTHLY Payroll Period

(a) SINGLE person (including head of household)—				(b) MARRIED person—			
If the amount of wages (after subtracting withholding allowances) is:		The amount of income tax to withhold is:		If the amount of wages (after subtracting withholding allowances) is:		The amount of income tax to withhold is:	
Not over $154		$0		Not over $481		$0	
Over—	But not over—		of excess over—	Over—	But not over—		of excess over—
$154	—$551 . .	$0.00 plus 10%	—$154	$481	—$1,275 . .	$0.00 plus 10%	—$481
$551	—$1,767 . .	$39.70 plus 12%	—$551	$1,275	—$3,706 . .	$79.40 plus 12%	—$1,275
$1,767	—$3,592 . .	$185.62 plus 22%	—$1,767	$3,706	—$7,356 . .	$371.12 plus 22%	—$3,706
$3,592	—$6,717 . .	$587.12 plus 24%	—$3,592	$7,356	—$13,606 . .	$1,174.12 plus 24%	—$7,356
$6,717	—$8,488 . .	$1,337.12 plus 32%	—$6,717	$13,606	—$17,148 . .	$2,674.12 plus 32%	—$13,606
$8,488	—$20,988 . .	$1,903.84 plus 35%	—$8,488	$17,148	—$25,481 . .	$3,807.56 plus 35%	—$17,148
$20,988	. . . .	$6,278.84 plus 37%	—$20,988	$25,481	. . . .	$6,724.11 plus 37%	—$25,481

TABLE 4—MONTHLY Payroll Period

(a) SINGLE person (including head of household)—				(b) MARRIED person—			
If the amount of wages (after subtracting withholding allowances) is:		The amount of income tax to withhold is:		If the amount of wages (after subtracting withholding allowances) is:		The amount of income tax to withhold is:	
Not over $308		$0		Not over $963		$0	
Over—	But not over—		of excess over—	Over—	But not over—		of excess over—
$308	—$1,102 . .	$0.00 plus 10%	—$308	$963	—$2,550 . .	$0.00 plus 10%	—$963
$1,102	—$3,533 . .	$79.40 plus 12%	—$1,102	$2,550	—$7,413 . .	$158.70 plus 12%	—$2,550
$3,533	—$7,183 . .	$371.12 plus 22%	—$3,533	$7,413	—$14,713 . .	$742.26 plus 22%	—$7,413
$7,183	—$13,433 . .	$1,174.12 plus 24%	—$7,183	$14,713	—$27,213 . .	$2,348.26 plus 24%	—$14,713
$13,433	—$16,975 . .	$2,674.12 plus 32%	—$13,433	$27,213	—$34,296 . .	$5,348.26 plus 32%	—$27,213
$16,975	—$41,975 . .	$3,807.56 plus 35%	—$16,975	$34,296	—$50,963 . .	$7,614.82 plus 35%	—$34,296
$41,975	. . . .	$12,557.56 plus 37%	—$41,975	$50,963	. . . .	$13,448.27 plus 37%	—$50,963

Source: Internal Revenue Service

Calculating Income Tax Withholding, *continued*

**Example 1:
Wage-Bracket
Method**

Assume that Wilson Smith is married and claims three withholding allowances. He is paid monthly and this month earned gross wages of $5,420.

Step	Action	Example
1	Refer to the wage-bracket method table that shows the correct filing status and pay period	Select the table for "Married Persons— Monthly Pay Period" (See Illustration 2.4)
2	Locate the wage range row for gross income in left columns.	Range: $5,390 – $5,430
3	Locate the column with number of allowances claimed. Follow the column down until it intersects with the row for step 2.	Three allowances Withholding: $377.

TIP

Current standard deductions (that are built into wage bracket tables):

- Single: $12,000
- Head of household: $18,000
- Married filing jointly: $24,000

TIP

An IRS withholding calculator is available online at: *https://www.irs.gov /individuals/irs-withholding-calculator.* The calculator is for new tax rates from the "Tax Cuts and Jobs Act" enacted December 2017.

continued ▶

Calculating Income Tax Withholding, *continued*

Illustration 2.4

Wage Bracket Method Tables for Income Tax Withholding

MARRIED Persons—**MONTHLY** Payroll Period

(For Wages Paid through December 31, 2018)

And the wages are—		And the number of withholding allowances claimed is—										
At least	But less than	0	1	2	3	4	5	6	7	8	9	10
		The amount of income tax to be withheld is—										
$3,710	$3,750	$300	$259	$217	$176	$138	$104	$69	$35	$0	$0	$0
3,750	3,790	305	264	222	181	142	108	73	39	4	0	0
3,790	3,830	310	268	227	185	146	112	77	43	8	0	0
3,830	3,870	315	273	232	190	150	116	81	47	12	0	0
3,870	3,910	320	278	237	195	154	120	85	51	16	0	0
3,910	3,950	324	283	241	200	158	124	89	55	20	0	0
3,950	3,990	329	288	246	205	163	128	93	59	24	0	0
3,990	4,030	334	292	251	209	168	132	97	63	28	0	0
4,030	4,070	339	297	256	214	173	136	101	67	32	0	0
4,070	4,110	344	302	261	219	178	140	105	71	36	2	0
4,110	4,150	348	307	265	224	182	144	109	75	40	6	0
4,150	4,190	353	312	270	229	187	148	113	79	44	10	0
4,190	4,230	358	316	275	233	192	152	117	83	48	14	0
4,230	4,270	363	321	280	238	197	156	121	87	52	18	0
4,270	4,310	368	326	285	243	202	160	125	91	56	22	0
4,310	4,350	372	331	289	248	206	165	129	95	60	26	0
4,350	4,390	377	336	294	253	211	170	133	99	64	30	0
4,390	4,430	382	340	299	257	216	174	137	103	68	34	0
4,430	4,470	387	345	304	262	221	179	141	107	72	38	3
4,470	4,510	392	350	309	267	226	184	145	111	76	42	7
4,510	4,550	396	355	313	272	230	189	149	115	80	46	11
4,550	4,590	401	360	318	277	235	194	153	119	84	50	15
4,590	4,630	406	364	323	281	240	198	157	123	88	54	19
4,630	4,670	411	369	328	286	245	203	162	127	92	58	23
4,670	4,710	416	374	333	291	250	208	167	131	96	62	27
4,710	4,750	420	379	337	296	254	213	171	135	100	66	31
4,750	4,790	425	384	342	301	259	218	176	139	104	70	35
4,790	4,830	430	388	347	305	264	222	181	143	108	74	39
4,830	4,870	435	393	352	310	269	227	186	147	112	78	43
4,870	4,910	440	398	357	315	274	232	191	151	116	82	47
4,910	4,950	444	403	361	320	278	237	195	155	120	86	51
4,950	4,990	449	408	366	325	283	242	200	159	124	90	55
4,990	5,030	454	412	371	329	288	246	205	163	128	94	59
5,030	5,070	459	417	376	334	293	251	210	168	132	98	63
5,070	5,110	464	422	381	339	298	256	215	173	136	102	67
5,110	5,150	468	427	385	344	302	261	219	178	140	106	71
5,150	5,190	473	432	390	349	307	266	224	183	144	110	75
5,190	5,230	478	436	395	353	312	270	229	187	148	114	79
5,230	5,270	483	441	400	358	317	275	234	192	152	118	83
5,270	5,310	488	446	405	363	322	280	239	197	156	122	87
5,310	5,350	492	451	409	368	326	285	243	202	160	126	91
5,350	5,390	497	456	414	373	331	290	248	207	165	130	95
5,390	5,430	502	460	419	377	336	294	253	211	170	134	99
5,430	5,470	507	465	424	382	341	299	258	216	175	138	103
5,470	5,510	512	470	429	387	346	304	263	221	180	142	107
5,510	5,550	516	475	433	392	350	309	267	226	184	146	111
5,550	5,590	521	480	438	397	355	314	272	231	189	150	115
5,590	5,630	526	484	443	401	360	318	277	235	194	154	119
5,630	5,670	531	489	448	406	365	323	282	240	199	158	123
5,670	5,710	536	494	453	411	370	328	287	245	204	162	127
5,710	5,750	540	499	457	416	374	333	291	250	208	167	131
5,750	5,790	545	504	462	421	379	338	296	255	213	172	135
5,790	5,830	550	508	467	425	384	342	301	259	218	176	139
5,830	5,870	555	513	472	430	389	347	306	264	223	181	143
5,870	5,910	560	518	477	435	394	352	311	269	228	186	147
5,910	5,950	564	523	481	440	398	357	315	274	232	191	151
5,950	5,990	569	528	486	445	403	362	320	279	237	196	155
5,990	6,030	574	532	491	449	408	366	325	283	242	200	159
6,030	6,070	579	537	496	454	413	371	330	288	247	205	164
6,070	6,110	584	542	501	459	418	376	335	293	252	210	169
6,110	6,150	588	547	505	464	422	381	339	298	256	215	173
6,150	6,190	593	552	510	469	427	386	344	303	261	220	178
6,190	6,230	598	556	515	473	432	390	349	307	266	224	183
6,230	6,270	603	561	520	478	437	395	354	312	271	229	188
6,270	6,310	608	566	525	483	442	400	359	317	276	234	193
6,310	6,350	612	571	529	488	446	405	363	322	280	239	197

Source: Internal Revenue Service

Calculating Income Tax Withholding, *continued*

Example 2:
Wage-Bracket
Method

Jennifer Chang is single and claims one allowance. During her current monthly pay period she earned $4,125 of gross pay.

Step	Action	Example
1	Refer to the wage-bracket method table that shows the correct filing status and pay period	Select the table for "Single Persons—Monthly Pay Period" (See Illustration 2.5)
2	Locate the wage range row for gross income in left columns.	Range: $4,125 – $4,165
3	Locate the column with number of allowances claimed. Follow the column down until it intersects with the row for step 2.	One allowance Withholding: $430.

Other Table Issues

When using the wage-bracket table:

IF	THEN
There are more than 10 allowances,	▪ Withhold for only 10 allowances OR ▪ Switch to the percentage method OR ▪ Multiply number of allowances above 10 by the value of one allowance for that pay period Table 2.3, subtract the result from the gross wage, then use the adjusted gross wage and 10 allowances.
Gross wage exceeds the table limit,	switch to the percentage method

continued ▶

Calculating Income Tax Withholding, *continued*

Illustration 2.5

Wage Bracket Method Tables for Income Tax Withholding

SINGLE Persons—MONTHLY Payroll Period

(For Wages Paid through December 31, 2018)

And the wages are—		And the number of withholding allowances claimed is—										
At least	But less than	0	1	2	3	4	5	6	7	8	9	10
		The amount of income tax to be withheld is—										
$2,765	$2,805	$281	$240	$198	$157	$115	$75	$40	$6	$0	$0	$0
2,805	2,845	286	245	203	162	120	79	44	10	0	0	0
2,845	2,885	291	249	208	166	125	83	48	14	0	0	0
2,885	2,925	296	254	213	171	130	88	52	18	0	0	0
2,925	2,965	301	259	218	176	135	93	56	22	0	0	0
2,965	3,005	305	264	222	181	139	98	60	26	0	0	0
3,005	3,045	310	269	227	186	144	103	64	30	0	0	0
3,045	3,085	315	273	232	190	149	107	68	34	0	0	0
3,085	3,125	320	278	237	195	154	112	72	38	3	0	0
3,125	3,165	325	283	242	200	159	117	76	42	7	0	0
3,165	3,205	329	288	246	205	163	122	80	46	11	0	0
3,205	3,245	334	293	251	210	168	127	85	50	15	0	0
3,245	3,285	339	297	256	214	173	131	90	54	19	0	0
3,285	3,325	344	302	261	219	178	136	95	58	23	0	0
3,325	3,365	349	307	266	224	183	141	100	62	27	0	0
3,365	3,405	353	312	270	229	187	146	104	66	31	0	0
3,405	3,445	358	317	275	234	192	151	109	70	35	0	0
3,445	3,485	363	321	280	238	197	155	114	74	39	4	0
3,485	3,525	368	326	285	243	202	160	119	78	43	8	0
3,525	3,565	374	331	290	248	207	165	124	82	47	12	0
3,565	3,605	382	336	294	253	211	170	128	87	51	16	0
3,605	3,645	391	341	299	258	216	175	133	92	55	20	0
3,645	3,685	400	345	304	262	221	179	138	96	59	24	0
3,685	3,725	409	350	309	267	226	184	143	101	63	28	0
3,725	3,765	418	355	314	272	231	189	148	106	67	32	0
3,765	3,805	426	360	318	277	235	194	152	111	71	36	2
3,805	3,845	435	365	323	282	240	199	157	116	75	40	6
3,845	3,885	444	369	328	286	245	203	162	120	79	44	10
3,885	3,925	453	377	333	291	250	208	167	125	84	48	14
3,925	3,965	462	386	338	296	255	213	172	130	89	52	18
3,965	4,005	470	394	342	301	259	218	176	135	93	56	22
4,005	4,045	479	403	347	306	264	223	181	140	98	60	26
4,045	4,085	488	412	352	310	269	227	186	144	103	64	30
4,085	4,125	497	421	357	315	274	232	191	149	108	68	34
4,125	4,165	506	430	362	320	279	237	196	154	113	72	38
4,165	4,205	514	438	366	325	283	242	200	159	117	76	42
4,205	4,245	523	447	371	330	288	247	205	164	122	81	46
4,245	4,285	532	456	380	334	293	251	210	168	127	85	50
4,285	4,325	541	465	389	339	298	256	215	173	132	90	54
4,325	4,365	550	474	398	344	303	261	220	178	137	95	58
4,365	4,405	558	482	406	349	307	266	224	183	141	100	62
4,405	4,445	567	491	415	354	312	271	229	188	146	105	66
4,445	4,485	576	500	424	358	317	275	234	192	151	109	70
4,485	4,525	585	509	433	363	322	280	239	197	156	114	74
4,525	4,565	594	518	442	368	327	285	244	202	161	119	78
4,565	4,605	602	526	450	374	331	290	248	207	165	124	82
4,605	4,645	611	535	459	383	336	295	253	212	170	129	87
4,645	4,685	620	544	468	392	341	299	258	216	175	133	92
4,685	4,725	629	553	477	401	346	304	263	221	180	138	97
4,725	4,765	638	562	486	409	351	309	268	226	185	143	102
4,765	4,805	646	570	494	418	355	314	272	231	189	148	106
4,805	4,845	655	579	503	427	360	319	277	236	194	153	111
4,845	4,885	664	588	512	436	365	323	282	240	199	157	116
4,885	4,925	673	597	521	445	370	328	287	245	204	162	121
4,925	4,965	682	606	530	453	377	333	292	250	209	167	126
4,965	5,005	690	614	538	462	386	338	296	255	213	172	130
5,005	5,045	699	623	547	471	395	343	301	260	218	177	135
5,045	5,085	708	632	556	480	404	347	306	264	223	181	140
5,085	5,125	717	641	565	489	413	352	311	269	228	186	145
5,125	5,165	726	650	574	497	421	357	316	274	233	191	150
5,165	5,205	734	658	582	506	430	362	320	279	237	196	154
5,205	5,245	743	667	591	515	439	367	325	284	242	201	159
5,245	5,285	752	676	600	524	448	372	330	288	247	205	164
5,285	5,325	761	685	609	533	457	380	335	293	252	210	169
5,325	5,365	770	694	618	541	465	389	340	298	257	215	174
5,365	5,405	778	702	626	550	474	398	344	303	261	220	178

Source: Internal Revenue Service

Calculating Income Tax Withholding, *continued*

Withholding on Part-Year Earnings   For an employee who works only part of a year, either full-time or part-time, an employer has two choices:

- Calculate withholding in the normal manner as previously discussed.
- If the employee requests in writing to withhold tax by the "part-year employment method" to prevent over-withholding, then complete the following process, based on actual, not annual, earnings:

The request (in writing) must detail:

- Last day of employment with previous employer
- A declaration that the employee uses a calendar year accounting method
- A declaration that he or she will be employed for no more than 245 days of continuous employment during the current calendar year

Calculation procedure: Assume that Mark Williams was last employed on September 14 in the current calendar year. He begins employment with the new employer on November 4. He is paid weekly and earns $500 per week. His W-4 shows single with zero allowances. The tax withheld in the previous week was $16. For the second week ending November 18, the income tax withholding would be calculated as follows:

Step	Procedure	Example
1	Add current period wages to wages already paid in the current term of continuous employment.	$500 + $500 = $1,000
2	Add the number of payroll periods in step 1 to the number of payroll periods from last employment to the beginning of current employment. To find this second amount, divide the days between the last day of the previous employment (or the last December 31, if later) by the number of days in the current payroll period.	2 + (50/7) = 9 (Disregarding fractional periods)
3	Divide the step 1 amount by the total payroll periods calculated in step 2 (Average wages over the period)	$1,000/9 = $111.11

continued ▶

Calculating Income Tax Withholding, *continued*

Step	Procedure	Example
4	Find the tax on step 3 using a withholding table for the appropriate period. (here weekly, no allowances)	See Illustration 2.6 below: $4
5	Multiply step 4 by total payroll periods from step 2.	$4 × 9 = $36
6	Subtract from step 5 the tax already withheld in previous periods of the current continuous employment.	$36 – $16 = $20

Illustration 2.6

Wage Bracket Method Tables for Income Tax Withholding

SINGLE Persons—**WEEKLY** Payroll Period

(For Wages Paid through December 31, 2018)

And the wages are—		And the number of withholding allowances claimed is—										
At least	But less than	0	1	2	3	4	5	6	7	8	9	10
		The amount of income tax to be withheld is—										
$ 0	$75	$0	$0	$0	$0	$0	$0	$0	$0	$0	$0	$0
75	80	1	0	0	0	0	0	0	0	0	0	0
80	85	1	0	0	0	0	0	0	0	0	0	0
85	90	2	0	0	0	0	0	0	0	0	0	0
90	95	2	0	0	0	0	0	0	0	0	0	0
95	100	3	0	0	0	0	0	0	0	0	0	0
100	105	3	0	0	0	0	0	0	0	0	0	0
105	110	4	0	0	0	0	0	0	0	0	0	0
110	115	4	0	0	0	0	0	0	0	0	0	0
115	120	5	0	0	0	0	0	0	0	0	0	0
120	125	5	0	0	0	0	0	0	0	0	0	0
125	130	6	0	0	0	0	0	0	0	0	0	0
130	135	6	0	0	0	0	0	0	0	0	0	0
135	140	7	0	0	0	0	0	0	0	0	0	0
140	145	7	0	0	0	0	0	0	0	0	0	0
145	150	8	0	0	0	0	0	0	0	0	0	0
150	155	8	0	0	0	0	0	0	0	0	0	0
155	160	9	1	0	0	0	0	0	0	0	0	0
160	165	9	1	0	0	0	0	0	0	0	0	0
165	170	10	2	0	0	0	0	0	0	0	0	0

Source: Internal Revenue Service

Withholding Based on Quarterly Average Earnings   An employer may withhold income tax by estimating total quarterly gross earnings. The employer divides the total gross amount by the number of payroll periods in the quarter to determine average earnings per period. If the withholding is not equal to the amount that should have been withheld based on actual earnings, a withholding adjustment will be necessary at some point during the quarter. This method is not available for tip earnings.

Calculating Income Tax Withholding, *continued*

Withholding Based on Annualized Earnings

An employer may withhold based on annualized gross earnings. The percentage method is used to calculate the withholding. The procedure is shown below. Assume that John Anderson is married with four allowances and has a gross salary of $2,950 semi-monthly.

Step	Procedure	Example
1	Determine the number of wage periods in a year.	$2 \times 12 = 24$
2	Multiply the result from step one by the gross wages per pay period.	$2,950 \times 24$ = $70,800
3	Calculate the value of the allowances on an annual basis. (See Table 2.3 on page 68, annual allowance amount.)	$4,150 \times 4$ = $16,600
4	Calculate the "excess amount".	$70,800 - $16,600 = $54,200
5	Calculate the annual tax (Illustration 2.7 below)	Calculation: .12 $\times$ ($54,200 - $30,600) + $1,905 = $4,737
6	Calculate the amount to withhold per pay period.	$4,737/24 = $197.38

Illustration 2.7

TABLE 7—ANNUAL Payroll Period

(a) SINGLE person (including head of household)—

If the amount of wages (after subtracting withholding allowances) is:		The amount of income tax to withhold is:	of excess over—
Not over $3,700		$0	
Over—	But not over—		
$3,700	—$13,225 . .	$0.00 plus 10%	—$3,700
$13,225	—$42,400 . .	$952.50 plus 12%	—$13,225
$42,400	—$86,200 . .	$4,453.50 plus 22%	—$42,400
$86,200	—$161,200 . .	$14,089.50 plus 24%	—$86,200
$161,200	—$203,700 . .	$32,089.50 plus 32%	—$161,200
$203,700	—$503,700 . .	$45,689.50 plus 35%	—$203,700
$503,700	. . . .	$150,689.50 plus 37%	

(b) MARRIED person—

If the amount of wages (after subtracting withholding allowances) is:		The amount of income tax to withhold is:	of excess over—
Not over $11,550		$0	
Over—	But not over—		
$11,550	—$30,600 . .	$0.00 plus 10%	—$11,550
$30,600	—$88,950 . .	$1,905.00 plus 12%	—$30,600
$88,950	—$176,550 . .	$8,907.00 plus 22%	—$88,950
$176,550	—$326,550 . .	$28,179.00 plus 24%	—$176,550
$326,550	—$411,550 . .	$64,179.00 plus 32%	—$326,550
$411,550	—$611,550 . .	$91,379.00 plus 35%	—$411,550
$611,550	. . . .	$161,379.00 plus 37%	—$611,550

Source: Internal Revenue Service

continued ▶

Calculating Income Tax Withholding, *continued*

Withholding Based on Cumulative Wages

When an employee's gross wages varies significantly during a year, the employee may want to prevent annual under-withholding or over-withholding by requesting the cumulative wages method of withholding. An employee must make the request in writing, the employee's payroll periods must remain constant during the year, and the method applies for the remainder of the calendar year, using the percentage method tables.

For example, John Taylor is married, claims no allowances, is paid monthly, and had gross wages of only $500 per month in January and February, but then earned $5,700 in March and $6,200 each month in April and May. In June, he requests that his employer use the cumulative wages withholding method for the rest of the year. His June gross wages are $6,100. His total withholding through May 31 using the wage bracket method was $1,732. The table below illustrates an employer's withholding calculation procedure.

Step	Procedure	Example
1	Determine the number of wage periods to-date, including the current period.	January - June = 6
2	Calculate the average pay per payroll period by dividing the total earnings to date by the result from Step 1.	$25,200/6 = $4,200
3	Calculate the withholding on the amount is Step 1, using the percentage withholding method.	From 4(b): (no allowances) $4,200 – $2,550 = $1,650 ($1,650 × .12) + $158.70 = $356.70
4	Multiply the withholding from Step 3 by the number of payroll periods from Step 1.	$356.70 × 6 = $2,140.20
5	Withholding for June: Subtract withholding to-date from the amount in Step 4. (Note: A negative result means over-withholding to-date and no withholding is required for the current period.)	$2,140.20 – $1,732. = $408.20. (Would have been $584 using wage-bracket table.)

Calculating Income Tax Withholding, *continued*

Other Methods

The withholding methods discussed here are not exhaustive. Other methods are permitted as follows:

- Any other methods and tables for withholding taxes can be used, as long as the amount of tax withheld is consistently about the same as it would be as discussed under the *Percentage Method* in Publication 15.
- Combined Federal Income Tax, Employee Social Security Tax, and Employee Medicare Tax Withholding Table (Not available for nonresident aliens.) See Publications 15 and 15-A for further details.

Withholding on Supplemental Wages

Supplemental wages are gross amounts for employees that are not part of regular wages. Examples include bonuses, commissions, overtime, awards, taxable fringe benefits, back pay, severance pay, tips treated as wages, and vacation pay added to regular pay during a vacation period. Use the following table to determine withholding. Also see page 115 for "grossing up" a payment so that an employee receives a specified amount after withholding.

IF	THEN
Total supplemental gross pay during the year exceeds one million dollars,	withhold the excess (above one million) at the top marginal individual tax rate.
The amount is one million or less,	see the table below.

IF	THEN
The supplemental payment is combined with regular wages (not separately identified), then to figure tax on the supplemental amount,	withhold income tax on the single amount in the normal manner used for regular payments in the payroll period.

continued ▶

Calculating Income Tax Withholding, *continued*

IF	THEN
The supplemental payment is identified separately from regular wages, then to figure tax on the supplemental amount,	the employer can do either one of the following: ■ Withhold 22% of the supplemental amount ■ If the supplemental payment is made concurrently with regular wages, add them and figure the tax. Then subtract the regular wages withheld or that would be withheld. OR: If not concurrent, combine the supplemental amount with either wages paid in the most recent pay period or paid or to be paid in the current period, figure the withholding on the total, and subtract the regular wage withholding amount. (See Pub. 15)

Note: Supplemental wages are also generally subject to Social Security and FUTA taxes.

Part IV: Employer Payroll Tax and Benefits Expenses

Overview

Summary and Types

In addition to gross pay expense, employers also incur a second type of payroll expense: employer payroll taxes. These kinds of payroll taxes apply only to an employer and add to an employer's total employment costs. Employer payroll taxes are assessed on a calendar-year basis. The types of employer payroll tax expenses are:

■ Employer Social Security taxes
■ Federal and state unemployment taxes
■ Other state and local payroll taxes

continued ▶

Overview, *continued*

These are taxes paid only by an employer; they should not be confused with payroll taxes that an employee pays and that are deducted from an employee's gross pay.

Social Security

Employer Matching

As previously indicated, Social Security Tax (OASDI and Medicare) is paid both by employee and employer. The amounts are equal; in other words, an employer matches the tax paid by an employee. An exception to the matching requirement is the .9% additional Medicare tax on high-income employees. Only the employee pays this tax; it is *not* matched the employer.

The OASDI and Medicare tax calculations were discussed on pages 47–49.

Unemployment Taxes

Overview

Both federal and state authorities have passed unemployment tax laws. At the federal level, the Federal Unemployment Tax Act (FUTA) was created by Congress in 1939. This law, imposed only on employers, is intended to ensure unemployment benefits to workers who lose jobs even though the workers are able and qualified. The annual FUTA wage base is currently $7,000 of gross pay (for each employee) and the FUTA tax rate is 6%. However, the law allows a 5.4% credit against the FUTA tax for employers that pay state unemployment tax. (See below). All states currently impose unemployment taxes, so the effective federal rate therefore is usually .6%, subject to certain exceptions (See below). The federal tax is generally used to cover administrative expenses of federal and state unemployment programs.

Employers Covered by FUTA

The general definition of "employer" for FUTA purposes is the same as we have previously discussed (See page 6.) . However, FUTA also has three specific tests for employers to determine if they are "FUTA employers"; that is, responsible for meeting FUTA requirements. An employer qualifies if:

- **General test:** The employer has paid wages of at least $1,500 or more in any calendar quarter during the current and preceding year to employees who are not farmworkers or household workers,
  or
  The employer had one or more employees for at least some part of a day in any 20 or more different calendar weeks (7 consecutive days beginning on

continued ▶

Unemployment Taxes, *continued*

Sunday) in the current or preceding year. The employees can be the same or different persons and they can be full time, part-time or seasonal.

- **Household employer test:** At least $1,000 was paid to household employees in any calendar quarter in the current year or preceding year. A "household employee" for this purpose is an employee who performs domestic services work such as cooking, cleaning, gardening, caretaking, etc. in a private home, college club, fraternity, or sorority.
- **Farmworker employer test:** 1) The employer paid at least $20,000 to farmworkers during any calendar quarter in the current year or preceding year, or 2) The employer had 10 or more farmworkers during at least some part of a day during any 20 or more different calendar weeks in the current year or preceding year.

Upon satisfying a "FUTA employer" test, an employer retains that status for FUTA purposes during the entire calendar year in which the test was satisfied.

Example: FUTA and SUTA Calculation Procedure

Assume that a business has three employees: John, Bill, and Mary. From January 1 to March 31 John had total gross pay of $5,100, Bill had $6,500 and Mary had $7,200. John's April gross pay is $1,700, Bill's is $1,700 and Mary's April gross pay is $3,150. The table below shows the three calculation steps to calculate FUTA and state unemployment tax (SUTA) for the April payroll. SUTA is 5.4% on the first $7,000.

Step 1
For each employee, subtract the cumulative gross pay from the wage base.
If the result is **zero or positive**, cumulative pay is still below the limit, so all of the current gross pay is taxable. Go to Step 3. **If** the result is **negative**, cumulative pay has exceeded the limit and this excess is not taxable. Some or all of the current gross pay is excluded. Go to Step 2.

Example:

John		Bill	
Wage base	$7,000	Wage base	$7,000
Cumulative gross pay	6,800	Cumulative gross pay	8,200
Go to Step 3	$200	Go to Step 2	($1,200)

Mary		*Note: these calculations are for both FUTA and SUTA. If SUTA wage base were different, a separate SUTA calculation would be needed.*
Wage base	$7,000	
Cumulative gross pay	10,350	
Go to Step 2	($3,350)	

Unemployment Taxes, *continued*

Step 2

Offset the negative amount (the amount excluded) against the current gross pay to find the taxable portion of the current gross pay (but not less than zero). Then go to Step 3.

Example:

FUTA	SUTA
John: not applicable—all taxable Bill: $1,700 – $1,200 = $500 taxable Mary: $3,150 – $3,350 = $0 taxable	John: not applicable—all taxable Bill: $1,700 – $1,200 = $500 taxable Mary: $3,150 – $3,350 = $0 taxable

Step 3

Multiply the taxable portion of the current gross pay times the tax rate, and add the results.

Example:

FUTA	SUTA
John: $1,700 × .006 = $10.20 Bill: $500 × .006 = $ 3.00 Mary: $0 × .006 = –0– Total FUTA tax $13.20	John: $1,700 × .054 = $91.80 Bill: $500 × .054 = $27.00 Mary: $0 × .054 = –0– Total SUTA tax $118.80

Employees Covered by FUTA

The definition of "employee" for FUTA purposes is essentially the same as we have previously discussed; that is, for FUTA purposes most workers are considered employees based on common law. However, FUTA expands the definition of "employee" to include the following:

- An agent or commission driver. Duties are to deliver food, beverages (other than milk), laundry, or dry cleaning for the provider of these items.
- A traveling salesperson who works full time for one firm or person, taking orders for merchandise for resale or supplies for use in the customer's business. Additional incidental part-time work does change the worker's status.

Notice that these are the same as two or the four statutory employee categories under FICA. The other two categories of life insurance sales persons and home workers (not the same thing as domestic/household employees) are not included for FUTA.

Unemployment Taxes, *continued*

FUTA Wages	As with FICA, "wages" is a general term that means any form of compensation, unless specifically exempt by law.
Payments Exempt From FUTA	FUTA exempts specific payment categories. The table below shows common employment categories and types of payments that are exempt from FUTA.

Table 2.4: Payments Exempt From FUTA Tax

Exempt Item	Description
Achievement Awards	Exempt up to $1,600 for qualified awards and $400 for non-qualified awards.
Agricultural Labor	Farmworkers may or may not be exempt. An employer of agricultural employees must pay tax under FUTA if: ■ The employer paid cash wages of at least $20,000 to farmworkers in any calendar quarter in the current or preceding year, OR ■ The employer employed at least 10 farmworkers for part of at least one day during any 20 or more different calendar weeks during the current of preceding calendar year. The above does not apply to exempt services from family members.
Business Expense Reimbursements	Exempt if under an accountable plan
Deceased Worker	Exempt for wages paid to estate after calendar year of worker's death
Dependent Care	Employer payments to employees or by third parties for dependent care under a qualified dependent care assistance program and/or the value of employer-maintained dependent care facilities use to a maximum of $5,000 ($2,500 married filing separately) are exempt.
Education	Annual payments up to $5,250 made by an employer under an education assistance plan to maintain or improve employee job skills are exempt to both active and prior employees. Undergraduate and graduate tuition reduction by an educational institution is also generally exempt.
Emergency Workers	Exempt
Employee Discounts	Subject to certain limitations, employer discounts on property other than real estate, stocks, and bonds purchased by employees are exempt.

Unemployment Taxes, *continued*

Table 2.4: Payments Exempt From FUTA Tax *continued*

Exempt Item	Description
Family Employee	1) Child employed by parent: exempt under age 21 if work is for a sole proprietorship or partnership is which each partner is a parent 2) Parent employed by child: exempt 3) Spouse employed by spouse: exempt if services are *not* in a trade or business
Foreign Affiliates	Foreign affiliates of American employers.
Government Employee	Exempt
Health Savings Accounts	Employer payments under qualified plans exempt up to contribution limits.
Homeworker	Exempt if a statutory employee.
Hospital Employee	Exempt
Household Employee	▪ Domestic service in private homes: exempt if paid less than $1,000 in cash in any quarter in the current or preceding year ▪ Domestic service in college clubs, fraternities, and sororities exempt if paid less than $1,000 in cash in any quarter in the current or preceding year Note that a household employee is not someone who works in your trade or business or is a homeworker, or who is an independent contractor with their own business.
Insurance	Employee accident and health insurance premiums are exempt. Life insurance is also exempt.
Meals and Lodging	The value of meals and lodging provided for the convenience of the employer are exempt if furnished on employer's business premises. Lodging must be a condition of employment. Occasional light meals (coffee, snacks, etc.) are exempt.
Military Service Differential Pay	The amount paid by an employer for the difference between military pay for employees called to active service exceeding 30 days and regular employee compensation is exempt. (This applies to FUTA but not income tax.)
Non-profit organizations	Non-profits qualifying under 501(c)(3) are exempt from FUTA (but not SUTA, unless they self-insure).
Newspaper Carriers And Vendors	Exempt based on same rules as for income tax withholding
No-Additional-Cost Services	Employer services provided to employees when no substantial additional cost will be incurred because of excess capacity are exempt.

continued ▶

Table 2.4: Payments Exempt From FUTA Tax *continued*

Exempt Item	Description
Railroad Retirement Act	Exempt for employees subject to this act
Religious Exemption	A charitable organization exempt from federal income tax under section 501(c)(3) is also exempt from FUTA.
Retirement Planning Services	Exempt
Retirement Plans	1) Exempt for employer contributions to a qualified plan (except for amounts contributed under a SEP salary reduction agreement) 2) Exempt for distributions from qualified retirement plans and 403(b) annuities. Note: Employee wages (gross pay) is subject to the employer FUTA at the time they are earned, even though some is tax- deferred for income tax purposes because of contributions."
Sick Pay	Payments made by or on behalf of an employer to an employee for sickness or personal injury after the first six continuous calendar months following the last month of employment are exempt. Payments must be according to a plan between employee and employer.
Statutory Non-Employees	Exempt
Students Enrolled And Regularly Attending Classes	1) Exempt for domestic services in college clubs, fraternities, or sororities while working as a regular student; also exempt if paid less than $100 per year by income tax-exempt school. 2) Generally exempt when performing services for a school, college, or university not for academic credit—some exceptions may apply. 3) Student nurses performing part-time services at hospitals for nominal charge as part of training.
Tips	Tips of less than $20 per month are exempt. See pages 36 and 55 for required employee and employer tip reporting.
Workers' Compensation	Employer payments for workers' compensation insurance, either into state funds or by private insurance contract, are exempt. Workers' compensation benefit payments are also exempt.
Working Condition Benefits	Working condition benefits are services or property provided to an employee by an employer so that the employee is able to perform his or her duties. Examples are company-provided car, cell phone, computers, and training.

Unemployment Taxes, *continued*

Overview: State Unemployment Tax

As previously discussed, individual states are the direct payers of unemployment benefits to their residents.

Employers pay state unemployment insurance (usually called SUTA, sometimes called SUI), which assesses a tax on at least the first $7,000 of wages (a "wage base") that a worker has received during a calendar year; this tax is also paid by the employer*, as is FUTA. Most states have a higher wage base. The wage base applies to each employee for each employer.

A state unemployment tax is a percentage of the annual wage base. All states maintain an unemployment compensation experience rating system. This means that the state maintains a record of each employer's contributions* into a state unemployment compensation fund (maintained in an account with the U.S. Treasury) as well as the fund's expenditures on behalf of employees from the employer. Employers with stable employment that requires lower fund expenditures are charged a lower percentage tax rate, and vice versa. In some states employers can make voluntary contributions to increase their fund balances and thereby reduce their tax rates.

* Three states—Alaska, New Jersey, and Pennsylvania—also require SUTA contributions from employees.

Determining the FUTA Credit

An employer can receive up to a maximum of 5.4% (90% × 6%) credit against the 6% FUTA tax. This is a fixed percentage (except for Title XII advances—see below). If an employer pays a lower SUTA rate than 5.4% into a state fund (because stability of employment history lowers the state rate), the 5.4% credit will not decrease. Likewise, if an employer pays a higher SUTA rate to a state than 5.4%, the FUTA 5.4% credit does not increase.

The $7,000 wage base is used for the FUTA calculation; however, most states have a higher wage base for calculating contributions into their state unemployment insurance funds. Even though these higher bases will often result in a higher dollar tax (than using a $7,000 base) at the state rate, this does not affect the FUTA 5.4% credit or $7,000 wage base.

Title XII Advances and FUTA Credit Reduction

In the event that a state does not have sufficient funds to make unemployment benefit payments to workers, it can borrow the funds from the federal government. The funds loaned to a state for this purpose are called "Title XII advances", from Title XII (12) of the Social Security Act.

In general, a state has until November 10 of the second year following the loan to repay the borrowed funds; if it does not, beginning in the second year after

continued ▶

Unemployment Taxes, *continued*

the loan, the FUTA tax credit is reduced by .3% per year, subject to a maximum reduction depending on state solvency. In this way, the loan funds are indirectly repaid through a higher effective FUTA tax rate on employers in the state.

SUTA Wages

For the purpose of SUTA, "wages" are for the most part defined the same as for FUTA. However, individual states do have variations and may consider certain additional activities as taxable wages and exempt other activities. Therefore, an employer should review state unemployment tax guidelines

Interstate Employees

In some situations an employee will work in more than one state for the same employer. States conform to a system that provides the criteria to determine to which location (i.e. which state) unemployment tax should apply. The criteria, as applied in sequence if a prior test is not determinative, are:

1) Where the work primarily, not incidentally, takes place
2) The base of operations to which the employee regularly begins and ends his/ her work and to which he/she reports.
3) The location from which directions are issued.
4) The employee's state of residence.

TIP

What is your true payroll cost? Consider the following: Gross wages (includes bonuses, commissions, overtime, sick leave, vacation and compensatory time), employer payroll taxes, workers' compensation, and fringe benefits. Ancillary costs would include payroll services and software and—hopefully not—penalties.

Benefits Expenses

Overview

In addition to gross pay and the employer payroll taxes, employers may also incur a third type of payroll expense. This expense is generally called **benefits expense** or *fringe benefits*. This refers to additional compensation in various forms other than wages. There are numerous kinds of benefits; some of the more common ones are explained and listed here. If the benefits are provided under a plan approved by federal and/or state taxing authorities, the benefits also can be tax free or tax deferred to the employee while the employer records an expense deduction. (Also see pages 52–55).

Benefits Expenses, *continued*

Insurance

Probably for most employees the key benefit types are health, life, and disability insurance, followed by some kind of retirement plan.

- **Medical insurance:** This refers to a medical insurance plan that pays all or the majority of the cost of employee medical costs; however, medical coverage can vary widely between plans. Less expensive plans can still expose employees to potentially unaffordable medical costs should a severe chronic illness or devastating illness or accident occur.

Employers should also be aware of the federal Affordable Care Act (also called the "ACA" or "Obama Care". Full name: Patient Protection and Affordable Care Act). The ACA does not require employers to provide employee medical insurance; however, it imposes penalties on larger employers (At least 50 full-time equivalent employees in the previous year) who do not provide employee medical insurance coverage. Illustration 2.8 on page 90 provides a basic employer compliance outline.

The purpose of this complex law is to create a large insurance pool that is sufficient to provide widespread medical coverage. In effect, this means medical insurance coverage for most people, particularly directed to people who are otherwise unable to obtain coverage, generally because they do not work for an employer who provides medical insurance, or because they cannot afford to pay for medical insurance, or because they do not qualify for Medicare.

Passage of this law created many new benefits as well as wide-ranging financial effects; also, continued changes are likely for both economic and political reasons. Both employees and employers should maintain awareness of changes in this law.

- **Life Insurance:** This insurance provides a cash payment (usually to a designated family member) in the case of death of the insured employee. Group term life insurance above $50,000 is taxable to the employee and requires withholding.
- **Disability insurance:** Medical insurance does not cover the costs of being disabled (which is typically also associated with the loss of income) as a result of accident or illness. Disability insurance covers loss of income.
- **Workers' compensation insurance:** See below, page 91.

continued ▶

Benefits Expenses, *continued*

Illustration 2.8: Affordable Care Act Employer Compliance Procedure

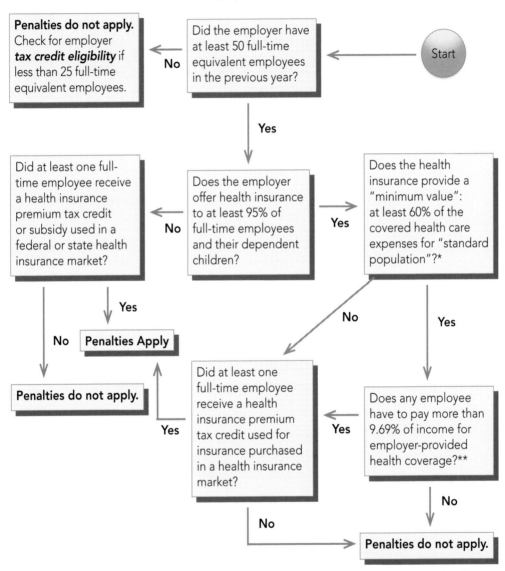

 * Minimum value for a standard population can be determined by: 1) Using the Health and Human Services (HHS) website calculator, 2) Contacting an employee benefits insurance company
** Refers to employee household income. Check current rate and guidelines. At this time, employer can apply 9.56% against these guidelines to determine household income for self-coverage: 1) Current federal poverty level for a single person calculated monthly, 2) Employee's W-2 box 1 current year-end reported wages, per month (however, difficult to determine before year-end), 3) Hourly rate of pay at 130 monthly hours or regular salary at beginning of coverage period. Note that percentage is annually inflation adjusted.

Benefits Expenses, *continued*

Retirement Plan

A retirement plan is an arrangement in which the employer provides for payments to employees after they retire (a pension plan) or creates a tax-deferred plan in which the employee and/or employer make contributions into a fund, for which the contributions are non-taxable to the employee. A plan can be designed to require defined contributions or to provide defined benefits. A ***plan administrator*** is a company that specializes in designing pension plans and supervising the administration and investments of the plan. An employer can make contributions directly to the plan administrator, and these payments are recorded as an operating expense. See pages 57–60 for a summary of qualified (deferred tax to beneficiary) plans.

Vacation Pay

Vacation pay means that an employee is being compensated, normally at their regular rate, while employed but taking time off from work in a manner agreed between employer and employee. Vacation pay is not required under the FLSA; however, vacation requirements may apply for government contractors under Service Contract and Labor Standards and the Davis-Bacon Act. (See page 11.) Also check state and local requirements. The calculation for vacation pay is discussed beginning on page 98. Payroll tax and withholding apply to vacation pay when paid.

Workers' Compensation Insurance

In all but two states (Texas and Oklahoma), workers' compensation insurance is a compulsory employer expense. With some variation in policies, workers' compensation insurance coverage pays workers who are injured, disabled, or killed on the job. Although coverage in most states is mandatory, the method of purchasing insurance varies. Most states permit employers to either purchase private insurance (provided coverage and insurance company rating meet state requirements) or purchase the insurance through a state fund. The cost of the insurance is generally calculated as a rate per $100 of annual gross compensation of individual job categories, based on a risk rating of each job category. This in turn may be adjusted by an experience loss rating based on loss history. The method of payment varies. A common procedure is for the employer to make an initial payment based on a beginning of the year estimate. At year-end the cost is finalized based on actual employment and the premium cost is adjusted, requiring either an additional payment or a rebate.

continued ▶

Benefits Expenses, *continued*

Example: ABC company has two job categories: office and construction. The actual annual gross wages are: office category, $185,000 and repair services, $500,000. The rate for office is $.22 per $100 and the rate for repair services is $2.75 per $100. The company has had minimal losses, so has a .9 overall loss rating. The annual cost is:

$$[(\$185,000/100) \times \$.22] + [(\$500,000/100) \times \$2.75] = \$14,157 \times .9 = \$12,741.30$$

In return for providing this insurance, the insurance becomes the sole remedy for work-related injury. Employees do not need to incur the cost and substantial risk of suing employers for job-related injuries, and employers do not become parties to lawsuits.

TIP

Check with state workers' compensation requirements regarding overtime pay. Some dollar payroll calculation states do not require that the calculation include overtime premiums.

Benefits Expenses, *continued*

Other Benefit
Types

Table 2.5 shows other common types of employee benefits.

Table 2.5: Common fringe benefits

Employee Fringe Benefit	Taxable (Y/N)
Achievement awards	N*
Athletic or health club membership if located and used at place of business	N*
Bonus	Y
De minimis fringe benefits-small gifts and food, etc.	N*
Employee discounts	N*
Employee stock options	Y
Work-related frequent flyer miles converted to cash by employee	Y
Work-related frequent flyer miles used for personal travel	N
Group term life insurance coverage in excess of $50,000	Y
Meals for convenience of employer on business premises	N
Lodging for convenience of employer on business premises-condition of employment	N
Moving expenses paid by employer in excess of actual expenses	Y
No-additional cost services	N
Qualified adoption assistance	N*
Qualified dependent care assistance	N*
Qualified employer-paid child and dependent care services	N*
Qualified health, accident, disability and long-term care insurance plans	N*
Qualified spending accounts such as medical flexible spending account	N*
Qualified retirement accounts	N*
Qualified tuition reduction plan	N*
Qualified transportation service	N*
Retirement planning services	N*
Vacation pay	Y
Vehicle owned by employer, used for personal purposes	Y
Working condition fringe benefits used only at work	N

* Exempt to a limit

Section 3 Record the Payroll

Introduction   Recording payroll is primarily an accounting function, rather than involving compliance questions, as in Section 2. This section discusses the typical accounting procedures that are required each time that a payroll is calculated.

Overview

General Procedures

After the correct gross wages, employee withholding, employer payroll taxes, and benefits have been calculated, these amounts must be recorded in the accounting records. This requires an understanding of basic accounting procedures such as the use of debits and credits, journals, and ledgers. The content presented in this section assumes an understanding of these topics.

Four Basic Parts

The process of recording the payroll involves four basic parts:

- Record the gross wages expense and related accounts
- Record the employer payroll taxes expense and related accounts
- Record the benefits expense and related accounts
- Update each employee's earnings record

Summarize the Information

As a preliminary step to starting the process, the employer must first summarize and organize the payroll information. This is usually accomplished by using a *payroll register* (also called a payroll record or payroll journal). A payroll register is an informal summary tool that is used each payroll period to show the individual and total amounts of gross earnings, deductions, and net pay for that particular payroll period.

TIP

Employee salaries and wages are normally operating expenses that are also tax-deductible; in other words, they reduce business taxable income. However, there is a situation where this does not happen! It is called a "golden parachute" payment, and happens when a company has a change in control. If certain officers, shareholders, or highly compensated individuals receive large payments as a result of the change in control, the company will not be able to use most or a large part of the payment as a deductible expense, and the individual receiving payment pays an extra 20% excise tax. Search "golden parachutes" online for more details.

Journal Entry for the Gross Pay Expense

Overview

The first step in recording payroll is the journal entry for the gross pay expense. This journal entry consists of recording the current gross pay, the related deductions, and the net pay. *The payroll register totals are the sources of information for this journal entry.* Refer to the payroll register on the next two pages..

Example

The example below shows a journal entry for the gross pay expense. The total debits to office salaries and wages is $4,964, which is the total of the gross pay column, classified by type of pay. The credit to Wages Payable is the total of the net pay column, and the other payables are totals of deductions columns.

March 14	Office Salaries Expense	1,700.00	
	Wages Expense	3,264.00	
	Federal Income Tax Payable		765.00
	State Income Tax Payable		148.00
	FICA Payable		379.75
	Health Insurance Payable		87.00
	Union Dues Payable		26.25
	Salaries and Wages Payable		3,558.00

Withholding Liabilities

Notice that all the withholding deductions are recorded as credits to various liabilities. All of these are current liabilities. The employer is simply acting as a collection agent and is obligated to remit the amounts withheld to other parties in a timely manner. For example, the federal income tax and FICA withheld must be paid to the United States Treasury Department within a prescribed period of time.

Journal Entry for the Employer Payroll Tax Expense

Overview

The second step in recording payroll is the journal entry for the employer payroll tax expense. This journal entry consists of recording the employer FUTA, SUTA, and FICA payroll taxes, plus any other state payroll taxes, if applicable. The dollar amounts subject to these taxes are the totals shown in the payroll register in "current gross taxable for . . ." columns. Remember that these taxes only apply to the employer; the employees make no payments.

Example

The example on page 98 shows a journal entry for the employer payroll tax expense. FUTA is .006 × $1,420 = $8.52; SUTA is .054 × $1,420 = $76.68; FICA/Medicare is the same as the employee withholding = $379.75.

continued ▶

The Payroll Register Illustrated

Example

On this page and the next page is an example of a completed payroll register.

						Payroll Register for the		
Employee Name	Total Hours	Earnings				Current Gross Taxable for ...		
		Regular	Over-time	Current Gross	Year to Date Gross	FUTA/ SUTA	OASDI
Acevedo, Baxter	40	600.00		600.00	7,200.00	400.00	600.00
Dunwitty, Betty	40	720.00		720.00	7,920.00	–0–	720.00
Heintz, Marilyn	44	600.00	90.00	690.00	7,150.00	540.00	690.00
Onishi, James		800.00		800.00	8,800.00	–0–	800.00
Sanders, Emily	40	480.00		480.00	5,350.00	480.00	480.00
Van Arsdale, Robert	42	720.00	54.00	774.00	7,900.00	–0–	774.00
Washington, Ellie		900.00		900.00	9,900.00	–0–	900.00
Totals		4,820.00	144.00	4,964.00	54,220.00	1,420.00	4,964.00

Detailed Explanation

Each of the following items relates to highlighted items in the reference boxes shown on the illustrated payroll register.

1) **Earnings:** For wage employees, earnings are calculated at an hourly rate; for salaried employees (Onishi and Washington), earnings are a fixed amount. Gross earnings in the current period includes both the regular and overtime pay. For example, Marilyn Heintz earned $600 regular pay, so her regular rate must be $600/40 = $15 per hour. Therefore, her overtime rate is $15 × 1.5 = $22.50 per hour. Because she worked 4 hours in excess of 40, she earns overtime of $22.50 × 4 = $90.

2) **Year to date gross:** This is an optional column that helps identify the cumulative amount of employee gross pay that includes the current payroll. Cumulative amounts are part of each employee's individual earnings record.

3) **Current gross taxable for FUTA/SUTA and OASDI:** This is the amount of the gross pay in the current period that is subject to these taxes. *Example:* The FUTA/SUTA limit is $7,000. Baxter Acevedo's current period gross pay is $600 and this amount exceeded the limit by $200. This means that only $400 of his current gross pay ($600 – $200) is subject to FUTA/SUTA taxes. The OASDI limit of $128,400 is much greater than his cumulative gross pay, so it is easy to see that all of his current gross pay is taxable for OASDI.

The Payroll Register Illustrated, *continued*

Week Ended March 14, 2018

		Deductions				Payment		Acct. Debited	
Federal Inc. Tax	State Inc. Tax	OASDI/ Medicare	Health Insurance	Union Dues	Total	Net Pay	Ck. #	Office Salaries	Wages
89.00	18.00	45.90	12.00	5.25	170.15	429.85	857		600.00
108.00	22.00	55.08	9.00	5.25	199.33	520.67	858		720.00
104.00	21.00	52.79	15.00	5.25	198.04	491.96	859		690.00
120.00	24.00	61.20	11.00	–0–	216.20	583.80	860	800.00	
48.00	10.00	36.72	18.00	5.25	117.97	362.03	861		480.00
116.00	23.00	59.21	12.00	5.25	215.46	558.54	862		774.00
180.00	30.00	68.85	10.00	–0–	288.85	611.15	863	900.00	
765.00	148.00	379.75	87.00	26.25	1,406.00	3,558.00		1,700.00	3,264.00

4) **Deductions:** These are the withholding deductions for each employee. For example, Baxter Acevedo has a total of $170.15 of deductions, consisting of federal and state income taxes, FICA, health insurance contributions, and union dues.

5) **Net Pay:** This shows the net amount of pay each employee will receive and, when paid, the check number of the payroll check written to the employee. Net pay is current gross pay minus the total deductions.

6) **Account debited:** These columns classify the gross wage expense. In this case, gross wages are classified as either office salaries or wages. Different companies use different classifications.

Register Format

The payroll register can vary somewhat in format. Some companies use a completely separate payroll register, whereas others make it part of their cash payments journal. Also, the column titles vary somewhat. Some formats include a column on the left side for the gross amount of accrued vacation pay being used and an "other" column in the deductions section for miscellaneous deductions.

Journal Entry for the Employer Payroll Tax Expense, *continued*

March 14	Payroll Tax Expense	464.95	
	FICA Payable		379.75
	FUTA Payable		8.52
	SUTA Payable		76.68

Journal Entry for the Benefits Expense

Overview   If the employer provides benefits, then the third step in recording payroll is the journal entry for the benefits expense. This journal entry consists of accruing the expense and liability for each type of benefit.

Example   The example below shows a journal entry for benefits expense consisting of vacation pay, health insurance, and workers, compensation expenses.

March 14	Vacation Pay Expense	225.00	
	Medical Benefits Expense	350.00	
	Workers, Compensation Expense	150.00	
	Vacation Pay Payable		225.00
	Health Insurance Payable		350.00
	Work. Comp. Ins. Payable		150.00

What Is Total Payroll Cost?   The total cost of this payroll is the gross pay expense, the employer payroll tax expense, and the benefits expense. For the three examples above, this is: $4,964.00 + $464.95 + $725.00 = $6,153.95.

More on Vacation Pay

Overview   Vacation pay (also called "Paid Time Off" or "PTO" with other compensated absences), although not required absent a contractual agreement, is a common form of compensation. In the example above, we can see that $225 of vacation pay expense was accrued for the March 14 payroll period. However, this does not fully explain how the amount was caculated, which is discussed below.

More on Vacation Pay, *continued*

Vacation Pay Accrual

Vacation pay usually accrues according to the amount of time an employee has worked. Some organizations require that an employee work full time for a minimum period of time before vacation pay begins to be earned. Vacation pay does not change total annual wages; it is simply a portion of the annual wages that an employee receives without working. For proper accounting, this portion is accrued as an expense over the part of the year that the employee is working.

Example: Beautiful Designs Company gives two weeks of paid vacation to its employees per year. Dave Smith earns $78,000 annual pay, which is $1,500 per week wages expense if recorded over 52 weeks. However, Dave will be working only 50 weeks, not 52. Therefore, $3,000 (two weeks of vacation pay) must be added to the working 50 weeks by accruing at $3,000/50 = $60 per week. The company will add $60 per week classified as vacation pay expense to its payroll expense for a total of $1,560 per week wages and vacation pay expense. A quicker way to visualize this is that 2/50 = an additional 4% added to each payroll. Vacation pay also can be accrued hourly, daily, weekly or based on any other metric. Sick leave and other PTO works in a similar manner. As a result of turnover or "use it or lose it" policy, if a company expects that not all vacation pay will be used, the accrual can be reduced by some percentage factor.

A record is maintained for each employee; when an employee uses vacation pay, the company's vacation pay liability is reduced: debit vacation pay liability, credit various withholding liabilities, and credit cash. Generally, though not required, if an employee's pay rate changes, for example with a raise, the liability is adjusted to a higher amount because it is the rate the employee would expect when vacation time is used. As always, check state and local requirements.

continued

Employee Earnings Records

Overview

Every employer is required by law to maintain a permanent record of the wages and withholding for each employee. The primary purpose of these earnings records is to provide the information necessary to report the annual gross pay and withholding to each employee at year end on form **W-2**. Employees use the W-2 information for preparing their income tax returns as well as for other purposes, such as loan applications. The employer must also provide the same information to government taxing authorities.

Example

The example below is a partial employee *earnings record* that shows information for the month of March. Notice that the record is updated after each payroll period. Think of each record as a subsidiary ledger for each employee's earnings history. The example you see here has a cumulative gross pay column so the wage base limits can be identified. It also provides information for required quarterly payroll reports.

Tropics Travel Company
Employee Earnings Record
For the Year 2018

Employee: Van Arsdale, Robert
S.S.#: 123-45-6789
Employment Date: July 11, 2013
Termination Date:
Address: 80 Sunshine Ct, Denver, CO 80229

Filing Status: Single
Exemptions: 1

Pay Rate: $18 hourly
Job Title: Staff Assistant

		Earnings				Deductions							
2017 Week Ended	Total Hrs.	Reg. Pay	O.T. Pay	Gross Pay	Cum. Gross Pay	Fed. Income Tax	State Income Tax	OASDI/ Medcr.	Health Ins.	Union Dues	Total	Net	Check No.
3/7	40	720.00		720.00	7,126.00	108.00	22.00	55.08	12.00	5.25	202.33	517.67	755
3/14	42	720.00	54.00	774.00	7,900.00	116.00	23.00	59.21	12.00	5.25	215.46	558.54	862
3/21	44	720.00	108.00	828.00	8,728.00	133.00	26.00	63.34	12.00	5.25	239.59	588.41	912
3/28	43	720.00	81.00	801.00	9,529.00	129.00	25.00	61.28	12.00	5.25	232.53	568.47	988
March		2,880.00	243.00	3,123.00		486.00	96.00	238.91	48.00	21.00	889.91	2,233.09	
First Quarter		8,750.00	810.00	9,560.00		1,590.00	312.00	731.34	144.00	63.00	2,840.34	6,719.66	

Note: The source of this information is the payroll register. For example, the March 14 (highlighted) entry comes from the March 14 payroll register example.

Employee Earnings Records, *continued*

Reconciling the ***Payroll Register*** ***and Employee*** ***Pay Records***	Each payroll period, the payroll department must reconcile the totals on the payroll register to the total amounts on the employee earnings records. For example, if the gross pay on the payroll register is $4,964.00, then adding up the gross pay shown on each of the employee earnings records for all the employees for the same date should also result in a total of $4,964.00. This reconciliation is also done for each deduction item and net pay. A computerized payroll system should perform this function automatically.

Payments Overview

Introduction	After the payroll is calculated and approved, payroll checks are prepared, signed, and distributed. However, payroll-related payments involve more than just payments to employees. This section explains the payment process.

Payments to ***Whom?***	Payroll-related payments are made to the following parties:

- Employees
- Government taxing authorities
- Benefits providers
- Other designated recipients

Payments to Employees

Journal Entry	The journal entry to record payment to employees is shown below:

March 13	Salaries and Wages Payable	3,558.00	
	Cash		3,558.00

continued

Payments to Employees, *continued*

Payroll Checks

The credit to cash represents the total of all the payroll checks that employees receive. This is the total net pay. Most companies use special checks for payroll. Each check has a detachable portion called a ***statement of earnings*** that shows the gross pay, withholding, and net pay for the period that corresponds to the amount of the check received by an employee. The source of this information is the payroll register. Before the check is cashed, the statement of earnings should be detached and filed by the employee.

Electronic Funds Transfer

Many employees ask their employers to have the net pay automatically deposited in the employee's checking account. This results in a quicker deposit and eliminates the risk of losing the check. The employee still receives a statement of earnings with each payroll.

Payments to Taxing Authorities

Journal Entry

The journal entry to record payment to taxing authorities is shown below. This entry has two components. The example you see below consists of:

- Payment of the withholding liability for federal and state income tax and FICA.
- Payment of the employer payroll tax liability.

Notice that the employer portion of FICA is part of the $759.50 debit that includes both employee and employer portions of $379.75 each.

March 19	Federal Income Tax Payable	765.00	
	State Income Tax Payable	148.00	
	FICA Payable	759.50	
	SUTA Payable	76.68	
	FUTA Payable	8.52	
	Cash		1,757.70

Payroll Deposit Deadlines

Taxing authorities have strict payment deadlines for when the employer must make payroll deposits. Depending on the size of the payroll and kind of tax, payment deadlines range from annual to semi-weekly (the bigger the payroll, the quicker the deadline). See Publication 15.

continued ▶

Payments to Taxing Authorities, *continued*

If payment deadlines are not met, significant late payment penalties will be imposed.

> *Note:* The government considers its receipts from the employer's payroll tax deposits as an important source of cash flow. It takes the obligation to make these deposits very seriously. When the author was in school, he had a part-time bookkeeping job for a small business that was constantly late with payroll deposits and that had ignored a catch-up payment agreement with the IRS. The author returned from lunch one day to find two IRS agents changing the lock on the door (after seizing the assets).

How Payments Are Made

EFT: All employers must use an electronic funds transfer system (EFT) to automatically transfer payroll deposits to designated government accounts. This system is free and is called "EFTPS."

Payments to Other Parties

Overview

In general, payments to third parties are made according to the contractual agreement with each party. An exception is court-ordered withholding such as wage garnishments for child support, which have fixed payment dates.

Journal Entry

Journal entries to record payment to third parties are shown below:

March 25	Health Insurance Payable	350.00	
	Cash		350.00
March 31	Pension Plan Payable	150.00	
	Cash		150.00

Constructive Receipt

When are Wages Paid?

Determination of the day that wages are paid can have important consequences. These consequences most often materialize at the end of a calendar year when tax rates or wage bases change from one year to the next. Wages are considered paid on the day of actual physical payment to

continued ▶

an employee (such as when employee receives a check) or when funds are "constructively received", which means became available, set aside, or credited to the account of an employee, such that the employee has access to the funds. The date on a check has no effect on the application of the rule. The rule also applies in the case of overpayment.

For example, an employee performs services in December of 2018, and the employer makes the payroll check available to the employee on Monday, December 31. The employee picks up the check the following week in January 2019. The employee was constructively paid in 2018, and 2018 payroll tax rules apply to the employer and the income is taxable to the employee in 2018. If the check or other payment had not been available to the employee until Wednesday January 2, 2019, payment would be considered made in 2019 and 2019 tax rules would apply even though the services were performed in 2018.

The Use of Computers in Payroll

Overview

Introduction

Because of detailed calculations and potentially large amounts of data, payroll procedures are an excellent application for the use of a computer. In fact, one of the first computer applications that a small business wants to use is often the preparation of payroll (for businesses that do not use an independent payroll service).

What a Computerized Payroll System Does

A fully integrated computerized payroll system performs the following functions:

- Maintains a database of employee information and current payroll tax rates, wage bases, and other information needed for calculations
- Performs all payroll calculations
- Prints payroll checks
- Performs accounting and record-keeping functions
- Prints all payroll forms and tax returns
- Provides management with summary analysis reports

Input Is Required

Of course, the computer system cannot perform these payroll functions unless data are entered into the computer. For example, hours worked by employees must be calculated and recorded for each payroll period, and then they must be entered into the computer with employee identification codes. Additionally,

Overview, *continued*

the database of employee information frequently must be updated, and entering this information is not an automated procedure.

The journal entries created by the payroll software should interface with the general ledger software, so these entries are recorded with a single command.

Hidden Costs

A computerized payroll system has numerous hidden costs; therefore, the volume of calculations and reports should be large enough to create a time savings that offsets the other hidden costs. Some of these costs are:

- Substantial training and practice time is required to understand and efficiently operate a computerized accounting system.
- Annual updates of payroll software are required.
- Recurring updates of employee database information are required.
- Software support services from the vendor may be an additional charge.
- Special payroll forms are required.
- Upgrades of computer hardware will be needed, particularly if the size of the software program increases.

Internal Control Issues

Computerized payroll systems create special internal control issues. The primary concerns are about access and separation of duties.

- Because a single payroll computer module can perform virtually all the payroll functions, one person with access to the payroll program can essentially control all payroll functions.
- Pay rates and critical data can be altered, and unauthorized program changes can be made. This means that overpayments as well as fictitious employees can easily be created.
- Small- to moderate-sized business are particularly vulnerable because only one or two people regularly use the computer accounting system.

Internal Control

Overview

As discussed earlier and above, internal control means the policies and procedures that a business uses to safeguard its assets, particularly against theft and mismanagement, and to ensure compliance with regulations. Internal control also applies to other aspects of payroll. These are discussed below.

---

continued ▶

Internal Control, *continued*

Separation of Duties

When a single person has responsibility and authority for multiple duties, the opportunity for fraud greatly increases because the opportunity for evaluation and review decreases. It is important to remain aware of the key activities involved in the payroll process and separate the duties of each step among different people. Key duties are discussed below. In a small business with limited staff, the owner must assume some or all of these duties.

Processing Controls

- Payroll processing calculations are performed as a separate duty, independent from all other payroll duties.
- Staff performing processing duties cannot input or change time card or hours worked data. Processing staff receives employee status information from the human resources department but does not have access to or cannot change from the human resources department data.
- Staff performing payroll-processing duties must report to accounting but does not have access to accounting system (journals, ledgers). Accounting staff independently records payroll information from data provided by payroll processing.

Record Keeping

- Accounting department exclusively inputs data into accounting system. Payroll entries are approved by accounting supervisor.
- Accounting department performs compliance reporting (required forms, etc.).
- Accounting maintains documents under physical and software security: passwords, lockouts for sensitive files, firewalls, etc. (Note: some commonly-used government forms prepared online such as Form 941 can be password protected. As well, these forms can be downloaded, copies made and then password protected.)
- Physical time cards are stored securely and never returned to employee or supervisor. New timecards are physically controlled and pre-numbered. Payroll reports are stored securely and require authorized access.

Payment Controls

- Create a separate payroll checking account. This simplifies the reconciliation of cash balances and limits access to cash via payroll disbursements.
- A manager authorized to sign checks is independent and not involved in payroll processing or accounting functions.
- Physical checks should be handed to employees by someone other than an immediate supervisor. Person delivering checks requires employee ID and does not work in human resources and does not have access to human resource records. (Note: direct deposit eliminates the need for physical checks

Internal Control, *continued*

but requires human resources to regularly monitor employee status as active employees.)

- Wage payments are prompt per state laws (compliance).
- Deposit requirements are timely met (compliance) per federal and state/local law. This requires information from the accounting department, but deposits (and access to cash) should not be made by the accounting department.

Calculation and Verification Controls

- Employee payroll data input to processing is checked and verified by supervisor. Employee and supervisor approve with signature.
- Calculations are checked, at least on a random sample basis, by payroll supervisor.
- Benefit rates and amounts are verified with Human Resources.
- Payroll processing output is checked for accuracy, at least on a random sample basis, by independent party not working in payroll processing department.
- An independent party (not in payroll processing) reconciles the payroll checking account.

Authorization Controls

- Hiring, pay rate, classification, etc. is performed by the human resources department.
- Authorization is required for signing checks.
- Authorization is required for distributing checks.
- Vacation time and special leave is pre-authorized.
- Comp time must be authorized.
- Access to designated data is pre-authorized.

Reporting

Designated individuals in the accounting department are responsible for either preparing payroll forms or reviewing the forms, signing and submitting required forms and reports (compliance requirements), internal analysis as required, and preparing financial statements.

Payroll Audit

Payroll functions are regularly internally and/or externally audited to check calculations, evaluate above procedures, match accounting records and reporting documents to payroll data, and review and improve internal control procedures.

Internal Control, *continued*

Outsourcing: Use of Payroll Processing Services

Some banks and specialized companies offer payroll-processing services. The use of these services can relieve employers of some of the record-keeping and virtually all of the physical processing and form preparation functions in payroll. However, the other procedures listed above are still required. Employers should very carefully monitor all authorized payments made by processing services (if any). In some cases funds are prematurely frozen for a period before payment is really required. In other cases, actual fraud has occurred with processors reporting deposits that were never made and stealing funds from employers.

Record-Keeping

It is recommended that as a general rule for IRS purposes, all payroll records be kept for at least four years after the date tax becomes due or is paid, whichever is later. Keep records indefinitely if a return is not filed. (Keep returns for at least six years in case you materially (25% or more of income) under-report income—but seven years for a margin of error—that should be reported.)

Summary of Accounts Used

Overview

The following lists show the accounts that are typically used (if both federal and state income tax applies) when recording each of the three elements of payroll transactions. Account names may vary somewhat with different organizations.

Recording Gross Wages and Withholding

Account	Description
■ Wages Expense/ Salaries Expense	An operating expense that is the gross amount paid to employees for wages, salaries, and other compensation such as bonuses.
■ Federal Income Tax Payable	A current liability resulting from amounts withheld from employees for federal income tax
■ State Income Tax Payable	A current liability resulting from amounts withheld from employees for state income tax
■ FICA Payable	A current liability resulting from amounts withheld from employees for OASDI and Medicare

Summary of Accounts Used, *continued*

Account	Description
■ Health Insurance Payable	A current liability resulting from amounts withheld from employees if they share the cost of medical insurance premiums
■ Union Dues Payable*	A current liability resulting from amounts withheld from employees and payable to their union
■ Salaries and Wages Payable	A current liability for the net amount due employees after subtracting withholding

* There may also be other voluntary withholding items

Recording Employer Payroll Tax Expense

Account	Description
■ Payroll Tax Expense	An operating expense resulting from all the payroll tax obligations of the employer
■ FICA Payable	A current liability resulting from amounts withheld from employees for OASDI and Medicare
■ FUTA Payable	A current liability resulting from the employer's federal unemployment tax obligation
■ SUTA Payable	A current liability resulting from the employer's state* unemployment tax obligation

* There may also be other state-related payroll tax expenses

continued

Summary of Accounts Used, *continued*

*Recording
Benefits Expense*

Account	Description
▪ Vacation Pay Expense	An operating expense that records the vacation pay accrued to employees
▪ Medical Benefits Expense	An operating expense that records the cost of medical insurance premiums paid by the employer
▪ Workers Compensation Insurance Expense	An operating expense that records the cost of workers compensation insurance
▪ Sick Pay Expense	An operating expense that records the sick pay accrued to employees
▪ Vacation Pay Payable	A current liability that records the amount of vacation pay due employees.
▪ Health Insurance Payable	A current liability that records the amount of health insurance obligation
▪ Workers Comp. Insurance Payable	A current liability that records the amount of workers compensation insurance obligation

Section 4 Make Payments

Introduction

Several types of payments are required after a payroll is calculated. This discussion focuses on federal rules; in most cases the timing of state deposit requirements parallels federal. This is a compliance area in which a tax calendar becomes essential.

Review of Payment types and Procedures

Types of Payments

Employers are required to make various types of payments that are related to the normal payroll process. The most common and recurring payment types are:

1) Wages to employees
2) Benefits payments to benefit administrators
3) Employee income and payroll tax withholding to taxing authorities
4) Employer payroll taxes to taxing authorities

Wage payments to employees (which includes commissions, bonuses, etc.) and benefit payments to administrators are also included in the above discussion about recording the payroll. Other types of payments are miscellaneous withholding items paid to other parties, such as for wage garnishments, union dues, and voluntary employee withholding. Unfortunately, many employers also incur unnecessary compliance penalty payments for failing to satisfy various taxing authority or other legal requirements.

What we have not yet discussed is the important issue of deposit requirements imposed by federal and state (and sometimes local) taxing authorities. Payroll withholding and employer payroll tax deposits are an important source of cash flow for government budgets, and failing to meet deposit requirements is a common reason for employer penalties. We discuss deposit requirements below in the context of federal requirements.

Employee Payments

This requirement is relatively straightforward. Aside from state frequency of payment requirements, usually the only other consideration is the manner of payment. The most cost-effective payment is direct deposit to an employee checking or savings account. Physical checks are also still frequently used. Cash payments should not be made. Note: refer to internal control issues in Section 3.

continued ▶

Tax Deposit Requirements and Procedures

Overview of Deposit Procedures

Federal tax authorities require regular and timely deposits for FICA and income tax withheld, reported quarterly by most employers on form 941. (Also similar but slightly different deposit rules apply to filers of forms 943, 944, and 945. See section 5 and summary on page 139 for a discussion of these forms.) For form 941, the first step to determine deposit requirements is to create a "lookback" period.

FICA and Employee Income Tax: Lookback Period

On the first business day of a calendar year, an employer determines a 4-quarter lookback period by referring to the 941 forms filed as follows:

- 3rd and 4th quarters of the second preceding calendar year, plus
- 1st and 2nd quarter of the preceding calendar year.

Example: for 2018 the lookback period is July 1–September 30 and October 1–December 31 of 2016, plus January 1–March 31 and April 1–June 30 of 2017.

Step	IF	THEN
1	Total tax is less than $2,500 for the current quarter or was less than $2,500 in the prior quarter, AND there was not a $100,000 or more undeposited tax liability on any day in the current deposit period,	Pay the amount due at the time of a timely filed Form 941. Also use 941-V payment voucher. Note: If the employer is not qualified from the prior quarter and unsure about current quarter, it is safer to make monthly or semi-weekly deposits.
2	The employer reported tax of $50,000 or less during the lookback period OR the employer is in the first year of a new business,	The employer is a **monthly** depositor. Tax for a month must be deposited by the 15th day of the following month.
3	The employer reported tax of more than $50,000 during the lookback period,	The employer is a **semi-weekly** depositor. The following schedule applies: ■ Payday is on Wednesday, Thursday, and/or Friday: Deposit is on the **next Wednesday**. ■ Payday is on Saturday, Sunday, Monday, and/or Tuesday: Deposit is on the **next Friday**.

continued ▶

Tax Deposit Requirements and Procedures, *continued*

4	Regardless of the above schedules, on any day in the current deposit period there is a $100,000 or more under-deposited tax liability,	▪ The tax must be deposited by the **next business day** AND ▪ The employer becomes a semiweekly depositor for the remainder of the current calendar year and all of the next calendar year.
5	Any deposit day falls on a non-business day,	The deposit is considered timely if made by the next business day (Any weekday except Saturday, Sunday, or a federal holiday).
---	**New Employers**	A new employer becomes a **monthly** depositor until a lookback period is established.

Reminder: If employer is unsure about exceeding the $2,500 limit to allow payment with timely filed return, it is safer to at least make monthly deposits.

FUTA Deposits   FUTA (and SUTA) employer payroll taxes require separate reporting and have their own deposit requirements. The FUTA deposit requirements are shown below.

Step	IF	THEN
1	The cumulative unpaid FUTA tax is more than $500 by the end of a calendar quarter,	Deposit the tax no later than the last day of the month following the quarter.*
2	Carry the liability forward until it is more than $500 and deposit as in Step 1.	Carry the liability forward until it is more than $500 and return to Step 1, unless it is the last quarter of the year, then go to Step 3.
3	The liability is $500 or less for the year,	Deposit the amount of with filing of Form 940 by January 31.

continued ▶

As with other payroll tax deposits, electronic filing is generally required. The electronic federal tax payment system (EFTPS) can be used at no charge.

Accuracy of Deposit Rule (A "Safety Net")

The IRS generally requires that 100% of every withheld FICA and income tax deposit be timely made in order to avoid a penalty. But there is an exception, if both of these conditions are met:

- A deposit shortfall does not exceed $100 or 2% of the amount due,
- The deposit shortfall is deposited by the applicable shortfall makeup deposit date.

Deposit shortfall makeup dates:

- For monthly depositors: No later than the due date of the return for the period for which the shortfall occurred.
- For semi-weekly depositors: The earlier of:

  1) The first Wednesday or Friday on or after the 15th of the month following the month in which the shortfall occurred, or
  2) The due date of the return to which the shortfall is related. (IRC §31.6302-1(f))

How to Make Deposits

Except for payments that can be made with filing of a return, employment taxes must be deposited by EFT (Electronic Funds Transfer). This is a system that will electronically transfer amounts from an employer's bank account to the Treasury Department.

With this system, payments can be made online, by phone (a voice-response and touch-tone system) or by batch software processing for tax professionals. The system used is called "EFTPS". It is a free service for all types of federal government tax payments; to obtain more information go to www.eftps.gov or call 1-800-555-4477.

Enrollment in the system can be completed online or with Form 9779. Payment can also be made through third-party processors, but this may involve fees.

For a new business, if deposits are required and the employer has applied for but not yet received an EIN (Employer Identification Number) deposits can be mailed to the IRS with a copy of the application and a brief explanation.

First Quarterly Deposit Penalty Waiver

Summary

The IRS may waive deposit penalties applicable to a first quarter in the following circumstances:

- If an employer timely filed the applicable employment tax return, the IRS may waive deposit penalties if the employer inadvertently failed to make a timely deposit and it was the first quarter that the employer was required to deposit any employment tax.
- If an employer inadvertently failed to timely make the first deposit after the deposit frequency changed, the IRS may also waive penalties.

Limitations: A business cannot have more than 500 employees or a net worth exceeding 7 million dollars. (IRC §6656(c))

Deposit Penalties

As previously mentioned, payroll deposits are an important source of cash flow to federal, state, and some local governments. As with all types of filing and tax payment requirements, penalties are imposed if deposit requirements are not met. See page 145 for a summary of payroll-related penalties.

TIP

Did you know..? Late payroll deposits and payments are costly to small businesses. About 40% of small business are fined an average of $850 per year for not making timely payments.

Source: SCORE (Service Corps of Retired Executives)

"Grossing Up" a Net Amount

There are occasions when a supplemental payment is made to an employee and the intention is for the employee to receive a specified net amount. However, this can be complicated by the fact that usually withholding reduces what an employee receives. A supplemental payment requires both: 1) a calculation of gross pay before withholding is applied, and 2) conforming to IRS supplemental payment rules (See page 79). A method to determine gross pay so that an employee receives a specified net amount is to use the following formula, which defines the net amount in terms of a net percent:

- *[Desired Take-Home Amount / (1 – total withholding percentage)]*
- *(Any fixed dollar amount withheld is separately calculated as above and added.)*

Usually the gross amount of a supplemental wage payment is not intended to cover pre-tax deductions such as tax-deferred retirement contributions; if so, a higher pre-contribution gross amount would be calculated, subject to additional FICA, as in Example #3 below.

continued ▶

Payment Types and Procedures, *continued*

Finally, if a supplemental wage payment requires certain withholding rules as previously discussed, such as combining regular gross pay plus supplemental pay to determine withholding, or if the gross amount causes cumulative gross wages to exceed the OASDI limit in the current period, an iterative method that requires the use of software can be applied.

Procedure and Example #1

Macon Enterprises is giving its star salesperson, Mary Smith, a bonus. They want her to receive an amount of $5,000, but need to determine the correct amount of gross pay before withholding so that she receives the $5,000. Mary's year-to-date gross pay will be within the annual OASDI limit. Based on tax tables, her federal income tax rate is 22% and her state tax rate is 7%.

Step	Procedure	Example
1	Calculate the net income tax rate after the tax-deferred annuity percent.	FICA: .0765 FIT: .2200 SIT: .0700 Total .3665
2	Subtract from 1.	1 – .3665 = .6335
3	For gross pay, divide desired take-home amount by the result from Step 2.	$5,000/.6335 = $7,892.66
4	Determine amounts for accounting purposes.	FICA: $7,892.66 × .0765 = $603.79 FIT: $7,892.66 × .22 = $1,736.38 SIT: $7,892.66 × .07 = $552.49
5	Verify net payment amount.	$7,892.66 – $603.79 – $1,736.38 – $552.49 = $5,000.

Note: $7,892.66 will be a debit to wages expenses and $603.79, $1,736.38, and $552.49 will be withholding liabilities that result in net wages payable of $5,000.

Payment Types and Procedures, *continued*

Procedure and Example #2

Atwater Company is making a supplemental payment to Walter Thompson for a production enhancement. The company wants Walter to receive $20,000 after all amounts are deducted. Walter's gross pay will be within the OASDI wage base limit. His federal tax rate is 22% and his state rate is 4%. $50 of union dues must also be withheld.

Step	Procedure	Example
1	Combine the applicable withholding percentages.	FICA: .0765 FIT: .2200 SIT: .0400 Total .3365
2	Subtract from 1.	1 – .3365 = .6635
3	Divide desired take-home amount by the result from Step 2.	$20,000/.6635 = $30,143.18
4	Repeat the procedure for the $50.	$50/.6635 = $75.36
5	Combine the totals for gross pay.	$30,143.18 + $75.36 = $30,218.54
6	Determine amounts for accounting purposes and verify net payment amount.	See example in the above table.

Payment Types and Procedures, *continued*

Procedure and
Example #3

Suppose that in Example #1 the employer wishes to calculate a gross amount that will include a 5% qualified retirement plan contribution that will be withheld from the supplemental gross amount.

Step	Procedure	Example
1	Combine the tax withholding percentages, with income tax percentages adjusted to a net rate relative to gross.	FICA: .0765 FIT: (.22 × .95) = .2090 SIT: (.07 × .95) = .0665 Total .3520
2	Subtract Step 1 amount from net taxable rate.	.95 − .3520 = .5980
3	Divide desired take-home amount by the result from Step 2 for gross pay.	$5,000/.5980 = $8,361.20
4	Determine withholding amounts for accounting purposes.	Contribution: $8,361.20 × .05 = $418.06 FICA: $8,361.20 × .0765 = $639.63 FIT: $8,361.20 × .2090 = $1,747.49 SIT: $8,361.20 × .0665 = $556.02
5	Verify net payment amount.	$8,361.20 − $418.06 − $639.63 − $1,747.49 − $556.02 = $5,000.

Note the following: The amounts of ($8,361.20 × .95) = $7,943.14 and $8,361.20 (wages for income tax and FICA-taxable wages) create a difference of $418.06 between boxes 1 and 3 on Form W-2. The $8,361.20 would also be used for employer payroll taxes calculations (FICA, FUTA, SUTA). For accounting purposes, the total debit to wages expense will be $8,361.20 before withholding liabilities to arrive at a net pay of $5,000.

Section 5 Submit Forms and Reports

Introduction

Submitting required forms and reports is a regular and unavoidable aspect of the payroll process, and like deposit requirements, can be the the source of expensive and unnecessary penalaties. The use of a tax calendar is also important here.

Quarterly Reporting

Overview

Employers are generally required to make regular quarterly reports to the Internal Revenue Service to report wages, tips, employee and employer FICA, income tax withheld and deposits made. State authorities require similar reporting. The federal report most commonly used is form 941, filed quarterly. We discuss form 941 below.

Exceptions:

- Employers of farm workers subject to federal income tax and/or FICA must separately file annual Form 943 for the farm workers instead of the quarterly Form 941 used for non-agricultural workers.
- Employers with an annual deposit obligation of $1,000 or less can annually file Form 944 instead of Form 941.
- Employers of household employees generally file schedule H with their own annual Form1040, individual tax return. (See Publication 926).
- Seasonal employers may not have to file Form 941every quarter. (See Form 941 instructions).

   Note: Other withholding, such as backup withholding (e.g. employer has not received employee social security number) and non-employee withholding (pensions, annuities, investments, etc.) is annually reported on Form 945.

Who Files Form 941?

The purpose of these reports is to inform tax authorities each quarterly period of: 1) FICA: employer and employee liability 2) Employee income tax: how much was withheld 3) Any related adjustments or credits 4) Deposits: All deposits made and when they were made.

continued ▶

Quarterly Reporting, *continued*

Employers must file Form 941 if any of the below items apply, unless one of the above exceptions apply:

- There are employees who receive wages and/or tips
- There is withheld income tax
- Form 941 was previously filed, even if there are no current wages or withholding amounts, unless a final return was previously filed.

Federal forms resource: All current federal forms can be accessed online at http://www.irs.gov/formspubs/.

Form 941 Due Dates

Form 941 reports are required for calendar quarters, as follows:

- 1st quarter: January, February, March
- 2nd quarter: April, May, June
- 3rd quarter: July, August, September,
- 4th quarter: October, November, December

IF...	THEN...	OTHERWISE...
Timely deposits are made in full payment of amounts due,	File by the 10th day of the second month following the end of the quarter.	File by the last day of the month following the end of the quarter.

Sources of Form 941 Information

The employee earnings records (see page 100 example) are primary sources of Form 941 information. Supplemental records and reporting will provide tips information if not incorporated into individual earnings records. Form 8974 can assist the calculation of the qualified small business tax credit that may be used to reduce employer payroll tax or income tax resulting from research activities.

An employer should especially note the importance of maintaining consistency between internal records and reporting. For example, employee earnings records, W-2s, and quarterly 941 forms must all show consistent amounts. The Social Security Administration checks W-2s and the annual total of quarterly reports for consistency. The IRS also matches the total reported on Form W-3 with the annual total of four quarterly 941 reports.

Quarterly Reporting, *continued*

TIP

IRS Electronic Payment and Filing Systems:

- For payment—EFTPS (Electronic Federal Tax Payment System): This is a free system offered by the U.S. Treasury Department. Go to www.eftps.gov to enroll. Also see Publications 966 and 4990.
- For filing—Modernized e-File for Employment Taxes (MeF), a part of the updated IRS e-File system for most federal tax returns: This allows employers to electronically self-prepare federal employment tax returns through IRS-approved commercially available software and approved transmitter. See Publication 3112, IRS *e-file Application and Participation.*
- For filing—FIRE system: This is an IRS electronic system only for business filers of certain information returns. For employers, the returns applicable to FIRE would be W-2G, 1099, 1042-S, 3921, 3922, and 8027 and 8955.

continued

Quarterly Reporting, *continued*

Illustration 5.1: Form 941

Form **941 for 20**	: Employer's QUARTERLY Federal Tax Return	950117
(Rev. January 2017)	Department of the Treasury — Internal Revenue Service	OMB No. 1545-0029

Employer identification number (EIN) ☐☐ – ☐☐☐☐☐☐☐

Name *(not your trade name)* _____

Trade name *(if any)* _____

Address _____
Number   Street   Suite or room number

_____
City   State   ZIP code

_____
Foreign country name   Foreign province/county   Foreign postal code

Report for this Quarter of 2017
(Check one.)

☐ **1:** January, February, March

☐ **2:** April, May, June

☐ **3:** July, August, September

☐ **4:** October, November, December

Instructions and prior year forms are available at *www.irs.gov/form941*.

Read the separate instructions before you complete Form 941. Type or print within the boxes.

Part 1:   Answer these questions for this quarter.

1   Number of employees who received wages, tips, or other compensation for the pay period including: *Mar. 12* (Quarter 1), *June 12* (Quarter 2), *Sept. 12* (Quarter 3), or *Dec. 12* (Quarter 4)   **1** _____

2   Wages, tips, and other compensation . . . .   **2** _____

3   Federal income tax withheld from wages, tips, and other compensation . . . . . .   **3** _____

4   If no wages, tips, and other compensation are subject to social security or Medicare tax   ☐ Check and go to line 6.

		Column 1		Column 2
5a	Taxable social security wages . .	_____ .	× 0.124 =	_____ .
5b	Taxable social security tips . . .	_____ .	× 0.124 =	_____ .
5c	Taxable Medicare wages & tips. .	_____ .	× 0.029 =	_____ .
5d	Taxable wages & tips subject to Additional Medicare Tax withholding	_____ .	× 0.009 =	_____ .

5e   Add Column 2 from lines 5a, 5b, 5c, and 5d . . . .   **5e** _____ .

5f   Section 3121(q) Notice and Demand—Tax due on unreported tips (see instructions) . .   **5f** _____ .

6   Total taxes before adjustments. Add lines 3, 5e, and 5f . . . .   **6** _____ .

7   Current quarter's adjustment for fractions of cents . . . .   **7** _____ .

8   Current quarter's adjustment for sick pay . . . .   **8** _____ .

9   Current quarter's adjustments for tips and group-term life insurance . . . .   **9** _____ .

10   Total taxes after adjustments. Combine lines 6 through 9 . . . .   **10** _____ .

11   Qualified small business payroll tax credit for increasing research activities. Attach Form 8974   **11** _____ .

12   Total taxes after adjustments and credits. Subtract line 11 from line 10 . . . . . .   **12** _____ .

13   Total deposits for this quarter, including overpayment applied from a prior quarter and overpayments applied from Form 941-X, 941-X (PR), 944-X, or 944-X (SP) filed in the current quarter   **13** _____ .

14   Balance due. If line 12 is more than line 13, enter the difference and see instructions . . .   **14** _____ .

15   Overpayment. If line 13 is more than line 12, enter the difference _____ .   Check one: ☐ Apply to next return. ☐ Send a refund.

▶ **You MUST complete both pages of Form 941 and SIGN it.**   [Next ▶]

For Privacy Act and Paperwork Reduction Act Notice, see the back of the Payment Voucher.   Cat. No. 17001Z   Form **941** (Rev. 1-2017)

Source: Internal Revenue Service

Quarterly Reporting, *continued*

Illustration 5.1: Form 941, continued

950217

Name *(not your trade name)*	Employer identification number (EIN)

Part 2: Tell us about your deposit schedule and tax liability for this quarter.

If you are unsure about whether you are a monthly schedule depositor or a semiweekly schedule depositor, see section 11 of Pub. 15.

16 Check one: ☐ Line 12 on this return is less than $2,500 or line 12 (line 10 if the prior quarter was the fourth quarter of 2016) on the return for the prior quarter was less than $2,500, and you didn't incur a $100,000 next-day deposit obligation during the current **quarter.** If line 12 (line 10 if the prior quarter was the fourth quarter of 2016) for the prior quarter was less than $2,500 but line 12 on this return is $100,000 or more, you must provide a record of your federal tax liability. If you are a monthly schedule depositor, complete the deposit schedule below; if you are a semiweekly schedule depositor, attach Schedule B (Form 941). Go to Part 3.

☐ **You were a monthly schedule depositor for the entire quarter.** Enter your tax liability for each month and total liability for the quarter, then go to Part 3.

Tax liability: Month 1 [_____.__]

Month 2 [_____.__]

Month 3 [_____.__]

Total liability for quarter [_____.__] Total must equal line 12.

☐ **You were a semiweekly schedule depositor for any part of this quarter.** Complete Schedule B (Form 941), Report of Tax Liability for Semiweekly Schedule Depositors, and attach it to Form 941.

Part 3: Tell us about your business. If a question does NOT apply to your business, leave it blank.

17 If your business has closed or you stopped paying wages . . . . ☐ Check here, and

enter the final date you paid wages [/   /] .

18 If you are a seasonal employer and you don't have to file a return for every quarter of the year . . ☐ Check here.

Part 4: May we speak with your third-party designee?

Do you want to allow an employee, a paid tax preparer, or another person to discuss this return with the IRS? See the instructions for details.

☐ Yes. Designee's name and phone number [_____] [_____]

Select a 5-digit Personal Identification Number (PIN) to use when talking to the IRS. ☐☐☐☐☐

☐ No.

Part 5: Sign here. You MUST complete both pages of Form 941 and SIGN it.

Under penalties of perjury, I declare that I have examined this return, including accompanying schedules and statements, and to the best of my knowledge and belief, it is true, correct, and complete. Declaration of preparer (other than taxpayer) is based on all information of which preparer has any knowledge.

X Sign your name here [_____]

Print your name here [_____]

Print your title here [_____]

Date [/   /]

Best daytime phone [_____]

Paid Preparer Use Only Check if you are self-employed . . . ☐

Preparer's name	[_____]	PTIN	[_____]
Preparer's signature	[_____]	Date	[/ /]
Firm's name (or yours if self-employed)	[_____]	EIN	[_____]
Address	[_____]	Phone	[_____]
City	[_____] State [____]	ZIP code	[_____]

Page **2**

Form **941** (Rev. 1-2017)

Source: Internal Revenue Service

continued ▶

Quarterly Reporting, *continued*

Illustration 5.1: Form 941, continued

Schedule B (Form 941):

Report of Tax Liability for Semiweekly Schedule Depositors

960311

OMB No. 1545-0029

(Rev. January 2017)   Department of the Treasury — Internal Revenue Service

Employer identification number (EIN)

Name *(not your trade name)*

Calendar year   (Also check quarter)

Report for this Quarter...
(Check one.)

☐ **1:** January, February, March

☐ **2:** April, May, June

☐ **3:** July, August, September

☐ **4:** October, November, December

Use this schedule to show your TAX LIABILITY for the quarter; don't use it to show your deposits. When you file this form with Form 941 or Form 941-SS, don't change your tax liability by adjustments reported on any Forms 941-X or 944-X. You must fill out this form and attach it to Form 941 or Form 941-SS if you're a semiweekly schedule depositor or became one because your accumulated tax liability on any day was $100,000 or more. Write your daily tax liability on the numbered space that corresponds to the date wages were paid. See Section 11 in Pub. 15 for details.

Month 1

								Tax liability for Month 1
1		9		17		25		
2		10		18		26		
3		11		19		27		
4		12		20		28		
5		13		21		29		
6		14		22		30		
7		15		23		31		
8		16		24				

Month 2

								Tax liability for Month 2
1		9		17		25		
2		10		18		26		
3		11		19		27		
4		12		20		28		
5		13		21		29		
6		14		22		30		
7		15		23		31		
8		16		24				

Month 3

								Tax liability for Month 3
1		9		17		25		
2		10		18		26		
3		11		19		27		
4		12		20		28		
5		13		21		29		
6		14		22		30		
7		15		23		31		
8		16		24				

Fill in your total liability for the quarter (Month 1 + Month 2 + Month 3) ▶

Total must equal line 12 on Form 941 or Form 941-SS.

Total liability for the quarter

For Paperwork Reduction Act Notice, see separate instructions.   IRS.gov/form941   Cat. No. 11967Q   **Schedule B (Form 941)** (Rev. 1-2017)

Source: Internal Revenue Service

Annual Reporting

Finding Forms

As with many payroll issues, a good source of information is the IRS website at irs.gov. As well, an Internet search by topic or issue followed by the term "forms" can also be useful. Also, payroll software will normally generate the more frequently used forms as part of processing. In many cases, state forms are used for similar purposes as federal forms. For state forms, locate the online page of the state taxing authority for a forms list, description, and filing requirements. Also see page 144.

Annual Reporting: Form W-2

W-2 Basic Filing Requirements

An employer must annually prepare and submit a Form W-2 to the Social Security Administration for an employee if any of the following conditions exist:

- Any payment (cash or noncash) greater than $600 was paid to an employee for services in a trade or business regardless of whether any amounts were withheld or not.
- Any income tax, social security, or Medicare tax is withheld
- Income tax would have been withheld if the employee had not claimed more than one allowance or had not claimed to be exempt from withholding on Form W-4

Refer to instructions for Form W-2 for additional information.

A social security number verification service (SSNVS) is available online for authorized employers and other authorized users. Go to *socialsecurity .gov/employer/ssnv.htm* for further information.

continued

Annual Reporting: Form W-2, *continued*

Due Dates	Following December 31 of the current year:

- Provide to employees: no later than January 31
- Provide to taxing authorities: no later than January 31 (Exception: deadline for W-2G for gambling winnings is allowed a 30-day extension to federal taxing authorities.)
- A single 30-day extension of time may requested on Form 8809. IRS will grant extensions only under extraordinary circumstances.

Source of W-2 Information	The employee earnings records (See page 100 example.) are primary sources of W-2 information. Supplementary records and reporting will provide tips and benefits information if not incorporated into individual earnings records. An employer should especially note the importance of maintaining consistency between internal records and reporting.

For example, employee earnings records, W-2s, and quarterly 941 or 943 forms must all show consistent amounts. The Social Security Administration checks W-2s and the annual total of quarterly reports for consistency.

Specific Circumstances	Table 5.1 on the next page addresses specific circumstances that may be occur in connection with the preparation and/or filing of Form W-2.

TIP

Identify yourself!—Do you know the differences between the forms: SS-4, SS-5, W-4 and W-9?

- A Form SS-4 is filed with the Internal Revenue Service in order to obtain an employer identification number (EIN or "Tax ID").
- A Form SS-5 is filed with the Social Security Administration by an individual to obtain a social security number. A social security number is used by individuals and sole proprietors without employees as identification.
- A Form W-4 is used by employers to obtain employee information primarily to determine correct income tax withholding.
- A Form W-9 is used by business (also non-profits, pension plans, and government agencies) payers of income to obtain information from the recipient of the payments in order to determine possible withholding. This request usually applies to independent contractors and recipients of dividends and interest. The party making the payments uses the information on Form 1099.

Annual Reporting: Form W-2, *continued*

Table 5.1: Form W-2 Potential Issues

IF...	THEN...
a box on the form does not apply to an employee,	leave that box blank.
a W-2 has been lost or destroyed,	provide a substitute copy with the wording "reissued statement".
there are errors on W-2s that have been sent out,	immediately prepare and send out Form W-2c, "Corrected Wage and Tax Statement". (Illustration 5.4)
An employer refuses to issue a corrected W-2	employee may initiate a W-2 complaint with the IRS. 800-829-1040 or online taxpayer assistance.
An employee does not provide a social security number (SSN).	instruct the employee to complete an application Form SS-5. If the employee has applied but the number is not available at time of filing write "Applied For" in box 'a' or all zeros in number box for electronic filing.
an employer cannot locate an employee or successfully deliver a W-2 to the last known address,	retain the employee copy for four years.
an employee leaves the employer,	provide W-2 at any time after the employee leaves, but no later than the normal due dates.
an employee asks for a W-2 after leaving,	provide within 30 days of request or final wage payment.
an employee who previously left is rehired during the current calendar year,	provide W-2 according to normal due dates
250 or more W-2s are prepared,	filing must be done electronically.
an employer is going out business,	provide w-2s to employees no later than the due date of the final Form 941.
employee is deceased,	if payment made in year of death show wages paid in box 1 and wages paid plus all accrued compensation in boxes 3 and 5; if paid after year of death, only actual payments are shown. Also file 1099 and send to estate.

continued ▶

Annual Reporting: Form W-2, *continued*

Internet Delivery to Employees

An employer can provide W-2s to those employees who have affirmatively consented to Internet delivery of their W-2s. An employee's consent must be via the Internet and state that the employee has access. The website delivering the W-2s must be secure and use individual passwords. An employee must be notified of the W-2 availability and provided instructions on how to access it. Normal due dates apply, and the employer is required to keep W-2s available online until October 15 of the following calendar year.

Illustration 5.2: Form W-2

22222	Void ☐	a Employee's social security number	For Official Use Only ▶ OMB No. 1545-0008		
b Employer identification number (EIN)			1 Wages, tips, other compensation	2 Federal income tax withheld	
c Employer's name, address, and ZIP code			3 Social security wages	4 Social security tax withheld	
			5 Medicare wages and tips	6 Medicare tax withheld	
			7 Social security tips	8 Allocated tips	
d Control number			9 Verification code	10 Dependent care benefits	
e Employee's first name and initial	Last name	Suff.	11 Nonqualified plans	12a See instructions for box 12	
			13 Statutory employee ☐ Retirement plan ☐ Third-party sick pay ☐	12b	
			14 Other	12c	
				12d	
f Employee's address and ZIP code					
15 State Employer's state ID number	16 State wages, tips, etc.	17 State income tax	18 Local wages, tips, etc.	19 Local income tax	20 Locality name

Form **W-2** Wage and Tax Statement　　**20**　.

Copy A For Social Security Administration — Send this entire page with Form W-3 to the Social Security Administration; photocopies are **not** acceptable.

Do Not Cut, Fold, or Staple Forms on This Page

Department of the Treasury—Internal Revenue Service
For Privacy Act and Paperwork Reduction Act Notice, see the separate instructions.

Cat. No. 10134D

Source: Internal Revenue Service

Annual Reporting: Form W-2, *continued*

Table 5.2: Summary of Instructions for completing Form W-2

Box	Description
a	**Employee social security number:** This should be available on Form W-4. (Note: After 2018, current regulations permit "truncated" numbers on employee copies (only) as follows: each of the first five digits of a social security number is replaced with "X".)
Void	This box is used when there is an error on a single form that is corrected on a following single form on one entire sheet of forms that is being prepared for taxing authorities.
b	**Employer identification number:** An employer identification number (EIN) is assigned by the IRS. An EIN can be applied for by completing and sending in Form SS-4. If no number is available and it has been applied for, enter "Applied For" in this space.
c	**Employer name, address and zip code:** Use the same information as used on Form 941 or 943.
d	**Control number:** This is optional - use only by employers with an internal system that is designed to identify employees or individual W-2s by an ID number.
e	**Employee name:** Use the exact same name as shown on employee social security card. If that is not available, use exact same name as on Form W-4.
f	**Employee address and zip code:** This information should be available on Form W-4.
1	**Wages, tips, other compensation:** Include all employee taxable compensation including the following: 1) wages, tips reported to employer, commissions, bonuses, prizes, and awards 2) taxable fringe benefits 3) certain employee expense reimbursements (under a non-accountable plan) 4) the cost of accident and health insurance for 2% or more shareholder-employees of a subchapter-S corporation 5) taxable benefits from a cafeteria plan 6) employer contributions to a qualified long-term care plan to extent such coverage is already available through a flexible spending plan 7) cost of group-term life insurance coverage in excess of $50,000 8) payments for non-job-related education expenses or payments under a non-accountable plan 9) payments of employee social security, Medicare, or income tax withholding 10) all other compensation including taxable compensation for which federal income tax was not withheld
2	**Federal income tax withheld:** Show the total federal income tax withheld from the employee's wages for the year.

continued ▶

Table 5.2: Summary of Instructions for completing Form W-2 *continued*

Box	Description
3	**Social security wages:** Show the total wages paid (before payroll deductions) subject to employee social security tax (OASDI) but not including social security tips and allocated tips. If reporting these amounts in a subsequent year (due to lapse of risk of forfeiture), the amount must be adjusted by any gain or loss. See *Box 7—Social security tips and Box 8—Allocated tips.* Generally, noncash payments are considered to be wages. Include employee business expense reimbursements reported in box 1. If you paid the employee's share of social security and Medicare taxes rather than deducting them from wages, see *Employee's social security and Medicare taxes (or railroad retirement taxes, if applicable) paid by employer.* The total of boxes 3 and 7 cannot exceed the maximum social security wage base.)
	Report in box 3 elective deferrals to certain qualified cash or deferred compensation arrangements and to retirement plans described in box 12 (codes D, E, F, G, and S) even though the deferrals are not includible in box 1. Also report in box 3 designated Roth contributions made under a section 401(k) plan, under a section 403(b) salary reduction agreement, or under a governmental section 457(b) plan described in box 12 (codes AA, BB, and EE).
	Amounts deferred (plus earnings or less losses) under a section 457(f) or nonqualified plan or nongovernmental section 457(b) plan must be included in boxes 3 and/or 5 as social security and/or Medicare wages as of the later of when the services giving rise to the deferral are performed or when there is no substantial forfeiture risk of the rights to the deferred amount. Include both elective and non-elective deferrals for purposes of nongovernmental section 457(b) plans.
	Wages reported in box 3 also include: Signing bonuses an employer pays for signing or ratifying an employment contract. Taxable cost of group-term life insurance over $50,000 included in box 1. Cost of accident and health insurance premiums for 2%-or-more shareholder-employees paid by an S corporation, but only if not excludable under section 3121(a)(2)(B). Employee and non-excludable employer contributions to an MSA or HSA. However, do not include employee contributions to an HSA that were made through a cafeteria plan. Employee contributions to a SIMPLE retirement account.
4	**Social security tax withheld:** Show the total employee social security tax (OASDI) withheld (not employer share), including social security tax on tips. The amount should not exceed 6.2% x social security wage base. Include only taxes withheld (or paid by employer for the employee) for current year wages and tips.

Table 5.2: Summary of Instructions for completing Form W-2 *continued*

Box	Description
5	**Medicare wages and tips:** The wages and tips subject to Medicare tax are the same as those subject to social security tax (boxes 3 and 7) except that there is no wage base limit for Medicare tax. Enter the total Medicare wages and tips in box 5.
6	**Medicare tax withheld:** Enter the total employee Medicare tax (including any Additional Medicare Tax) withheld. Include only tax withheld for current year wages and tips.
7	**Social security tips:** Show the tips that the employee reported to employer even if employer did not have enough employee funds to collect the social security tax for the tips. (The total of boxes 3 and 7 should not be more than the maximum amount for the social security wage base for current year). Report all tips in box 1 along with wages and other compensation. Include any tips reported in box 7 in box 5 also.
8	**Allocated tips:** If employer operates a large food or beverage establishment, employer should show the tips allocated to the employee. Do not include this amount in boxes 1, 3, 5, or 7.
9	Blank
10	**Dependent care benefits:** Show the total dependent care benefits under a dependent care assistance program paid or incurred by you for your employee. Include the fair market value (FMV) of care in a daycare facility provided or sponsored by you for your employee and amounts paid or incurred for dependent care assistance in a cafeteria plan. Report all amounts paid or incurred (regardless of any employee forfeitures), including those in excess of the $5,000 exclusion. This may include (a) the FMV of benefits provided in kind by the employer, (b) an amount paid directly to a daycare facility by the employer or reimbursed to the employee to subsidize the benefit, or (c) benefits from the pre-tax contributions made by the employee under a dependent care flexible spending account. Include any amounts over $5,000 in boxes 1, 3, and 5.

continued ▶

Table 5.2: Summary of Instructions for completing Form W-2 *continued*

Box	Description
11	**Nonqualified plans:** The purpose of box 11 is for the Social Security Administration (SSA) to determine if any part of the amount reported in box 1 or boxes 3 and/or 5 was earned in a prior year. The SSA uses this information to verify that they have properly applied the social security earnings test and paid the correct amount of benefits. Report distributions to an employee from a nonqualified plan or nongovernmental section 457(b) plan in box 11. Also report these distributions in box 1. Make only one entry in this box. Distributions from governmental section 457(b) plans must be reported on Form 1099-R, not in box 1 of Form W-2. Under nonqualified plans or nongovernmental 457(b) plans, deferred amounts that are no longer subject to a substantial risk of forfeiture are taxable even if not distributed. Report these amounts in boxes 3 (up to the social security wage base) and 5. Do not report in box 11 deferrals included in boxes 3 and/or 5 and deferrals for current year services (such as those with no risk of forfeiture).
12	Complete and code this box for all code items described in IRS instructions for Form W-2. Do not enter more than four codes; if more than four codes are needed use an additional W-2.
13	Check all boxes that apply. Check statutory employee box for statutory employees whose earnings are subject to social security and Medicare taxes but not subject to federal income tax withholding. Do not check this box for common-law employees.
14	**Other:** Use this box for any other information that you want to give to your employee. Label each item.
15–20	**Boxes 15–20:** Use these boxes to report state and local income tax information. Enter the two-letter abbreviation for the name of the state.

Who Receives a W-2?

An employer provides W-2 copies to the following parties:

Copy A: To the Social Security Administration
Copy 1: To state and local taxing authorities
Copy B: To employees for filing federal income tax returns
Copy C: To employees for keeping in their records
Copy 2: To employees for filing state and local income tax returns
Copy D: Retained by the employer

Annual Reporting: Form W-2, *continued*

Form W-3
Transmittal Form

Form W-3 is a transmittal form that must accompany Form W-2 when filed with taxing authorities. A single Form W-3 accompanies all copies of Form W-2. A W-3c accompanies W-2c forms.

Internet Filing

The Social Security Administration strongly encourages filers to use electronic filing. Two methods are available:

- File uploads: Files must be properly formatted (according to Social Security Administration *Specifications for Filing Forms Electronically* (EFW2). As well, an employer must complete 4419, *Application for Filing Information Returns Electronically* (FIRE) and submit it to the Internal Revenue Service. See also: www.eftps.gov/eftps/.
- W-2 online: Online fill-in forms are available to fill in, save, print, and submit, to a maximum of 50 items at a time to the Social Security Administration. For further information see: www.SSA.gov/bso.

Illustration 5.3: Form W-3

DO NOT STAPLE

33333	a Control number	For Official Use Only ▶ OMB No. 1545-0008	

| b Kind of Payer (Check one) | 941 ☐ Military ☐ 943 ☐ 944 ☐ CT-1 ☐ Hshld. emp. ☐ Medicare govt. emp. ☐ | Kind of Employer (Check one) | None apply ☐ 501c non-govt. ☐ State/local non-501c ☐ State/local 501c ☐ Federal govt. ☐ | Third-party sick pay (Check if applicable) ☐ |

c Total number of Forms W-2	d Establishment number	1 Wages, tips, other compensation	2 Federal income tax withheld
e Employer identification number (EIN)		3 Social security wages	4 Social security tax withheld
f Employer's name		5 Medicare wages and tips	6 Medicare tax withheld
		7 Social security tips	8 Allocated tips
		9	10 Dependent care benefits
		11 Nonqualified plans	12a Deferred compensation
g Employer's address and ZIP code			
h Other EIN used this year		13 For third-party sick pay use only	12b
15 State Employer's state ID number		14 Income tax withheld by payer of third-party sick pay	
16 State wages, tips, etc.	17 State income tax	18 Local wages, tips, etc.	19 Local income tax
Employer's contact person		Employer's telephone number	For Official Use Only
Employer's fax number		Employer's email address	

Under penalties of perjury, I declare that I have examined this return and accompanying documents and, to the best of my knowledge and belief, they are true, correct, and complete.

Signature ▶   Title ▶   Date ▶

Form **W-3** Transmittal of Wage and Tax Statements   **20**   Department of the Treasury
Internal Revenue Service

continued ▶

Annual Reporting: Form W-2, *continued*

Illustration 5.4: Form W-2C

DO NOT CUT, FOLD, OR STAPLE THIS FORM

44444	For Official Use Only ▶ OMB No. 1545-0008		

a Employer's name, address, and ZIP code	c Tax year/Form corrected	d Employee's correct SSN
	/ W-2	
	e Corrected SSN and/or name (Check this box and complete boxes f and/or g if incorrect on form previously filed.) ☐	
	Complete boxes f and/or g only if incorrect on form **previously filed** ▶	
	f Employee's **previously reported** SSN	
b Employer's Federal EIN	g Employee's **previously reported** name	
	h Employee's first name and initial	Last name	Suff.

Note. Only complete money fields that are being corrected (exception: for corrections involving MQGE, see the General Instructions for Forms W-2 and W-3, under Specific Instructions for Form W-2c, boxes 5 and 6).

i Employee's address and ZIP code

Previously reported	Correct information	Previously reported	Correct information
1 Wages, tips, other compensation	1 Wages, tips, other compensation	2 Federal income tax withheld	2 Federal income tax withheld
3 Social security wages	3 Social security wages	4 Social security tax withheld	4 Social security tax withheld
5 Medicare wages and tips	5 Medicare wages and tips	6 Medicare tax withheld	6 Medicare tax withheld
7 Social security tips	7 Social security tips	8 Allocated tips	8 Allocated tips
9	9	10 Dependent care benefits	10 Dependent care benefits
11 Nonqualified plans	11 Nonqualified plans	12a See instructions for box 12	12a See instructions for box 12
13 Statutory employee ☐ Retirement plan ☐ Third-party sick pay ☐	13 Statutory employee ☐ Retirement plan ☐ Third-party sick pay ☐	12b	12b
14 Other (see instructions)	14 Other (see instructions)	12c	12c
		12d	12d

State Correction Information

Previously reported	Correct information	Previously reported	Correct information
15 State	15 State	15 State	15 State
Employer's state ID number	Employer's state ID number	Employer's state ID number	Employer's state ID number
16 State wages, tips, etc.	16 State wages, tips, etc.	16 State wages, tips, etc.	16 State wages, tips, etc.
17 State income tax	17 State income tax	17 State income tax	17 State income tax

Locality Correction Information

Previously reported	Correct information	Previously reported	Correct information
18 Local wages, tips, etc.	18 Local wages, tips, etc.	18 Local wages, tips, etc.	18 Local wages, tips, etc.
19 Local income tax	19 Local income tax	19 Local income tax	19 Local income tax
20 Locality name	20 Locality name	20 Locality name	20 Locality name

For Privacy Act and Paperwork Reduction Act Notice, see separate instructions.

Copy A—For Social Security Administration

Form **W-2c** (Rev. 8-2014)   **Corrected Wage and Tax Statement**   Cat. No. 61437D   Department of the Treasury Internal Revenue Service

Source: Internal Revenue Service

Annual Reporting: Form 1099

Form 1099-MISC

When annual payments by a business for nonemployee compensation are at least certain amounts the business and specified other entities (non-profits, qualified pension/profit-sharing plans, government agencies) must send a copy to recipient by January 31 for the prior calendar year. (1099-B, 1099-S, and 1099-MISC for only box 8 or 14 must be issued by February 15.) IRS copies of 1099-MISC must be filed by January 31 if an amount is reported in box 7. Other 1099-MISC payment types and other Form 1099 types must be filed by February 28 or March 31 if filed electronically. The minimum amounts and payment types that require reporting are:

- $10:

For: royalties and broker payments in lieu of dividends or tax-exempt interest (box 8)

- $600

For: Rents (box 1), services performed by a non-employee, fish purchased from a fishing trade or business (box 7), prizes and awards not to employees, and other income payments (box 3), medical and health care payments (box 6), crop insurance proceeds (box 10), payment to fishing boat crew members (box 5), payments to attorneys (box 14)

- $5,000:

For: Direct sales of consumer products to a buyer other than a permanent retail establishment for resale (box 9)

- Any amount of backup withholding of federal income tax (box 4)

Generally, payments to corporations (with limited exceptions, e.g. for health care or attorney fees) and payments for merchandise are exempt from 1099 filing requirements. Note that 1099 amounts are for nonemployee compensation; therefore, they would not be part of salaries and wages expense and salaries and wages payable, but rather accounts payable.

The multiple copies are similar to Form W-2, including copies sent to the Internal Revenue Service and the appropriate state tax authority. Further details, exceptions, and examples are available on the instructions for Form 1099-MISC. Also see the individual state 1099 requirements that may apply.

Other Common 1099 Forms

In addition to Form 1099-MISC, other types of 1099 forms report specific types of income. Common examples are:

- **1099-INT:** For interest income of $10 or more from banks, credit unions, credit unions, and similar investments. It also reports $600 or more of other types of interest.
- **1099-B:** For all income from a broker for stock and securities transactions.

continued ▶

Annual Reporting: Form 1099, *continued*

- **1099-C:** For cancellation of debt
- **1099-DIV:** For dividends of $10 or more and stock/securities payments.
- **1099-K:** For distributions of any amount from 3rd party network debit and credit cards transactions; any large 3rd party network transactions defined as certain amounts
- **1099-R:** For distributions of $10 or more from pensions, annuities, retirement plans, and life insurance companies.
- **1099-S:** For all payments for real estate transactions.
- **1099-G:** For government payments of $10 or more, most often tax refunds and unemployment compensation.
- **1099-PATR:** To report distributions of $10 or more from cooperatives. Also called "patronage dividends".

Illustration 5.5: Form 1099

Source: Internal Revenue Service

Form 1096 Transmittal Form

Just as W-2 form requires an accompanying transmittal document, so does Form 1099. This is Form 1096. One 1096 must accompany each specific group of 1099 forms sent to the IRS. For example, there would be one 1096 for all 1099-MISC copies, one 1096 for all 1099-INT copies, and so on.

Annual Reporting: Form 940

Form 940   Form 940 for annual reporting of FUTA is illustrated below.

Illustration 5.6: Form 940

Form **940 for 2017:** **Employer's Annual Federal Unemployment (FUTA) Tax Return**   850113
Department of the Treasury — Internal Revenue Service   OMB No. 1545-0028

Employer identification number (EIN)

Name (not your trade name)

Trade name (if any)

Address

Number   Street   Suite or room number

City   State   ZIP code

Foreign country name   Foreign province/county   Foreign postal code

Type of Return
(Check all that apply.)
- a. Amended
- b. Successor employer
- c. No payments to employees in 2017
- d. Final: Business closed or stopped paying wages

Go to www.irs.gov/Form940 for instructions and the latest information.

Read the separate instructions before you complete this form. Please type or print within the boxes.

Part 1:   Tell us about your return. If any line does NOT apply, leave it blank. See instructions before completing Part 1.

1a If you had to pay state unemployment tax in one state only, enter the state abbreviation .   1a
1b If you had to pay state unemployment tax in more than one state, you are a multi-state employer . . . .   1b ☐ Check here. Complete Schedule A (Form 940).

2 If you paid wages in a state that is subject to CREDIT REDUCTION . . . .   2 ☐ Check here. Complete Schedule A (Form 940).

Part 2:   Determine your FUTA tax before adjustments. If any line does NOT apply, leave it blank.

3 Total payments to all employees   3

4 Payments exempt from FUTA tax   4

Check all that apply: 4a ☐ Fringe benefits   4c ☐ Retirement/Pension   4e ☐ Other
4b ☐ Group-term life insurance   4d ☐ Dependent care

5 Total of payments made to each employee in excess of $7,000   5

6 Subtotal (line 4 + line 5 = line 6)   6

7 Total taxable FUTA wages (line 3 – line 6 = line 7). See instructions .   7

8 FUTA tax before adjustments (line 7 x 0.006 = line 8)   8

Part 3:   Determine your adjustments. If any line does NOT apply, leave it blank.

9 If ALL of the taxable FUTA wages you paid were excluded from state unemployment tax, multiply line 7 by 0.054 (line 7 x 0.054 = line 9). Go to line 12   9

10 If SOME of the taxable FUTA wages you paid were excluded from state unemployment tax, OR you paid ANY state unemployment tax late (after the due date for filing Form 940), complete the worksheet in the instructions. Enter the amount from line 7 of the worksheet . .   10

11 If credit reduction applies, enter the total from Schedule A (Form 940)   11

Part 4:   Determine your FUTA tax and balance due or overpayment. If any line does NOT apply, leave it blank.

12 Total FUTA tax after adjustments (lines 8 + 9 + 10 + 11 = line 12)   12

13 FUTA tax deposited for the year, including any overpayment applied from a prior year .   13

14 Balance due. If line 12 is more than line 13, enter the excess on line 14.
    • If line 14 is more than $500, you must deposit your tax.
    • If line 14 is $500 or less, you may pay with this return. See instructions   14

15 Overpayment. If line 13 is more than line 12, enter the excess on line 15 and check a box below   15
    ▶ You MUST complete both pages of this form and SIGN it.   Check one: ☐ Apply to next return. ☐ Send a refund.

Next ➡

For Privacy Act and Paperwork Reduction Act Notice, see the back of the Payment Voucher.   Cat. No. 112340   Form **940** (2017)

Source: Internal Revenue Service

Annual Reporting: Form 940, *continued*

Illustration 5.6: Form 940, continued

850212

Name *(not your trade name)*	Employer identification number (EIN)

Part 5: Report your FUTA tax liability by quarter only if line 12 is more than $500. If not, go to Part 6.

16 Report the amount of your FUTA tax liability for each quarter; do NOT enter the amount you deposited. If you had no liability for a quarter, leave the line blank.

16a **1st quarter** (January 1 – March 31) 16a

16b **2nd quarter** (April 1 – June 30) 16b

16c **3rd quarter** (July 1 – September 30) 16c

16d **4th quarter** (October 1 – December 31) 16d

17 **Total tax liability for the year** (lines 16a + 16b + 16c + 16d = line 17) 17   Total must equal line 12.

Part 6: May we speak with your third-party designee?

Do you want to allow an employee, a paid tax preparer, or another person to discuss this return with the IRS? See the instructions for details.

☐ **Yes.**   Designee's name and phone number

Select a 5-digit Personal Identification Number (PIN) to use when talking to IRS

☐ **No.**

Part 7: Sign here. You MUST complete both pages of this form and SIGN it.

Under penalties of perjury, I declare that I have examined this return, including accompanying schedules and statements, and to the best of my knowledge and belief, it is true, correct, and complete, and that no part of any payment made to a state unemployment fund claimed as a credit was, or is to be, deducted from the payments made to employees. Declaration of preparer (other than taxpayer) is based on all information of which preparer has any knowledge.

✗ **Sign your name here**

Print your name here

Print your title here

Date   /   /

Best daytime phone

Paid Preparer Use Only   Check if you are self-employed ☐

Preparer's name		PTIN	
Preparer's signature		Date	/ /
Firm's name (or yours if self-employed)		EIN	
Address		Phone	
City	State	ZIP code	

Form **940** (2017)

Source: Internal Revenue Service

Information Forms Summary

Common Information Forms Related to Payroll (Federal)

There are numerous types of information forms that must be submitted for different circumstances. Common federal payroll-related information forms are:

- **Schedule H:** Attach to personal or estate/trust tax return (1040, 1040NR or 1041) to report household employee payments, income tax withheld and payroll taxes, unless taxpayer has IRS approval for a third party to pay and report to taxpayer. If no personal return is filed, Schedule H must still be filed. If a sole proprietor, these amounts instead may be included on Form 941. Deposit requirement: Pay amounts due with personal tax filing unless included on Form 941. See Publication 926.
- **W-2:** Annual reporting of employee wages, withholding, and related items, unless a notice is received from IRS to submit specified employee W-2s.
- **W-3:** Transmittal form for W-2.
- **1099:** Annual reporting for independent contractor payments and various forms of miscellaneous income payments.
- **1096:** Transmittal form for 1099.
- **940:** Annual federal unemployment tax (FUTA) report for obligation and amounts paid. Only employers pay FUTA. Deposit requirement: If tax liability exceeds $500 at any point during a calendar quarter, a payment must be made by the last day of the month following the end of the quarter. Liability below $500 carries forward as part of the next quarter. For an annual total less than $500, pay the amount due with the annual filing of Form 940.
- **941:** Quarterly reports of federal income tax withholding and deposits, FICA employer and employee deposits required, and deposits. Deposit rules: page 112.
- **943:** Annual reports of agricultural employee income tax withholding and deposits (Publication 51). Deposits: Lookback period is second prior year. Follow same Form 941 steps 2-5 on pages 112-113. If tax is less than $2,500 for the year, pay with timely filed return.
- **944:** Annual reporting used instead of Form 941 for employers whose annual deposit requirement was less than $1,000 (after receiving IRS notice). Deposits: Lookback period is second prior year. Follow same Form 941 steps 2-5 on pages 112-113. If tax is less than $2,500 for the year, pay with timely filed return. If less than $2,500 for the last quarter, pay with timely filed return if prior current year deposits have been correct and timely.
- **945:** Annual reporting for other general withholding requirements such as backup withholding for independent contractors. Also used to report withholding on other income items. Deposits: Same as form 943 above.

continued ▶

Information Forms Summary, *continued*

- **1095-C:** Annual Medical insurance coverage disclosure from certain employers as required by the Affordable Care Act.
- **8027:** For annual reporting of total tips received and total receipts from business operations for large (averaging more than 10 employees working 80 hours daily for the prior year) food and beverage businesses. (See page 55). Tips are also reported as part of Form 941.

Illustration 5.7: Form 943

Form **943**	**Employer's Annual Federal Tax Return for Agricultural Employees**	OMB No. 1545-0035
Department of the Treasury Internal Revenue Service	▶ Go to *www.irs.gov/Form943* for instructions and the latest information.	20

Type or Print	Name (as distinguished from trade name)	Employer identification number (EIN)	If address is different from prior return, check here. ▶ □
	Trade name, if any		
	Address (number and street)		
	City or town, state or province, country, and ZIP or foreign postal code		
	If you don't have to file returns in the future, check here . . . . ▶ □		

1	Number of agricultural employees employed in the pay period that includes March 12, 2017 ▶	1	
2	Total wages subject to social security tax . . . . [2]		
3	Social security tax (multiply line 2 by 12.4% (0.124))	3	
4	Total wages subject to Medicare tax . . . . [4]		
5	Medicare tax (multiply line 4 by 2.9% (0.029))	5	
6	Total wages subject to Additional Medicare Tax withholding . . . . [6]		
7	Additional Medicare Tax withholding (multiply line 6 by 0.9% (0.009))	7	
8	Federal income tax withheld	8	
9	Total taxes before adjustments. Add lines 3, 5, 7, and 8	9	
10	Current year's adjustments	10	
11	Total taxes after adjustments (line 9 as adjusted by line 10)	11	
12	Qualified small business payroll tax credit for increasing research activities. Attach Form 8974 . .	12	
13	Total taxes after adjustments and credits. Subtract line 12 from line 11	13	
14	Total deposits for 2017, including overpayment applied from a prior year and Form 943-X . . .	14	
15	**Balance due.** If line 13 is more than line 14, enter the difference and see the instructions . ▶	15	
16	**Overpayment.** If line 14 is more than line 13, enter the difference ▶ $ _____ Check one:□ Apply to next return. □ Send a refund.		

- **All filers:** If line 13 is less than $2,500, **don't** complete line 17 or Form 943-A.
- **Semiweekly schedule depositors:** Complete Form 943-A and check here ▶ □ • **Monthly schedule depositors:** Complete line 17 and check here ▶ □

17	Monthly Summary of Federal Tax Liability. (**Don't** complete if you were a semiweekly schedule depositor.)		
	Tax liability for month	Tax liability for month	Tax liability for month
A January . . .	**F** June	**K** November . . .	
B February . . .	**G** July	**L** December . . .	
C March . . .	**H** August	**M** Total liability for year (add lines **A** through **L**) . . .	
D April . . .	**I** September . .		
E May	**J** October		

Third-Party Designee	Do you want to allow another person to discuss this return with the IRS? See separate instructions. □ Yes. Complete the following. □ No.		
	Designee's name ▶	Phone no. ▶	Personal identification number (PIN) ▶

Sign Here	Under penalties of perjury, I declare that I have examined this return, including accompanying schedules and statements, and to the best of my knowledge and belief, it is true, correct, and complete. Declaration of preparer (other than taxpayer) is based on all information of which preparer has any knowledge.		
	Signature ▶	Print Your Name and Title ▶	Date ▶

Paid Preparer Use Only	Print/Type preparer's name	Preparer's signature	Date	Check □ if self-employed	PTIN
	Firm's name ▶			Firm's EIN ▶	
	Firm's address ▶			Phone no.	

For Privacy Act and Paperwork Reduction Act Notice, see the separate instructions.   Cat. No. 11252K   Form **943** (2017)

Source: Internal Revenue Service

Information Forms Summary, *continued*

Illustration 5.8: Form 944

Form **944 for 2017:** **Employer's ANNUAL Federal Tax Return**

Department of the Treasury — Internal Revenue Service

OMB No. 1545-2007

Employer identification number (EIN) [ ][ ] – [ ][ ][ ][ ][ ][ ][ ]

Name *(not your trade name)*

Trade name *(if any)*

Address

Number   Street   Suite or room number

City   State   ZIP code

Foreign country name   Foreign province/county   Foreign postal code

Who Must File Form 944

You must file annual Form 944 instead of filing quarterly Forms 941 **only if the IRS notified you in writing.**

Go to *www.irs.gov/Form944* for instructions and the latest information.

Read the separate instructions before you complete Form 944. Type or print within the boxes.

Part 1: Answer these questions for this year. Employers in American Samoa, Guam, the Commonwealth of the Northern Mariana Islands, the U.S. Virgin Islands, and Puerto Rico can skip lines 1 and 2, unless you have employees who are subject to U.S. income tax withholding.

1 Wages, tips, and other compensation . . . . 1 [.]

2 Federal income tax withheld from wages, tips, and other compensation . . . . . 2 [.]

3 If no wages, tips, and other compensation are subject to social security or Medicare tax 3 ☐ Check and go to line 5.

4 Taxable social security and Medicare wages and tips:

	Column 1		Column 2
4a Taxable social security wages	[.]	× 0.124 =	[.]
4b Taxable social security tips	[.]	× 0.124 =	[.]
4c Taxable Medicare wages & tips	[.]	× 0.029 =	[.]
4d Taxable wages & tips subject to Additional Medicare Tax withholding	[.]	× 0.009 =	[.]

4e Add Column 2 from lines 4a, 4b, 4c, and 4d . . . . 4e [.]

5 Total taxes before adjustments. Add lines 2 and 4e . . . . 5 [.]

6 Current year's adjustments (see instructions) . . . . 6 [.]

7 Total taxes after adjustments. Combine lines 5 and 6 . . . . 7 [.]

8 Qualified small business payroll tax credit for increasing research activities. Attach Form 8974 . 8 [.]

9 Total taxes after adjustments and credits. Subtract line 8 from line 7 . . . . 9 [.]

10 Total deposits for this year, including overpayment applied from a prior year and overpayments applied from Form 944-X, 944-X (SP), 941-X, or 941-X (PR) . . . . . 10 [.]

11 Balance due. If line 9 is more than line 10, enter the difference and see instructions . . . . 11 [.]

12 Overpayment. If line 10 is more than line 9, enter the difference [.] Check one: ☐ Apply to next return. ☐ Send a refund.

▶ You MUST complete both pages of Form 944 and SIGN it.   [Next ▶]

For Privacy Act and Paperwork Reduction Act Notice, see the back of the Payment Voucher.   Cat. No. 39316N   Form **944** (2017)

Source: Internal Revenue Service

continued ▶

Information Forms Summary, *continued*

Illustration 5.8: Form 944, continued

Name *(not your trade name)*	Employer identification number (EIN)

Part 2: Tell us about your deposit schedule and tax liability for this year.

13 Check one: ☐ Line 9 is less than $2,500. Go to Part 3.

☐ Line 9 is $2,500 or more. Enter your tax liability for each month. If you are a semiweekly depositor or you accumulate $100,000 or more of liability on any day during a deposit period, you must complete Form 945-A instead of the boxes below.

	Jan.		Apr.		Jul.		Oct.
13a	▪	13d	▪	13g	▪	13j	▪
	Feb.		May		Aug.		Nov.
13b	▪	13e	▪	13h	▪	13k	▪
	Mar.		Jun.		Sep.		Dec.
13c	▪	13f	▪	13i	▪	13l	▪

Total liability for year. Add lines 13a through 13l. Total must equal line 9.   13m [   ] ▪

Part 3: Tell us about your business. If question 14 does NOT apply to your business, leave it blank.

14 If your business has closed or you stopped paying wages...

☐ Check here and enter the final date you paid wages. [   ]

Part 4: May we speak with your third-party designee?

Do you want to allow an employee, a paid tax preparer, or another person to discuss this return with the IRS? See the instructions for details.

☐ Yes. Designee's name and phone number [   ]   [   ]

Select a 5-digit Personal Identification Number (PIN) to use when talking to IRS. ☐ ☐ ☐ ☐ ☐

☐ No.

Part 5: Sign Here. You MUST complete both pages of Form 944 and SIGN it.

Under penalties of perjury, I declare that I have examined this return, including accompanying schedules and statements, and to the best of my knowledge and belief, it is true, correct, and complete. Declaration of preparer (other than taxpayer) is based on all information of which preparer has any knowledge.

✗ **Sign your name here** [   ]   Print your name here [   ]
Print your title here [   ]

Date [   ]   Best daytime phone [   ]

Paid Preparer Use Only   Check if you are self-employed ☐

Preparer's name	[ ]	PTIN	[ ]
Preparer's signature	[ ]	Date	[ ]
Firm's name (or yours if self-employed)	[ ]	EIN	[ ]
Address	[ ]	Phone	[ ]
City	[ ] State [ ]	ZIP code	[ ]

Form **944** (2017)

Source: Internal Revenue Service

Information Forms Summary, *continued*

Illustration 5.9: Form 945

Form **945**	**Annual Return of Withheld Federal Income Tax**	OMB No. 1545-1430
Department of the Treasury Internal Revenue Service	► For withholding reported on Forms 1099 and W-2G. ► For more information on income tax withholding, see Pub. 15 and Pub. 15-A. ► Go to *www.irs.gov/Form945* for instructions and the latest information.	20

Type or Print	Name (as distinguished from trade name)	Employer identification number (EIN)	If address is different from prior return, check here. ►
	Trade name, if any		
	Address (number and street)		
	City or town, state or province, country, and ZIP or foreign postal code		

A If you don't have to file returns in the future, check here ► ☐ and enter date final payments made. ► ------------------

1 Federal income tax withheld from pensions, annuities, IRAs, gambling winnings, etc. . . . . . | **1** |

2 Backup withholding . . . . | **2** |

3 **Total taxes.** If $2,500 or more, this must equal line 7M below or Form 945-A, line M . . . . . | **3** |

4 Total deposits for 2017, including overpayment applied from a prior year and overpayment applied from Form 945-X . . . . | **4** |

5 **Balance due.** If line 3 is more than line 4, enter the difference and see the separate instructions . | **5** |

6 **Overpayment.** If line 4 is more than line 3, enter the difference ► $ _____

Check one: ☐ Apply to next return. ☐ Send a refund.

• **All filers:** If line 3 is less than $2,500, **don't** complete line 7 or Form 945-A.
• **Semiweekly schedule depositors:** Complete Form 945-A and check here . . . . ► ☐
• **Monthly schedule depositors:** Complete line 7, entries A through M, and check here . . . . ► ☐

7 Monthly Summary of Federal Tax Liability. (Don't complete if you were a semiweekly schedule depositor.)

	Tax liability for month		Tax liability for month		Tax liability for month
A January . . .		**F** June		**K** November . .	
B February . .		**G** July		**L** December . .	
C March . . .		**H** August		**M** Total liability for year (add lines **A** through **L**) ►	
D April		**I** September . . .			
E May		**J** October			

Third-Party Designee Do you want to allow another person to discuss this return with the IRS? See separate instructions. ☐ Yes. Complete the following. ☐ No.

Designee's name ► | Phone no. ► | Personal identification number (PIN) ► | ☐☐☐☐☐

Sign Here Under penalties of perjury, I declare that I have examined this return, including accompanying schedules and statements, and to the best of my knowledge and belief, it is true, correct, and complete. Declaration of preparer (other than taxpayer) is based on all information of which preparer has any knowledge.

Signature ► | Print Your Name and Title ► | Date ►

Paid Preparer Use Only	Print/Type preparer's name	Preparer's signature	Date	Check ☐ if self-employed	PTIN
	Firm's name ►			Firm's EIN ►	
	Firm's address ►			Phone no.	

For Privacy Act and Paperwork Reduction Act Notice, see the separate instructions.   Cat. No. 14584B   Form **945** (2017)

Source: Internal Revenue Service

State and Local Taxes

Overview

Most states tax income and have income tax withholding requirements. (Exceptions are: Alaska, New Hampshire (taxes investment income), Nevada, Florida, South Dakota, Tennessee (taxes investment income), Texas, Washington, and Wyoming. Note: However, these states have high sales and property taxes.) For those states that do tax income, the use of withholding tables and the withholding process is generally similar to what has so far been discussed.

W-2 Reporting

State income tax is reported in box 16 and related withholding is reported in box 18. Generally, box 16 and box 1 would be the same amounts; however, there can be exceptions: 1) If the amount of pre-tax income recognized is different for state purposes than for federal, the amounts will be different (for example, a state does not recognize 401(k) contributions as deferred income). 2) For work in multiple states box 16 can reference multiple amounts depending on the states in which the employee worked. Note: If an employee wants a different number of allowances for state withholding, the employer should provide a state allowance form in addition to the federal form W-4.

State Reporting Requirements

- States generally require quarterly payroll tax reports that show the total wages paid and the calculation of state payroll taxes due. In most cases the filing dates are the last day of the month following the end of the quarter being reported.
- Some states require employee wage reports, typically filed quarterly. These reports list individual employees, their wages for the period, and other required state information.
- Some states require a notice identifying individual employee information upon their termination of employment.
- Some states require a notice of reduction in employment identifying individual employee information upon their reduced employment due to lack of work.

Interstate Employees

In some situations an employee will work in more than one state for the same employer. States conform to a system that provides the criteria to determine to which location (i.e. which state) the unemployment tax should apply. The criteria, as applied in sequence if a prior test is not determinative, are:

1) Where the work primarily, not incidentally, takes place
2) The base of operations to which the employee regularly begins and ends his/her work and to which he/she reports.
3) The location from which directions are issued.
4) The employee's state of residence.

State and Local Taxes, *continued*

State Deposit *** Requirements***	Deposit requirements vary by state. Employers must check individual state regulations.

Where to File Forms

Overview	Directions for filing forms are available on the instructions for the forms. You can do an Internet search by form number followed by "instructions".

Making Corrections

Overview	Forms 941-X, 943-X, 944-X and 945-X (945-A for liability corrections) are used for corrections to the following previously-filed employer forms:

- 941
- 941-SS (American Samoa, Guam, Northern Mariana, and U.S. Virgin Islands)
- 943
- 944
- 945

For Form W-2: Form W-2 c is used to make corrections for Form W-2. Also use a new transmittal Form W-3.

For Form 1099: On a new form, enter the correct information and check "corrected" box. Also use a new transmittal Form 1096.

Federal Penalties

Overview	All filing and payment requirements include penalties for failure to comply. The tables below show potential federal employer penalties for failure to conform to federal requirements for form and return filing and payment for some of the major items that we have discussed. States also impose penalties.

continued ▶

Federal Penalties, *continued*

Payee and Government Information Forms

Without Reasonable Cause, Failure to...	Penalty
Provide payee with form or correct form (W-2, 1099)	<ul><li>$100 per item</li><li>Intentional disregard: $260 per item</li><li>Criminal penalties: $5,000 and above, additional criminal penalties</li><li>Maximum: $1,500,000 ($500,000 small business)"</li></ul>
Provide the IRS with form or correct form	<ul><li>$50 per item, to a maximum of $187,500 or $536,000 depending on business size if corrected within 30 days</li><li>$100 per item, to a maximum of $536,000 or $1,609,000 depending on business size if corrected before August 1</li><li>Filed later than August 1: $260 per item to a maximum of $1,072,500 or $3,218,500 depending on business size</li><li>Intentional disregard: $530 per item, no limit</li></ul>

Federal Penalties, *continued*

Forms 940, 941, 943, 944 and 945

Without Rea-sonable Cause, Failure to...	Penalty
Make timely deposits	■ 1 to 5 days late: 2% of amount not timely deposited. ■ 6 to 15 days late: 5% of amount not timely deposited. ■ 16 or more days but at least 10 days before the date that first IRS was sent asking for payment: 10% of amount not timely deposited. ■ Amounts that should have been deposited but instead were sent directly to the IRS or paid with the return, or otherwise incorrectly deposited: 10% of amount not correctly deposited. ■ Amounts that remain unpaid more than 10 days after the date of the first notice sent by the IRS or the date a demand is received from the IRS, whichever is earlier: 15% Deposits are generally applied to the most recent amounts due. If a penalty notice is received employer can designate the order of application to minimize penalty.
Pay tax due per correct tax return	■ .5% per month of the tax due to a maximum of 25%, plus interest at the current IRS rate. Payments reduce penalty if made on or before the first day of a month. ■ Negligence: 20% of the underpayment ■ Willful failure: Penalty is assessed against any responsible individual(s) in an amount equal to the unpaid income taxes withheld plus employee's portion of FICA. This is also called the "Trust Fund Recovery Penalty" or "TFRP". The IRS can also assess criminal penalties up to $10,000, imprisonment up to 5 years, or both, for fraud and tax evasion. ■ Levy/seizure: A levy means seizure of property. The IRS can seize most property within 10 days of demand for payment, in order to obtain the value of unpaid tax.
File tax return	■ 5% per month or part of month of the tax due to a maximum of 25%. If both a failure to file and a failure to pay (above) are assessed, the failure to file penalty is reduced by the amount of the failure to pay penalty. The maximum combined penalty (excluding interest) for the first 5 months is 25% (4.5% failure to file and .5% failure to pay per month). The total maximum combined penalty is 47.5% (4.5% failure to file for 5 months = 22.5%) + (.5% failure to pay for 50 months = 25%). The minimum penalty if a return is over 60 days past due is the lesser of 100% of the tax due or $205. Penalties, but not interest, may be abated for reasonable cause.

continued   ▶

Federal Penalties, *continued*

"Other Penalties

- Frivolous Tax Returns: $5,000 (For returns with completely unsupported or frivolous methods)
- Accuracy-related: 20% of underpayment (Negligence or disregarding rules and regulations and/or substantial understatement, unless a reasonable basis for a position is taken. This penalty can be avoided if certain tax position standards are met that are called "substantial authority" and "more likely than not". This requires professional assistance.)
- Civil fraud: 75% of the underpayment
- Criminal fraud: civil fraud penalty plus fines and jail.

Abatement of Penalties and Tax

Overview

The term "abatement" means a reduction, decrease, or removal. In the context of our payroll topic, abatement refers to a reduction or removal of penalties and/or taxes imposed on an employer. Here, the most common circumstances to which abatement applies are reductions or removal of penalties imposed for failure to pay, failure to file, or failure to deposit. As well, in some cases the tax itself may also be abated. In this discussion, we will focus primarily on IRS penalty relief.

Rationale for Abatement of Penalty

Four categories of abatement rationale can apply. The first and probably most straightforward is statutory relief, which means that a law or regulation applies to specific circumstances such that a penalty should not be assessed. The second abatement category is administrative waiver (relief). This means that IRS administrative personnel address a policy by issuing a statement or news release clarifying or interpreting an IRS position on penalty assessment that provides relief from a penalty that might otherwise have been assessed. Third, a penalty may be abated by a taxpayer demonstrating reasonable cause for one of the failures stated above. The final category is correction of an IRS error in penalty or tax determination.

Statutory Abatement

In order to obtain penalty abatement for this category, a taxpayer should identify the provision granting relief and carefully identify how each element of the relief provision applies to the taxpayer's specific situation. Some examples of statutory penalty relief provisions are: disaster relief, war zone relief, and reliance on incorrect written IRS advice.

Abatement of Penalties and Tax, *continued*

First Time Penalty Abatement Waiver (FTA)

As described above, administrative abatement generally results from a policy change. The most frequently-used administrative abatement is probably the First Time Penalty Abatement Waiver, a policy established in 2001. The waiver allows taxpayers who are typically compliant to remove or reduce a penalty assessment. As applied to payroll taxes, this abatement allows a taxpayer that is first time non-compliant to abate the failure to pay, failure to file, and failure to deposit penalties for a single quarter. (Note: The FTA does not apply for Forms W-2 and W-3.) The requirements are:

- **Filing compliance:** The taxpayer must have filed all currently required returns or a valid extension, and there cannot be an outstanding IRS request for an unfiled return.
- **Payment compliance:** The taxpayer has paid, has received an extension to pay, or has arranged to pay via an installment agreement that is current, all taxes due. A taxpayer who is not in compliance with the above two requirements may be given the opportunity to comply in order to obtain an FTA before penalties are applied.
- **Penalty history:** The taxpayer cannot have had "significant" penalties assessed in the prior three years. If in doubt, when applying for relief, discuss this the IRS contact person. An amount under $100 is probably not disqualifying. An estimated tax penalty or a prior reasonable cause abatement is not disqualifying. Receiving an FTA more than years prior is also not disqualifying. If there is a series of penalties, an FTA should be requested for the first year.

An FTA can be requested by telephone or mail. For telephone, a taxpayer can use the toll-free number that is on the penalty notice; at times, the IRS may want a written request. If by mail, the taxpayer must write all relevant facts and circumstances is a clear, direct manner to the IRS service center where the taxpayer files paper returns. (If the penalty results from an audit, the request should go to the source of the audit.) A failure to pay penalty will continue to accrue until the tax is fully paid, so a taxpayer should verify that the IRS will apply the FTA after the tax is paid, or that an FTA should be applied for at that point. As with all tax-authority physical mail correspondence, a taxpayer should be sure to retain tracking and delivery information with a copy of the correspondence; a post office return-receipt letter is best.

As sometimes happens, an intial FTA may be denied; however, the IRS can make incorrect determinations, sometimes as the result of automated systems output. If a request is denied, particulary if a letter does not seem to properly address the facts, a taxpayer should ask to discuss the issue with the IRS

continued ▶

Abatement of Penalties and Tax, *continued*

representative's manager-level administrator. If this fails, a taxpayer has the right to an appeals-level review, which may then grant relief.

Reasonable Cause

Penalties (but not interest, except for interest accruing on penalties) may be abated as the result of what the IRS determines as "reasonable cause", and with no willful neglect. Reasonable cause, by its nature is subjective; therefore, taxpayer rationale must be demonstrable and compelling. Generally, lack of funds does not constitute reasonable cause in most cases. When contacted by a taxpayer requesting a reasonable cause abatement, the IRS considers the following guidelines:

- Fire, earthquake, flooding, and other natural disasters.
- Loss of access to records beyond the taxpayer's control
- Death, serious illness, and incapacity of taxpayer or immediate family member
- Other circumstances beyond taxpayer control despite taxpayer ordinary business care and prudence

In presenting the facts, a taxpayer should clearly address the following questions with adequate documentation:

- What happened, parties involved, and when did it happen?
- Why was taxpayer prevented from paying, filing, or deposting payroll tax?
- Did the circumstances affect the ability to carry on normal business activies?
- When circumstances changed, what actions did the taxpayer take and when (i.e. did taxpayer attempt to resolve issues and to meet obligations as soon as possible)?

The IRS also considers:

- Taxpayer compliance history and payment patterns
- Other tax filing (state and local)

As with other abatement categories, a taxpayer has the right to an appeals-level review, in which relief may be granted.

Error Correction

A penalty can be imposed as the result of IRS error. This can be due to a range of common issues such as calculation, coding, identification, document loss, file maintenance, or incorrect IRS advice. Detailed calculation and documentation must be provided by the taxpayer. As a matter of practice, IRS errors are rarely a source of penalties.

Abatement of Penalties and Tax, *continued*

Timing and Methods for Seeking Penalty Relief

Depending on circumstances, abatement potentially can be requested at any of the following points with the following methods:

- Before the IRS assesses a penalty: At the time a paper return is submitted, include a penalty nonassertion request with the return.
- After a penalty has been assessed, but before it is paid: Taxpayer requests a penalty abatement by calling or writing the IRS.
- After a penalty has been paid: Taxpayer requests a refund using form 843 *Claim for Refund and Request for Abatement*. The form must be filed within three years of the filing or the original return, or within two years of the date the tax was paid, whichever is later. The form should be filed at the IRS service center where paper forms are currently filed.

Statutory Relief for Payroll Tax Deposits

Two statutory relief provisions apply specifically to employment tax deposit requirements:

- Accuracy of deposit rule (page 114)
- First quarterly deposit or change in deposit schedule (page 115)

See pages 148–150 for further discussion.

If penalties are assessed due to late deposits, check to determine which periods the deposits have been applied to. The IRS may be applying subsequent deposits to earlier periods, thereby creating additional penalties in later periods. If this is the case, a taxpayer may be able to reduce penalties by exercising the right to designate the periods to which deposits should be applied.

Section 6 Employment of Non-U.S. Persons

Overview

Introduction

There is essentially a separate method of taxation for non-U.S. persons. This section provides an introduction to procedures related to wage compensation of non-U.S. persons. However, the reader should keep in mind that this topic is broad in scope, and there can be further complexities that potentially can affect both employers and employees. Non-U.S. persons should read Publication 519.

What are Non-U.S. (Foreign) Persons?

Wage payments to non-U.S. persons are also affected by tax withholding and tax reporting requirements. For tax purposes, a non-U.S. person is defined within the context of *tax residency*. For tax residency purposes, there are three categories of non-U.S. persons.

- **Resident alien:** A resident alien is generally taxed in the same manner as a U.S. citizen.
- **Non-resident alien:** A non-resident alien is a "Foreign Person". There are special tax rules for foreign person income earned in the United States.
- **Dual-status alien:** A dual-status alien is a person who has been both a non-resident alien and a resident alien within the same tax year.

An "alien" is defined as any individual who is not a U.S. citizen or U.S. national (a person born in American Somoa or a certain part of the Northern Mariana islands, and electing U.S. national status instead of citizenship.) Note that if someone is treated as a resident of a foreign country resulting from the terms of a tax treaty, they are automatically treated as U.S. non-resident aliens for tax purposes.

For federal income tax purposes, a resident alien is determined by either of two tests:

- Green card test
- Substantial presence test

FLSA

The Fair Labor Standards Act (FLSA) applies to all employment in the U.S. and District of Columbia, regardless of immigration status or lack of documentation.

Resident Aliens

Definition

A resident alien is a person who for *tax purposes* (not always the same as for immigration and employment authorizaiton purposes) has passed either the green card test or the substantial presence test for a full calendar year. The earlier of meeting either test begins the residency period. Note: it is also possible to be a resident alien for part of a year for a person who is a dual status alien. (See page 163)

Green Card Test

"Green card" refers to an alien registration card (Form I-551) from the U.S. Citizenship and Immigration Service granting a person approval to reside permanently in the United States as an immigrant. A person who lawfully possesses a valid green card and has not had residency status taken away or has not abandoned residency status is considered to have passed the green card test, is considered to be a lawful permanent resident of the United States, and is therefore for tax purposes clasified as a resident alien.

Substantial Presence Test

The following is required to satisfy the substantial presence test:

- Be physically present in the United States for at least 31 days in the current calendar year, and
- Be physically present in the Unites States (excluding U.S. possessions and airspace) for 183 days or part of a day during a three-year period that includes the current calendar year, the prior calendar year, and the second prior calendar year, counting:
  - all days present in the current year,
  - 1/3 of the days present in the prior year
  - 1/6 of the days present in the second prior year

The following are not counted as "days":

- Days commmunting to the U.S. from a residence in Canada or Mexico
- Days in the U.S. for less than 24 hours when in transit between two places outside of the U.S.
- Days as a crew member of a foreign vessel.
- Days unable to leave the U.S. because of a medical condition arising in the U.S.
- Days for which a person is classified as an "exempt" person according to certain visa status or as a visiting athlete to compete in a charitable sports event.
- Initial days do not count as days for which there was a closer connection to the home country than the United States.

Note: Some visa classifications (such as F-1 or J-1 student visas, Teacher/Researcher/Trainee J-1 or Q visas) are generally considered "exempt" persons.

continued ▶

Resident Aliens, *continued*

These exempt status classifications are temporarily exempt from the substantial presence test requirement, typically for five and two years, subject to additional guidelines. Time spent in this status does not count toward the 183 day requirement.

Employer Requirements

- **Status verification:** Employers must comply with the Immigration Reform and Control Act (IRCA). To demonstrate full compliance, employers must check authorization to work status of all new hires equally. This means asking for proof of citizenship or verification of lawful permanent residency (green card) or an employment authorization to work document (sometimes called a "work permit") or a visa that allows work for a particular employer . Employers must complete an Employment Eligibility Verification Form (Form I-9) for all new employees regardless of citizenship status. Employers also bear the resposibility of making a good-faith effort to examine documents of identity and eligibility to work and to determine if they appear to be genuine. Note: Under the law, a hiring policy of "U.S. citizens only" is illegal except where required under federal, state, or local law.
- **Withholding and payroll taxes:** Resident alien withholding is the same method as for U.S. citizens. Employers are subject to the same withholding and tax requirements as described earlier in this book for U.S. citizens. Resident aliens follow the same rules for completion of Form W-4 as U.S. citizens.
- **Identification numbers:** For a non-citizen who is eligible and desires to work in the United States, an unrestricted social security card or social security card authorizing work must be obtained and shown to the employer.

This means that non-U.S. citizens without green cards or work visas will require both a social security number and a work permit. (Generally, for a non-citizen to obtain a social security number proof of permission to work from the Department of Homeland Security (DHS) is required unless a government agency requires a social security number. Both items can be applied for simultaneously from DHS using Form I-765.)

For tax purposes, an employer requires a social security number and should not accept an Individual Taxpayer Identification Number (ITIN) in lieu of a social security number. An ITIN is only available to persons who are not eligible for U.S. employment and require tax identification for filing a return or other purposes. Note: An employer cannot withhold payment due to the absence of a social security number. The FLSA requires payment for all hours worked.

Non-Resident Aliens (NRA)

Overview   Non-resident aliens are generally subject to tax only on U.S. source income. Foreign source income may be taxable in limited circumstances. Table 6.1 below shows various determination of income sources for non-resident aliens.

Table 6.1: Determination of Income Source for Non-Resident Alien

Income Type	Determination of Source
Salaries and wages	Where services were performed
Other personal services	Where services were performed
Pension distribution	Where services were performed
Interest	Location of taxpayer residence
Dividends	Based on whether U.S. or foreign corporation, with some exceptions.
Rent	Location of property
Natural resources	Location of property
Sale of real estate	Location of property
Sale of purchased inventory	Location of sale
Sale of produced inventory	Technical allocation rules
Sale of depreciable personal property	Technical allocation rules
Sales of stocks, securities	Gains generally not taxable when trading for own account and not in trade or business in U.S. as a broker or securities dealer or connected with a U.S. trade or business, and individual is physically present less than 183 days or parts of days in the United States in a calendar year.

Note: Many of the above items (and others not listed) will require completion of forms 1042-S and 1042 by the entity making payments. Employers do not use these forms for employee wage compensation (Form W-2) or amounts reported on Form 1099 unless there is exempt income.

Employer Requirements for Non-Resident Aliens (NRA)

Employer

In respect to non-resident aliens, an "employer" includes:

- Any person paying wages to an NRA individual, or a foreign partnership or corporation not engaged in trade or business in the United States
- Any person who has *control* of the payments of wages for services performed for another person who does not have of payments
- IRS guidelines for determining employer-employee relationship remain applicable.

Status Verification

Employers must comply with the Immigration Reform and Control Act (IRCA). To demonstrate full compliance employers must check citizenship status of all new hires equally. This means asking for proof of citizenship or authorization to work from the Department of Homeland Security for non-citizens. Under the law a policy of "U.S. citizens only" is illegal except where required under federal, state, or local law. Employers must complete and retain an Employment Eligibility Verification Form (Form I-9) for all new employees regardless of citizenship status. Employers also bear the resposibility of making a good-faith effort to examine documents proving identity and eligibility to work to determine if they appear to be genuine.

Withholding

- An NRA is subject to a 30% tax on most U.S. source income; however, for wages, an NRA is subject to graduated withholding as normally done with U.S. citizens.
- Mandatory withholding is required at the time of payment unless exceptions (below) apply.

Form W-4

NRA employees must complete federal and state withholding allowance forms. For federal purposes, the following special rules apply:

- The box for "single" must be checked, regardless of marital status
- On line 6, "Nonresident alien" or "NRA"should be written above dotted line.
- An NRA cannot claim "exempt" on line 7.

Identification: For a non-citizen who is eligible and desires to work in the United States, an unrestricted social security card or social security card authorizing work must be obtained and shown to the employer.

This means that non-resident aliens will require both a social security number and a work permit. (Generally, for a non-citizen to obtain a social security number proof of permission to work from the Department of Homeland

Employer Requirements for Non-Resident Aliens (NRA), *continued*

Security (DHS) is required unless a government agency requires a social security number. Both items can be applied for simultaneously from DHS using Form I-765.)

For tax purposes, an employer requires a social security number and should not accept an Individual Taxpayer Identification Number (ITIN) in lieu of a social security number. An ITIN is only available to persons who are not eligible for U.S. employment and require tax identification for filing a return or other purposes. Note: An employer cannot withhold payment due to the absence of a social security number. The FLSA requires payment for all hours worked.

Special Withholding Procedures

- An NRA cannot claim the standard deduction; this rule requires an additional withholding amount adjustment by an employer (See below).
- Some NRAs are exempt or will have reduced withholding if tax treaties apply. See: *www.irs.gov/Individuals/ InternationalTaxpayers/TaxTreaties.* In this regard, an NRA must submit Form 8233 (or W-8BEN for other than personal services such as a scholarship) to the employer/withholding agent, who in turn must review for completeness and documentation, and sign and forward the form to the IRS within 5 days of receipt. Employers unable to reasonably determine completeness and documentation or specific elements of a treaty not determinable until the end of a tax year will withhold at otherwise required rates and the employee will be able to claim a refund for any overwithholding at year-end by filing their personal tax return.
- Note that state and local withholding requirements may be different and result in different amounts than federal on Form W-2.

Exceptions to Mandatory Withholding

Wages and non-employee compensation are exempt from mandatory federal income tax withholding if all three of the following apply:

- The NRA who performed the services is present in the United States for a total not exceeding 90 days in a calendar year.
- The compensation for the services does not exceed $3,000
- The NRA performed the services as an employee of or under contract for an NRA individual or foreign corporation or partnership not engaged in a trade or business in the United States or the foreign office of U.S. citizen, corporation or partnership, or resident alien.

continued ▶

Employer Requirements for Non-Resident Aliens (NRA), *continued*

Also:

Wages and non-employee compensation are exempt from mandatory federal income tax withholding if both of the following apply:

- The NRA is in the U.S. based on F, J, M, or Q visa status
- The compensation for services is paid an NRA individual or foreign corporation or partnership or the foreign office of U.S. citizen, corporation or partnership, or resident alien.

Also exempt from manadatory withholding:

1) Regular crew members of a foreign vessel, 2) Residents of Canada and Mexico engaged in transportation 3) Foreign agricultural workers on H-2A visas.

Withholding Adjustment

As indicated an NRA does not receive a standard deduction; however, the standard deduction is built into tax tables used for withholding. Therefore, to adjust for this, employers must adjust (increase) withholding for NRAs. This is done by use of a table shown in of table 6.2 below, and following this procedure:

Step	Action
1	Select the appropriate payroll period in Table 6.2 and add the adjustment amount to employee wages.
2	Determine the number of withholding allowances (usually one for an NRA) and multiply this times the value of an allowance (See table 6.3.).
3	Using the percentage method (See Illustration 6.1), reduce the income by the result from Step 2 and calculate the tax to withhold, OR:
4	If using the wage-bracket tables, use the amount from Step 1 and correct allowances to calculate the withholding.

Note: The above calculations are for income tax withholding only. They do not affect total income tax, FICA, or FUTA taxes.

Note: NRA students and business apprentices from India are exempt from this procedure by treaty.

continued ▶

Employer Requirements for Non-Resident Aliens (NRA), *continued*

Table 6.2: NRA Wage Adjustment

Payroll Period	Add $ Amount
Weekly	$ 151.00
Biweekly	301.90
Semi-monthly	327.10
Monthly	654.20
Quarterly	1,962.50
Semi-annual	3,925.00
Annual	7,850.00
Daily or miscellaneous	30.20

Table 6.3: Percentage Method (2018 Allowance Values) One Withholding Allowance

Payroll Period	One Withholding Allowance
Weekly	$ 79.80
Biweekly	159.60
Semimonthly	172.90
Monthly	345.80
Quarterly	1,037.50
Semiannually	2,075.00
Annually	4,150.00
Daily or Miscellaneous per Day	16.00

continued

Employer Requirements for Non-Resident Aliens (NRA), *continued*

Example Percentage Method

Jon Schmidt properly completed Form W-4 to show non-resident alien status and claims one allowance. He is single and earns $6,000 paid monthly.

Step	Action	Example
1	Determine the gross wages and add adjustment amount	$6,000 + $654.20 from table 6.2 = $6,654.20
2	Identify the value of one withholding allowance	From Table 6.3: For monthly pay period: $345.80
3	Multiply the number of allowances by step 2 value.	1 × $345.80 = $345.80
4	Subtract the step 3 amount from step 1 amount to find "excess".	$6,654.20 – $345.80 = $6,308.40
5	Determine withholding amount by reference to correct percentage method tax table for filing status and period (Illustration 6.1).	Gross wage range for "single", "monthly" table: $3,533 to $7,183 Calculation: .22 × ($6,308.40 – $3,533) + $371.12 = $981.71 monthly withholding

Employer Requirements for Non-Resident Aliens (NRA), *continued*

Illustration 6.1

Percentage Method Tables for Income Tax Withholding

(For Wages Paid in 2018)

TABLE 1—WEEKLY Payroll Period

(a) SINGLE person (including head of household)—				(b) MARRIED person—			
If the amount of wages (after subtracting withholding allowances) is:		The amount of income tax to withhold is:		If the amount of wages (after subtracting withholding allowances) is:		The amount of income tax to withhold is:	
Not over $71 . . . . $0				Not over $222 . . . . $0			
Over—	But not over—		of excess over—	Over—	But not over—		of excess over—
$71	—$254	$0.00 plus 10%	—$71	$222	—$588	$0.00 plus 10%	—$222
$254	—$815	$18.30 plus 12%	—$254	$588	—$1,711	$36.60 plus 12%	—$588
$815	—$1,658	$85.62 plus 22%	—$815	$1,711	—$3,395	$171.36 plus 22%	—$1,711
$1,658	—$3,100	$271.08 plus 24%	—$1,658	$3,395	—$6,280	$541.84 plus 24%	—$3,395
$3,100	—$3,917	$617.16 plus 32%	—$3,100	$6,280	—$7,914	$1,234.24 plus 32%	—$6,280
$3,917	—$9,687	$878.60 plus 35%	—$3,917	$7,914	—$11,761	$1,757.12 plus 35%	—$7,914
$9,687		$2,898.10 plus 37%	—$9,687	$11,761		$3,103.57 plus 37%	—$11,761

TABLE 2—BIWEEKLY Payroll Period

(a) SINGLE person (including head of household)—				(b) MARRIED person—			
If the amount of wages (after subtracting withholding allowances) is:		The amount of income tax to withhold is:		If the amount of wages (after subtracting withholding allowances) is:		The amount of income tax to withhold is:	
Not over $142 . . . . $0				Not over $444 . . . . $0			
Over—	But not over—		of excess over—	Over—	But not over—		of excess over—
$142	—$509	$0.00 plus 10%	—$142	$444	—$1,177	$0.00 plus 10%	—$444
$509	—$1,631	$36.70 plus 12%	—$509	$1,177	—$3,421	$73.30 plus 12%	—$1,177
$1,631	—$3,315	$171.34 plus 22%	—$1,631	$3,421	—$6,790	$342.58 plus 22%	—$3,421
$3,315	—$6,200	$541.82 plus 24%	—$3,315	$6,790	—$12,560	$1,083.76 plus 24%	—$6,790
$6,200	—$7,835	$1,234.22 plus 32%	—$6,200	$12,560	—$15,829	$2,468.56 plus 32%	—$12,560
$7,835	—$19,373	$1,757.42 plus 35%	—$7,835	$15,829	—$23,521	$3,514.64 plus 35%	—$15,829
$19,373		$5,795.72 plus 37%	—$19,373	$23,521		$6,206.84 plus 37%	—$23,521

TABLE 3—SEMIMONTHLY Payroll Period

(a) SINGLE person (including head of household)—				(b) MARRIED person—			
If the amount of wages (after subtracting withholding allowances) is:		The amount of income tax to withhold is:		If the amount of wages (after subtracting withholding allowances) is:		The amount of income tax to withhold is:	
Not over $154 . . . . $0				Not over $481 . . . . $0			
Over—	But not over—		of excess over—	Over—	But not over—		of excess over—
$154	—$551	$0.00 plus 10%	—$154	$481	—$1,275	$0.00 plus 10%	—$481
$551	—$1,767	$39.70 plus 12%	—$551	$1,275	—$3,706	$79.40 plus 12%	—$1,275
$1,767	—$3,592	$185.62 plus 22%	—$1,767	$3,706	—$7,356	$371.12 plus 22%	—$3,706
$3,592	—$6,717	$587.12 plus 24%	—$3,592	$7,356	—$13,606	$1,174.12 plus 24%	—$7,356
$6,717	—$8,488	$1,337.12 plus 32%	—$6,717	$13,606	—$17,148	$2,674.12 plus 32%	—$13,606
$8,488	—$20,988	$1,903.84 plus 35%	—$8,488	$17,148	—$25,481	$3,807.56 plus 35%	—$17,148
$20,988		$6,278.84 plus 37%	—$20,988	$25,481		$6,724.11 plus 37%	—$25,481

TABLE 4—MONTHLY Payroll Period

(a) SINGLE person (including head of household)—				(b) MARRIED person—			
If the amount of wages (after subtracting withholding allowances) is:		The amount of income tax to withhold is:		If the amount of wages (after subtracting withholding allowances) is:		The amount of income tax to withhold is:	
Not over $308 . . . . $0				Not over $963 . . . . $0			
Over—	But not over—		of excess over—	Over—	But not over—		of excess over—
$308	—$1,102	$0.00 plus 10%	—$308	$963	—$2,550	$0.00 plus 10%	—$963
$1,102	—$3,533	$79.40 plus 12%	—$1,102	$2,550	—$7,413	$158.70 plus 12%	—$2,550
$3,533	—$7,183	$371.12 plus 22%	—$3,533	$7,413	—$14,713	$742.26 plus 22%	—$7,413
$7,183	—$13,433	$1,174.12 plus 24%	—$7,183	$14,713	—$27,213	$2,348.26 plus 24%	—$14,713
$13,433	—$16,975	$2,674.12 plus 32%	—$13,433	$27,213	—$34,296	$5,348.26 plus 32%	—$27,213
$16,975	—$41,975	$3,807.56 plus 35%	—$16,975	$34,296	—$50,963	$7,614.82 plus 35%	—$34,296
$41,975		$12,557.56 plus 37%	—$41,975	$50,963		$13,448.27 plus 37%	—$50,963

Source: Internal Revenue Service

continued ▶

Employer Requirements for Non-Resident Aliens (NRA), *continued*

FICA Tax

In general, NRAs are subject to FICA, with the following exceptions, which are exempt status:

- A-visas: Employees, family members, servants of foreign governments if acting in official capacity as foreign government employees.
- D-visas: Crew members of a ship or aircraft if the vessel is foreign and the employer is foreign if services are performed outside of the United States.
- F, J, M, and Q-visas: NRA students, academics, trainees, researchers, and others in F-1, J-1, M-1, or Q-1/Q-2 immigrant status provided employment is compliant with status. There are certain detailed limitations on these exemptions.
- G-visas: Employees of international organizations
- H-visas: Non-immigrants in H-2 and H-2A status if either: 1) An H-2 resident of the Philippines who performs services in Guam 2) An H-2A admitted temporarily admitted to the United States to perform agricultural labor.

Note: because resident aliens do not have these exemptions, an employer must be aware if the residency status changes to avoid exempting employees who are ineligible.

FICA Totalization Agreements

The United States maintains bilateral agreements with countries that impose taxes that are similar in nature to FICA. These are called "totalization" agreements, and eliminate dual coverage and dual taxation. These agreements create exemptions for resident aliens, non-resident aliens, and even U.S. citizens in the circumstance when they relocate to the U.S. but still qualify as a resident of a signatory country. Totalization applies only to FICA and not FUTA.

FUTA Tax

In general, NRAs are subject to FUTA, with the following exceptions, which are exempt status:

- Compensation to agricultural workers
- Compensation to household employees
- Compensation for religious, charitable, educational activities, and specified" tax-exempt organizations
- Compensation to NRAs temporarily in the U.S. in F-1, J-1, Q-1/Q-2 nonimmigrant status

Foreign Source Income

Foreign source income (income form outside the U.S.) is generally not taxed to a non-resident alien. There are limited circumstances in which the income can become taxable because either the income is generated from a U.S. place of trade or business or relates to conduct of business within the U.S.

Dual-Status Aliens

General Guidlines   A dual-status alien is a person who has been both a non-resident alien and a resident alien within the same tax year. A dual-status alien is taxed on income from all sources for the part of the year the person is resient alien, and is taxed as an NRA on U.S.- source income for the part of the year the person is an NRA. An employer will follow the guidelines previously discussed in this section.

Form Filing Requirements

Summary   In general, all the filing requirements discussed in previous sections still apply, with the addition of filing requirements that may apply for employers of non-resident aliens.

Employers of NRAs may be required to file the following additional forms:

- Form 8233 received from an employee to claim exemption from from wage withholding due to tax treaty. Filed within 5 days of receipt from employee.
- Form 1042-S to report employee income paid to a foreign person for which a withholding exemption based on a tax treaty is claimed. (1042-S is also used to report other income related to foreign persons that is subject to withholding.) The form is due March 15 for the preceding year. An extension is available by filing form 8809 no later than March 5. Copy A is sent to the IRS with Form 1042-T, a transmittal form. Copies B, C, and D are sent to the employee (or recipient of other income) to be used in reporting their income (Form 1040 for resident alien, Form 1040NR for NRA). Note that an employee may receive both forms 1042-S and W-2 if some wages are exempt and some are not or certain kinds of income (such as certain scholarship income) has been earned.
- Form 1042 is filed (separately) to report tax withheld whenever a Form 1042-S is filed. The due dates are the same.

Undocumented Workers

Overview   As we discussed earlier in Section 1, employers have a legal responsibility to verify the identity, citizenship, and residency status of potential employees, including Form I-9 requirements. Employment authorization from the Department of Homeland Security must be verified. As well, employers must immediately notify an employee of a tentaive nonconfirmation and the Department of

Undocumented Workers, *continued*

Homeland Security of a final non-confirmation of eligibility (from E-Verify). Employers who violate these requirements are subject to fines and even criminal penalties (if there is a pattern of behavior).

Employer Tax Issues

Undocumented workers are subject to income tax, and employers must withhold tax on wages, using backup withholding rates if necessary (or unknowingly using a false social security numbers supplied by an undocumented person from Form W-4). Other reporting requirements as previously discussed in earlier sections also apply. Undocumented worker income is also subject to FICA and FUTA requirements.

Appendix I

Timekeeping

The Critical Function of Timekeeping

Overview

The timekeeping function is a key part of the second step in the payroll process: "Calculate the Payroll". Its effects are extensive. It is most directly connected to hourly employee wage calculations but also potentially affects employees receiving commissions, bonuses, tips, piecework, and even salaried employees, and sick leave and vacation pay. In turn, the amounts calculated will also affect and withholding and payroll tax reporting and payments. This appendix examines some of the key elements involved in timekeeping that underlie our earlier discussion in Section 2 concerning payroll calculation, with suggestions for best practices.

What is Timekeeping?

Typcal timekeeping functions are: 1) Compile and check accuracy of employee time reporting (such as time sheets, punch cards, electronic and online reports), 2) Review reporting for employee initials or other employee confirmation methods, 3) Review reporting for supervisor approvals and provide feedback to supervisors for time reporting errors, 4) Perform any other required verification functions, 5) Compute totals and create various reports and data analysis as required by management, such as by regular time, overtime (calculated in compliance with FLSA and state laws - see Section 2), double-time, time allocations by task, job, or department, leave balances, rest periods, and undocumented absence, 6) Record leaves, absences, and vacation time, 7) Provide feedback on timekeeping operations to management and systems personnel, particularly when a computer or online system is used.

What is on a timesheet (or equivalent)? The most essential information is hours worked. However, for billing and/or cost allocation and analysis purposes, work time can also be reported by job, by type of task or activity, by machine or work station, and by geographical location, including travel time.

Strictly speaking, the timekeeping function is separate from other payroll activities such as computing and/or changing withholding, printing paychecks, and performing minimum wage and overtime dollar calculations. However, in smaller businesses, all these activities may be condensed into a single department or

continued ▶

performed by just one individual. The more condensed the activities, the greater the need for active internal control (see below).

Legal Compliance

The Fair Labor Standards Act as well as other federal laws and a variety of state laws require organizational compliance that is verified by accurate and reliable timekeeping. At the heart of the compliance requirements are the issues of correct payments for minimum wage and of overtime, which can only determined by reference to hours worked, and a dependable timekeeping method.

Internal Control

The subject of internal control has appeared at earlier points in this book. Internal control essentially means the procedures and policies that are in place to prevent fraud and theft losses, and secondarily, loss due to mismanagement. The payroll function, and particularly timekeeping, must be an important focus of interal control efforts, in order to prevent overstatement and misallocation of hours worked. Secondly, good internal control procedures will also assist in satisfying compliance requirements, and the accurate determination of minimum wage and overtime compensation.

Timekeeping Best Practices Summary

Overview

Best practices relate to policies and procedures. Payroll policies, which are an indicator of management objectives in this context, should be comprehensive, clear, and available to all employees. Following such a standard will prove to useful should the need at some point arise to demonstrate compliance with applicable laws. Procedures typically result from policies. Procedures usually involve a checklist of actions that must be taken.

Timekeeping Policies

Policies are created with objectives in mind. In the matters of payroll and timekeeping, policies revolve around compliance and internal control. The most basic requirement of a payroll policy is awareness – management should be able to demonstrate that all policies are documented and that employees have been made aware of policies and changes in policies. Key policies that should be included (that affect the timekeeping function) are:

- Integrity: Honesty in all aspects of recording work hours and job time is expected and required.
- Accuracy: Precision in the timekeeping process is required to ensure correct compensation to employees and correct expense to employer. "Precision" is defined in all applicable contexts, (e.g. hours rounded to a tenth of an hour).

- Documentation: All data that are part of or used in timekeeping must be recorded.
- Security: All recorded data is kept secure with procedures in place for limited access by specified employee classifications (e.g. in a small business, only the owner has access).
- Verification: Verification means obtaining proof of accuracy or evidence of an event. In the context of timekeeping this generally means periodic physical checking or electronic verification, such as for presence at work.
- Approvals: Approvals by a designated authority are required for specified events.
- Limitations: Limitations may placed on activities, such as a limitation on overtime.
- Errors/Corrections: All timekeeping errors must be corrected upon discovery with approval.
- Meals and rest periods: Periods are set for specified employees.
- Work away from the office: Notice and approval are required.
- Leaves (paid and unpaid): Times are identified and reported to payroll.
- Employee privacy: Privacy matters are identified and procedures are implemented (e.g. paycheck amounts).
- Procedure enforcement: Procedures must be followed and enforcement standards are set in coordination with potential disciplinary actions.
- Disciplinary actions: Events requiring disciplinary actions are clearly identified and the action(s) that may be taken are identified.

Timekeeping Internal Control Procedures

Overview

Timekeeping best practices should include the timekeeping internal control procedures that are described below. These should be part of every timekeeping activity; however, the list is not exhaustive. Essential procedures apply in most situations, but specific circumstances may dictate additional required procedeures. Note: internal control procedures related to hours worked applies primarily to non-exempt employees.

Employee Recording and Supervisor Approval

However time is recorded, each employee must record his or her total time (recording on a daily basis is DOL-required), should identify in-and-out times, and confirm totals with a signature, initial, or other recordable method. The time should also be reviewed by supervisor(s) for approval. A supervisor should not approve a report that contains blank spaces above initials or signature or allows

continued ▶

any further data input after approval. The purpose of supervisor approval is to check for reasonableness and appropriateness for required work duties; other internal control methods (below) are also available as a check on time reporting fraud. Time submission and supervisor review must be timely; payroll cannot and **should not be processed** without supervisor-approved verification.

Password Use

Electronic time sheet systems should require passwords and require password changes at regular intervals. Supervisor approvals should require separate passwords. Passwords should not be shared for spreadsheets or be accessible for any other reason. Password requirements and input control apply at all levels of the payroll process.

Separation of Duties

For a small business, the timekeeping and the payroll calculation and recording duties are often performed by a single person. In this case "separation of duties" means that payroll preparation is separated from all other activities, and no other person is authorized to enter any data, calculate the payroll, or perform any other payroll activity, except authorized management for supervisory purposes. This key internal control procedure helps prevent collusion between employees or undue influence or data entry by non-payroll employees. In a larger business with more employees and a higher volume of work, the timekeeping duties are further separated from other duties within the payroll department. In all cases, output of any kind should be reviewed and approved by someone not part of the activity creating the output.

Small Business Risks and Owner Reviews

In a small business it is often the case that one person performs not only timekeeping, but all payroll duties. Frequently this is done through a computerized payroll system. This creates a significant internal control issue, when a single person has access to timekeeping, employee database information, paycheck creation, deposit and filing duties, performs payroll checking account reconciliation and payroll expense reports and probably has access to general ledger accounts. In this circumstance it is essential for the owner(s) to carefully review each payroll element with every payroll, and regularly review employee database information.

Retention and Delivery to Timekeeping

If a paper-based system is in use, no employee should have access to other employee timesheets after supervisor approval. A supervisor should collect and retain timesheets and deliver them to timekeeping.

Exceptions Reports

Exceptions reports should be created to identify varitions from policy relating to such items as total hours, overtime, leave, and absences. For many items exceptions flagging features are available as part of automated timekeeping and payroll systems.

Changes Approval

Changes to any timekeeping output must be reviewed by an independent party. All changes should be included on an exceptions report.

Document Security

All timekeeping source data must be retained and protected. In the case of paper data, physical security and controlled access is necessary. In the case of electronic information proper off-site file storage should be required. Orginal data become very important, for example, in the case of Department of Labor audits to evaluate labor law compliance. Suggested retention time is four years from date of document, unless state and local law requires more. (Note: ERISA, regarding employee benefit programs, requires a 6 year retention period.)

Federal and State Data Requiremnts

Timekeeping must provide data that can demonstrate compliance with federal and state employment law requirements. This is particularly essential for minimum wage calculations and overtime calculations. This can apply to not only designated duties, but time for rest periods, training time, orientation time, on-call time, and away from office time.

Periodic Payroll Audits

Payroll, including the timekeeping function, should be periodically audited and internal controls reviewed by competent internal or external independent parties.

Time Data Acquisition and Processing Methods

Overview

The timekeeping process begins with a time recording, usually performed by each employee. The available methods are paper systems, timeclock systems, computerized hybrid systems, online systems, and RFID, NFC, and biometric technologies.

Paper Systems

The most basic timekeeping method is the use of timesheets, in which an employee records total time, and frequently by job, client, or other categories.

continued ▶

Timesheets often require not only total hours for each item, but also beginning and ending times. Timesheets are turned in directly to a supervisor by each employee (which may reduce fraud) or the employee enters data directly into a computer system or online. There is no independent evidence of time worked, so fraud is not difficult to engineer. As well, if daily employee activity is assigned to a variety of different tasks, jobs, or departments, errors can be material.

Timeclock Systems

In a traditional timeclock system, which is relatively inexpensive, each employee uses a paper card that is inserted into a mechanical device that stamps the date and time on the card at the beginning and end of a shift ("punching in and punching out"). At the end of a payroll period, the stamped cards are used by the timekeeping department to determine hours worked. This system at least provides evidence of arrival and departure times; however, it is usually difficult to identify who has actually used a card, and workers can have a co-worker punch in or punch out (known as "buddy punching") for them when not at work. The use of badges or PIN numbers can reduce this, but of course these can still be shared. Timeclocks can also be connected to central computer systems and used with coded employee cards that identify employees as well as any relevant work limitations, such as proper shift and break times, as well hours logged in and out.

A variation of the timeclock system is the use of either a local area computer network system at the business location or an online system allowing cell phone use. In these systems, an employee logs in and logs out for timekeeping purposes on a computer or an online interface. These systems can provide the same contols as the computer-connected timeclocks descraibed above. They reduce processing times but suffer from the same internal control shortcomings as described above. Personal passwords can reduce the problem (because some employees may not like to share passwords that make other data accessible), but these can also be shared. Additionally, unless computer time settings are locked in some manner, they can be changed to fraudulently report additional time.

Computerized Hybrid Systems

These systems simply use accumlatd paper timesheet or punchcard data that are input into a computer system by a worker physically coding and keying in the data. Although there may be some processing time savings, the manual data input is a significant bottleneck and is relatively inefficient, particularly if hours result from different tasks, departments or jobs that must be seperately coded and identified. The manual input also is subject to high error rates .

Time Data Acquisition and Processing Methods, *continued*

RFID and NFC Technology	RFID stands for "Radio Frequency Identification". This technology imbeds a chip into an ID card that signals an arrival or departure when the card holder comes into close proximity to a reader device. Similarly, NFC ("Near Field Communication") can be designed into a cell phone (which may be less likely to be shared) which is then used to signal arrival or departure when in close proximity to a reader device.
Biometrics	Biometric devices identify indivuals by fingerprint recognition and/or facial recognition. An employee must be physically present in front of the device to determine recognition prior to being recorded as present. These systems can virtually eliminate the buddy punching fraud issue.

Cost and Efficiency Considerations

Costs and Efficiency	The costs associated with timekeeping (and payroll in general) are numerous. Timekeeping procedures inherently involve a significant number of processing steps and are easily subjected to fraudulent data input. Therefore a starting premise might be to set an objective that automates processing as much as possible and reduces the possiblity of fraudulent data entry at various points in the process.
	Prior to undertaking changes, management should make an effort to identify current and potential timekeeping expense activities. Generally, the greater the manual hours, the greater the long-term expenses incurred. When employee hours have to be identified with (allocated to) different tasks, jobs, or departments, automated systems can save significant time. For analysis, identify the items, hours and costs involved in each activity. These are some typical expense activities: employee recording hours, supervisor checking and approval, securely transferring data, manual data input, calculating and allocating time, error corrections, management reports, and... losses from fraud. If fraudulent employee time recording is an issue (It's not an uncommon occurrence in many businesses), does it result in small, moderate, or large costs and to what extent can these be reduced by a new system, which will incur significant up-front costs, and new expenses (e.g. employee re-training to understand system procedures and perform data analysis, and software upgrades)?
	Automated processing can remove a great deal of processing time and associated expense, but it comes with its own issues. For example, notice that individual employee time input in a computerized system bypasses supervisor

continued ▶

review, or requires input first to a supervisor for review, who then finalizes the input procedure. When subject to fraudulent activity, automated system fraud can be more difficult to detect and result in greater losses than manual processing. Automated processing places much more control in the hands of fewer employees. Clearly, automated systems will magnify the need for internal control procedures, which of course, is an additional expense.

Can timekeeping be outsourced? Yes, there are third-party services that provide the technology on a subscription basis. This avoids the substantial up-front costs of developing and implementing a new system, although employee retraining will still be required.

What About Exempt Employees?

Still Record
Their Time?

Exempt employees – for the most part, salaried employees (see Section 2) - are not subject to timekeeping needs for minimum wage and overtime requirements... generally. Why "generally"? Because if errors are made and an exempt employee turns into a nonexempt employee following an audit, then years of hourly data for that employee become necessary. For salaried employees who may not be currently exempt but could be in the future, it may be worthwhile to record all hours –above and below 40, depending on the hourly calculation method used to determine overtime hours.

Finally, other timekeeping needs may apply to exempt employees, such as task and job hours alloctions, accrual of sick leave hours, vacation pay, and severance pay.

Appendix II

Employer Identification Number

If there are one or more employees, obtain an Employer Identification Number (EIN) online by searching for the form online or at https://www.irs.gov/pub/irs-pdf/fss4.pdf or simply search "obtain EIN". The form is filed as follows:

- Business location is in one of the 50 states or District of Columbia: Use the following address: Internal Revenue Service, Attn: EIN Operation, Cincinnati, OH, 45999. Fax number: 855-641-6935.
- No legal residence, principal place of business or office in any state: Use the following address: Internal Revenue Service, Attn: EIN International Operation, Cincinnati, OH, 45999. Fax number: 855-215-1627 (in the U.S) or 304-707-9471 (outside the U.S.

States also require employer identification numbers. Be sure to check identification requirements for your own state.

Electronic Payment System

Because federal payroll-related payments generally must be made electronically, an Electronic Federal Tax Payment System (EFTPS) should be created. For enrollment instructions and procedures go to the online address at https://www.eftps.gov. If you obtain an employer identification number (above) you will automatically be enrolled in eftps. However, it is still necessary to access the site to have information validated, receive a personal identification numbe (PIN), and access instructions. Instructions are also available in Publications 966 and 4990. Be sure to check state requirement and resources, which may be different.

Tax Calendar

This is easy, but essential. Go online to locate Publication 509 for federal deadlines. Also determine state and local deadlines from your own state. Refer to the calendar(s) often. Some of the most common reasons for payroll tax penalties are late filing and payment.

Pay Period	Every business with employees must have a regular pay period(s) –different pay periods are also permitted for different employee classifications. There is no one single best period; deciding on a pay period is a question of optimizing alternatives. See page 32 for a summary of the alternatives and pros and cons.
Deposit Schedule	For federal purposes a new business generally has a monthly payroll tax deposit schedule until a lookback period (see page 112) can be established. Be sure to double-check your own case, and check state and local requirements.
Human Resources Functions	Most new businesses will not have the resources to create a human resources department; however, human resource department-type activities are essential and include legal compliance requirements. See page 14 for a human resources checklist for a small or new business.
Insurance Requirements	Most states require some form of workers' compensation. Check state requirements and select from whatever options are available for businesses in your state.
Direct Deposit for Employees	Setting up a direct deposit link for each employee will save substantial time over the long run, and provide some internal control safeguards. Try to communicate all the advantages of this to employees so they will enroll.
Software Systems	Payroll functions are excellent applications for computerized systems, and there are numerous software systems available that can eliminate a great deal of manual time related to processing and calculation functions, especially as the number of employees increases. However, purchase of these systems requires research, and there are both upfront investments and software updating costs, and training time.
Employment Laws	There are numerous payroll laws that create a complex web of potential compliance requirements, which are often unexpected. Pages 10–12 provide a summary. If after review you are in doubt about compliance requirements, you can do your own inexpensive research by contacting the Department of Labor, the IRS, the Social Security Administration, and other administrative agencies; however, also consider obtaining professional legal assistance.

New Business Payroll Checklist, *continued*

Professional Help   Professional assistance includes numerous alternatives at varying costs. These
are some options:

- Outsourcing to payroll services: Some banks as well as specialized payroll
  companies provide payroll processing services. An advantage of this approach is that costs described above are avoided and payroll processing
  work is reduced. However, this approach still requires company timekeeping
  and data management work needed for input. See page 108 regarding these
  services.
- Outsourcing to accounting firms: Small to moderate-size accounting firms
  frequently provide payroll processing services. An advantage of using these
  services is that accounting firms, particularly CPAs, is the building of a relationship with a resource that also provides other necessary services such as
  accounting systems setup, financial statement preparation, and tax advice.
  Payroll processing costs might higher than payroll processing companies;
  however, sometimes a combination of services can be negotiated.
- Legal advice: Although this can be expensive, an intial consultation may be
  advisable for a new business in order to ensure that all compliance issues
  will be properly addressed. Select attorneys that specialize in payroll matters.

Appendix III

Tax Tables

Percentage Method Tables for Income Tax Withholding

(For Wages Paid in 2018)

TABLE 1—WEEKLY Payroll Period

(a) SINGLE person (including head of household)—				(b) MARRIED person—			
If the amount of wages (after subtracting withholding allowances) is:		The amount of income tax to withhold is:		If the amount of wages (after subtracting withholding allowances) is:		The amount of income tax to withhold is:	
Not over $71		$0		Not over $222		$0	
Over—	But not over—		of excess over—	Over—	But not over—		of excess over—
$71	—$254	$0.00 plus 10%	—$71	$222	—$588	$0.00 plus 10%	—$222
$254	—$815	$18.30 plus 12%	—$254	$588	—$1,711	$36.60 plus 12%	—$588
$815	—$1,658	$85.62 plus 22%	—$815	$1,711	—$3,395	$171.36 plus 22%	—$1,711
$1,658	—$3,100	$271.08 plus 24%	—$1,658	$3,395	—$6,280	$541.84 plus 24%	—$3,395
$3,100	—$3,917	$617.16 plus 32%	—$3,100	$6,280	—$7,914	$1,234.24 plus 32%	—$6,280
$3,917	—$9,687	$878.60 plus 35%	—$3,917	$7,914	—$11,761	$1,757.12 plus 35%	—$7,914
$9,687		$2,898.10 plus 37%	—$9,687	$11,761		$3,103.57 plus 37%	—$11,761

TABLE 2—BIWEEKLY Payroll Period

(a) SINGLE person (including head of household)—				(b) MARRIED person—			
If the amount of wages (after subtracting withholding allowances) is:		The amount of income tax to withhold is:		If the amount of wages (after subtracting withholding allowances) is:		The amount of income tax to withhold is:	
Not over $142		$0		Not over $444		$0	
Over—	But not over—		of excess over—	Over—	But not over—		of excess over—
$142	—$509	$0.00 plus 10%	—$142	$444	—$1,177	$0.00 plus 10%	—$444
$509	—$1,631	$36.70 plus 12%	—$509	$1,177	—$3,421	$73.30 plus 12%	—$1,177
$1,631	—$3,315	$171.34 plus 22%	—$1,631	$3,421	—$6,790	$342.58 plus 22%	—$3,421
$3,315	—$6,200	$541.82 plus 24%	—$3,315	$6,790	—$12,560	$1,083.76 plus 24%	—$6,790
$6,200	—$7,835	$1,234.22 plus 32%	—$6,200	$12,560	—$15,829	$2,468.56 plus 32%	—$12,560
$7,835	—$19,373	$1,757.42 plus 35%	—$7,835	$15,829	—$23,521	$3,514.64 plus 35%	—$15,829
$19,373		$5,795.72 plus 37%	—$19,373	$23,521		$6,206.84 plus 37%	—$23,521

TABLE 3—SEMIMONTHLY Payroll Period

(a) SINGLE person (including head of household)—				(b) MARRIED person—			
If the amount of wages (after subtracting withholding allowances) is:		The amount of income tax to withhold is:		If the amount of wages (after subtracting withholding allowances) is:		The amount of income tax to withhold is:	
Not over $154		$0		Not over $481		$0	
Over—	But not over—		of excess over—	Over—	But not over—		of excess over—
$154	—$551	$0.00 plus 10%	—$154	$481	—$1,275	$0.00 plus 10%	—$481
$551	—$1,767	$39.70 plus 12%	—$551	$1,275	—$3,706	$79.40 plus 12%	—$1,275
$1,767	—$3,592	$185.62 plus 22%	—$1,767	$3,706	—$7,356	$371.12 plus 22%	—$3,706
$3,592	—$6,717	$587.12 plus 24%	—$3,592	$7,356	—$13,606	$1,174.12 plus 24%	—$7,356
$6,717	—$8,488	$1,337.12 plus 32%	—$6,717	$13,606	—$17,148	$2,674.12 plus 32%	—$13,606
$8,488	—$20,988	$1,903.84 plus 35%	—$8,488	$17,148	—$25,481	$3,807.56 plus 35%	—$17,148
$20,988		$6,278.84 plus 37%	—$20,988	$25,481		$6,724.11 plus 37%	—$25,481

TABLE 4—MONTHLY Payroll Period

(a) SINGLE person (including head of household)—				(b) MARRIED person—			
If the amount of wages (after subtracting withholding allowances) is:		The amount of income tax to withhold is:		If the amount of wages (after subtracting withholding allowances) is:		The amount of income tax to withhold is:	
Not over $308		$0		Not over $963		$0	
Over—	But not over—		of excess over—	Over—	But not over—		of excess over—
$308	—$1,102	$0.00 plus 10%	—$308	$963	—$2,550	$0.00 plus 10%	—$963
$1,102	—$3,533	$79.40 plus 12%	—$1,102	$2,550	—$7,413	$158.70 plus 12%	—$2,550
$3,533	—$7,183	$371.12 plus 22%	—$3,533	$7,413	—$14,713	$742.26 plus 22%	—$7,413
$7,183	—$13,433	$1,174.12 plus 24%	—$7,183	$14,713	—$27,213	$2,348.26 plus 24%	—$14,713
$13,433	—$16,975	$2,674.12 plus 32%	—$13,433	$27,213	—$34,296	$5,348.26 plus 32%	—$27,213
$16,975	—$41,975	$3,807.56 plus 35%	—$16,975	$34,296	—$50,963	$7,614.82 plus 35%	—$34,296
$41,975		$12,557.56 plus 37%	—$41,975	$50,963		$13,448.27 plus 37%	—$50,963

Percentage Method Tables for Income Tax Withholding (continued)

(For Wages Paid in 2018)

TABLE 5—QUARTERLY Payroll Period

(a) SINGLE person (including head of household)—
If the amount of wages (after subtracting withholding allowances) is:
Not over $925 . . . . $0

Over—	But not over—	The amount of income tax to withhold is:	of excess over—
$925	—$3,306	$0.00 plus 10%	—$925
$3,306	—$10,600	$238.10 plus 12%	—$3,306
$10,600	—$21,550	$1,113.38 plus 22%	—$10,600
$21,550	—$40,300	$3,522.38 plus 24%	—$21,550
$40,300	—$50,925	$8,022.38 plus 32%	—$40,300
$50,925	—$125,925	$11,422.38 plus 35%	—$50,925
$125,925		$37,672.38 plus 37%	—$125,925

(b) MARRIED person—
If the amount of wages (after subtracting withholding allowances) is:
Not over $2,888 . . . . $0

Over—	But not over—	The amount of income tax to withhold is:	of excess over—
$2,888	—$7,650	$0.00 plus 10%	—$2,888
$7,650	—$22,238	$476.20 plus 12%	—$7,650
$22,238	—$44,138	$2,226.76 plus 22%	—$22,238
$44,138	—$81,638	$7,044.76 plus 24%	—$44,138
$81,638	—$102,888	$16,044.76 plus 32%	—$81,638
$102,888	—$152,888	$22,844.76 plus 35%	—$102,888
$152,888		$40,344.76 plus 37%	—$152,888

TABLE 6—SEMIANNUAL Payroll Period

(a) SINGLE person (including head of household)—
If the amount of wages (after subtracting withholding allowances) is:
Not over $1,850 . . . . $0

Over—	But not over—	The amount of income tax to withhold is:	of excess over—
$1,850	—$6,613	$0.00 plus 10%	—$1,850
$6,613	—$21,200	$476.30 plus 12%	—$6,613
$21,200	—$43,100	$2,226.74 plus 22%	—$21,200
$43,100	—$80,600	$7,044.74 plus 24%	—$43,100
$80,600	—$101,850	$16,044.74 plus 32%	—$80,600
$101,850	—$251,850	$22,844.74 plus 35%	—$101,850
$251,850		$75,344.74 plus 37%	—$251,850

(b) MARRIED person—
If the amount of wages (after subtracting withholding allowances) is:
Not over $5,775 . . . . $0

Over—	But not over—	The amount of income tax to withhold is:	of excess over—
$5,775	—$15,300	$0.00 plus 10%	—$5,775
$15,300	—$44,475	$952.50 plus 12%	—$15,300
$44,475	—$88,275	$4,453.50 plus 22%	—$44,475
$88,275	—$163,275	$14,089.50 plus 24%	—$88,275
$163,275	—$205,775	$32,089.50 plus 32%	—$163,275
$205,775	—$305,775	$45,689.50 plus 35%	—$205,775
$305,775		$80,689.50 plus 37%	—$305,775

TABLE 7—ANNUAL Payroll Period

(a) SINGLE person (including head of household)—
If the amount of wages (after subtracting withholding allowances) is:
Not over $3,700 . . . . $0

Over—	But not over—	The amount of income tax to withhold is:	of excess over—
$3,700	—$13,225	$0.00 plus 10%	—$3,700
$13,225	—$42,400	$952.50 plus 12%	—$13,225
$42,400	—$86,200	$4,453.50 plus 22%	—$42,400
$86,200	—$161,200	$14,089.50 plus 24%	—$86,200
$161,200	—$203,700	$32,089.50 plus 32%	—$161,200
$203,700	—$503,700	$45,689.50 plus 35%	—$203,700
$503,700		$150,689.50 plus 37%	—$503,700

(b) MARRIED person—
If the amount of wages (after subtracting withholding allowances) is:
Not over $11,550 . . . . . . $0

Over—	But not over—	The amount of income tax to withhold is:	of excess over—
$11,550	—$30,600	$0.00 plus 10%	—$11,550
$30,600	—$88,950	$1,905.00 plus 12%	—$30,600
$88,950	—$176,550	$8,907.00 plus 22%	—$88,950
$176,550	—$326,550	$28,179.00 plus 24%	—$176,550
$326,550	—$411,550	$64,179.00 plus 32%	—$326,550
$411,550	—$611,550	$91,379.00 plus 35%	—$411,550
$611,550		$161,379.00 plus 37%	—$611,550

TABLE 8—DAILY or MISCELLANEOUS Payroll Period

(a) SINGLE person (including head of household)—
If the amount of wages (after subtracting withholding allowances) divided by the number of days in the payroll period is:
Not over $14.20 . . . . $0

Over—	But not over—	The amount of income tax to withhold per day is:	of excess over—
$14.20	—$50.90	$0.00 plus 10%	—$14.20
$50.90	—$163.10	$3.67 plus 12%	—$50.90
$163.10	—$331.50	$17.13 plus 22%	—$163.10
$331.50	—$620.00	$54.18 plus 24%	—$331.50
$620.00	—$783.50	$123.42 plus 32%	—$620.00
$783.50	—$1,937.30	$175.74 plus 35%	—$783.50
$1,937.30		$579.57 plus 37%	—$1,937.30

(b) MARRIED person—
If the amount of wages (after subtracting withholding allowances) divided by the number of days in the payroll period is:
Not over $44.40 . . . . $0

Over—	But not over—	The amount of income tax to withhold per day is:	of excess over—
$44.40	—$117.70	$0.00 plus 10%	—$44.40
$117.70	—$342.10	$7.33 plus 12%	—$117.70
$342.10	—$679.00	$34.26 plus 22%	—$342.10
$679.00	—$1,256.00	$108.38 plus 24%	—$679.00
$1,256.00	—$1,582.90	$246.86 plus 32%	—$1,256.00
$1,582.90	—$2,352.10	$351.47 plus 35%	—$1,582.90
$2,352.10		$620.69 plus 37%	—$2,352.10

Wage Bracket Method Tables for Income Tax Withholding

SINGLE Persons—**WEEKLY** Payroll Period

(For Wages Paid through December 31, 2018)

And the wages are—		And the number of withholding allowances claimed is—										
At least	But less than	0	1	2	3	4	5	6	7	8	9	10
		The amount of income tax to be withheld is—										
$ 0	$75	$0	$0	$0	$0	$0	$0	$0	$0	$0	$0	$0
75	80	1	0	0	0	0	0	0	0	0	0	0
80	85	1	0	0	0	0	0	0	0	0	0	0
85	90	2	0	0	0	0	0	0	0	0	0	0
90	95	2	0	0	0	0	0	0	0	0	0	0
95	100	3	0	0	0	0	0	0	0	0	0	0
100	105	3	0	0	0	0	0	0	0	0	0	0
105	110	4	0	0	0	0	0	0	0	0	0	0
110	115	4	0	0	0	0	0	0	0	0	0	0
115	120	5	0	0	0	0	0	0	0	0	0	0
120	125	5	0	0	0	0	0	0	0	0	0	0
125	130	6	0	0	0	0	0	0	0	0	0	0
130	135	6	0	0	0	0	0	0	0	0	0	0
135	140	7	0	0	0	0	0	0	0	0	0	0
140	145	7	0	0	0	0	0	0	0	0	0	0
145	150	8	0	0	0	0	0	0	0	0	0	0
150	155	8	0	0	0	0	0	0	0	0	0	0
155	160	9	1	0	0	0	0	0	0	0	0	0
160	165	9	1	0	0	0	0	0	0	0	0	0
165	170	10	2	0	0	0	0	0	0	0	0	0
170	175	10	2	0	0	0	0	0	0	0	0	0
175	180	11	3	0	0	0	0	0	0	0	0	0
180	185	11	3	0	0	0	0	0	0	0	0	0
185	190	12	4	0	0	0	0	0	0	0	0	0
190	195	12	4	0	0	0	0	0	0	0	0	0
195	200	13	5	0	0	0	0	0	0	0	0	0
200	210	13	5	0	0	0	0	0	0	0	0	0
210	220	14	6	0	0	0	0	0	0	0	0	0
220	230	15	7	0	0	0	0	0	0	0	0	0
230	240	16	8	0	0	0	0	0	0	0	0	0
240	250	17	9	1	0	0	0	0	0	0	0	0
250	260	18	10	2	0	0	0	0	0	0	0	0
260	270	20	11	3	0	0	0	0	0	0	0	0
270	280	21	12	4	0	0	0	0	0	0	0	0
280	290	22	13	5	0	0	0	0	0	0	0	0
290	300	23	14	6	0	0	0	0	0	0	0	0
300	310	24	15	7	0	0	0	0	0	0	0	0
310	320	26	16	8	0	0	0	0	0	0	0	0
320	330	27	17	9	1	0	0	0	0	0	0	0
330	340	28	18	10	2	0	0	0	0	0	0	0
340	350	29	20	11	3	0	0	0	0	0	0	0
350	360	30	21	12	4	0	0	0	0	0	0	0
360	370	32	22	13	5	0	0	0	0	0	0	0
370	380	33	23	14	6	0	0	0	0	0	0	0
380	390	34	24	15	7	0	0	0	0	0	0	0
390	400	35	26	16	8	0	0	0	0	0	0	0
400	410	36	27	17	9	1	0	0	0	0	0	0
410	420	38	28	18	10	2	0	0	0	0	0	0
420	430	39	29	20	11	3	0	0	0	0	0	0
430	440	40	30	21	12	4	0	0	0	0	0	0
440	450	41	32	22	13	5	0	0	0	0	0	0
450	460	42	33	23	14	6	0	0	0	0	0	0
460	470	44	34	24	15	7	0	0	0	0	0	0
470	480	45	35	26	16	8	0	0	0	0	0	0
480	490	46	36	27	17	9	1	0	0	0	0	0
490	500	47	38	28	18	10	2	0	0	0	0	0
500	510	48	39	29	20	11	3	0	0	0	0	0
510	520	50	40	30	21	12	4	0	0	0	0	0
520	530	51	41	32	22	13	5	0	0	0	0	0
530	540	52	42	33	23	14	6	0	0	0	0	0
540	550	53	44	34	24	15	7	0	0	0	0	0
550	560	54	45	35	26	16	8	1	0	0	0	0
560	570	56	46	36	27	17	9	2	0	0	0	0
570	580	57	47	38	28	18	10	3	0	0	0	0
580	590	58	48	39	29	20	11	4	0	0	0	0
590	600	59	50	40	30	21	12	5	0	0	0	0
600	610	60	51	41	32	22	13	6	0	0	0	0
610	620	62	52	42	33	23	14	7	0	0	0	0
620	630	63	53	44	34	24	15	8	0	0	0	0
630	640	64	54	45	35	26	16	9	1	0	0	0

Wage Bracket Method Tables for Income Tax Withholding

SINGLE Persons—**WEEKLY** Payroll Period

(For Wages Paid through December 31, 2018)

And the wages are–		And the number of withholding allowances claimed is—										
At least	But less than	0	1	2	3	4	5	6	7	8	9	10
		The amount of income tax to be withheld is—										
$640	$650	$65	$56	$46	$36	$27	$17	$10	$2	$0	$0	$0
650	660	66	57	47	38	28	19	11	3	0	0	0
660	670	68	58	48	39	29	20	12	4	0	0	0
670	680	69	59	50	40	30	21	13	5	0	0	0
680	690	70	60	51	41	32	22	14	6	0	0	0
690	700	71	62	52	42	33	23	15	7	0	0	0
700	710	72	63	53	44	34	25	16	8	0	0	0
710	720	74	64	54	45	35	26	17	9	1	0	0
720	730	75	65	56	46	36	27	18	10	2	0	0
730	740	76	66	57	47	38	28	19	11	3	0	0
740	750	77	68	58	48	39	29	20	12	4	0	0
750	760	78	69	59	50	40	31	21	13	5	0	0
760	770	80	70	60	51	41	32	22	14	6	0	0
770	780	81	71	62	52	42	33	23	15	7	0	0
780	790	82	72	63	53	44	34	25	16	8	0	0
790	800	83	74	64	54	45	35	26	17	9	1	0
800	810	84	75	65	56	46	37	27	18	10	2	0
810	820	86	76	66	57	47	38	28	19	11	3	0
820	830	88	77	68	58	48	39	29	20	12	4	0
830	840	90	78	69	59	50	40	31	21	13	5	0
840	850	92	80	70	60	51	41	32	22	14	6	0
850	860	94	81	71	62	52	43	33	23	15	7	0
860	870	97	82	72	63	53	44	34	25	16	8	0
870	880	99	83	74	64	54	45	35	26	17	9	1
880	890	101	84	75	65	56	46	37	27	18	10	2
890	900	103	86	76	66	57	47	38	28	19	11	3
900	910	105	88	77	68	58	49	39	29	20	12	4
910	920	108	90	78	69	59	50	40	31	21	13	5
920	930	110	92	80	70	60	51	41	32	22	14	6
930	940	112	94	81	71	62	52	43	33	23	15	7
940	950	114	97	82	72	63	53	44	34	25	16	8
950	960	116	99	83	74	64	55	45	35	26	17	9
960	970	119	101	84	75	65	56	46	37	27	18	10
970	980	121	103	86	76	66	57	47	38	28	19	11
980	990	123	105	88	77	68	58	49	39	29	20	12
990	1,000	125	108	90	78	69	59	50	40	31	21	13
1,000	1,010	127	110	92	80	70	61	51	41	32	22	14
1,010	1,020	130	112	94	81	71	62	52	43	33	23	15
1,020	1,030	132	114	97	82	72	63	53	44	34	25	16
1,030	1,040	134	116	99	83	74	64	55	45	35	26	17
1,040	1,050	136	119	101	84	75	65	56	46	37	27	18
1,050	1,060	138	121	103	86	76	67	57	47	38	28	19
1,060	1,070	141	123	105	88	77	68	58	49	39	29	20
1,070	1,080	143	125	108	90	78	69	59	50	40	31	21
1,080	1,090	145	127	110	92	80	70	61	51	41	32	22
1,090	1,100	147	130	112	94	81	71	62	52	43	33	23
1,100	1,110	149	132	114	97	82	73	63	53	44	34	25
1,110	1,120	152	134	116	99	83	74	64	55	45	35	26
1,120	1,130	154	136	119	101	84	75	65	56	46	37	27
1,130	1,140	156	138	121	103	86	76	67	57	47	38	28
1,140	1,150	158	141	123	105	88	77	68	58	49	39	29
1,150	1,160	160	143	125	108	90	79	69	59	50	40	31
1,160	1,170	163	145	127	110	92	80	70	61	51	41	32
1,170	1,180	165	147	130	112	95	81	71	62	52	43	33
1,180	1,190	167	149	132	114	97	82	73	63	53	44	34
1,190	1,200	169	152	134	116	99	83	74	64	55	45	35
1,200	1,210	171	154	136	119	101	85	75	65	56	46	37
1,210	1,220	174	156	138	121	103	86	76	67	57	47	38
1,220	1,230	176	158	141	123	106	88	77	68	58	49	39
1,230	1,240	178	160	143	125	108	90	79	69	59	50	40
1,240	1,250	180	163	145	127	110	92	80	70	61	51	41
1,250	1,260	182	165	147	130	112	95	81	71	62	52	43
1,260	1,270	185	167	149	132	114	97	82	73	63	53	44
1,270	1,280	187	169	152	134	117	99	83	74	64	55	45
1,280	1,290	189	171	154	136	119	101	85	75	65	56	46

| $1,290 and over | | Use Table 1(a) for a SINGLE person on page 46. Also see the instructions on page 44. |

Wage Bracket Method Tables for Income Tax Withholding

MARRIED Persons—WEEKLY Payroll Period

(For Wages Paid through December 31, 2018)

And the wages are— At least	But less than	And the number of withholding allowances claimed is— 0	1	2	3	4	5	6	7	8	9	10
		The amount of income tax to be withheld is—										
$ 0	$225	$0	$0	$0	$0	$0	$0	$0	$0	$0	$0	$0
225	235	1	0	0	0	0	0	0	0	0	0	0
235	245	2	0	0	0	0	0	0	0	0	0	0
245	255	3	0	0	0	0	0	0	0	0	0	0
255	265	4	0	0	0	0	0	0	0	0	0	0
265	275	5	0	0	0	0	0	0	0	0	0	0
275	285	6	0	0	0	0	0	0	0	0	0	0
285	295	7	0	0	0	0	0	0	0	0	0	0
295	305	8	0	0	0	0	0	0	0	0	0	0
305	315	9	1	0	0	0	0	0	0	0	0	0
315	325	10	2	0	0	0	0	0	0	0	0	0
325	335	11	3	0	0	0	0	0	0	0	0	0
335	345	12	4	0	0	0	0	0	0	0	0	0
345	355	13	5	0	0	0	0	0	0	0	0	0
355	365	14	6	0	0	0	0	0	0	0	0	0
365	375	15	7	0	0	0	0	0	0	0	0	0
375	385	16	8	0	0	0	0	0	0	0	0	0
385	395	17	9	1	0	0	0	0	0	0	0	0
395	405	18	10	2	0	0	0	0	0	0	0	0
405	415	19	11	3	0	0	0	0	0	0	0	0
415	425	20	12	4	0	0	0	0	0	0	0	0
425	435	21	13	5	0	0	0	0	0	0	0	0
435	445	22	14	6	0	0	0	0	0	0	0	0
445	455	23	15	7	0	0	0	0	0	0	0	0
455	465	24	16	8	0	0	0	0	0	0	0	0
465	475	25	17	9	1	0	0	0	0	0	0	0
475	485	26	18	10	2	0	0	0	0	0	0	0
485	495	27	19	11	3	0	0	0	0	0	0	0
495	505	28	20	12	4	0	0	0	0	0	0	0
505	515	29	21	13	5	0	0	0	0	0	0	0
515	525	30	22	14	6	0	0	0	0	0	0	0
525	535	31	23	15	7	0	0	0	0	0	0	0
535	545	32	24	16	8	0	0	0	0	0	0	0
545	555	33	25	17	9	1	0	0	0	0	0	0
555	565	34	26	18	10	2	0	0	0	0	0	0
565	575	35	27	19	11	3	0	0	0	0	0	0
575	585	36	28	20	12	4	0	0	0	0	0	0
585	595	37	29	21	13	5	0	0	0	0	0	0
595	605	38	30	22	14	6	0	0	0	0	0	0
605	615	39	31	23	15	7	0	0	0	0	0	0
615	625	40	32	24	16	8	0	0	0	0	0	0
625	635	42	33	25	17	9	1	0	0	0	0	0
635	645	43	34	26	18	10	2	0	0	0	0	0
645	655	44	35	27	19	11	3	0	0	0	0	0
655	665	45	36	28	20	12	4	0	0	0	0	0
665	675	46	37	29	21	13	5	0	0	0	0	0
675	685	48	38	30	22	14	6	0	0	0	0	0
685	695	49	39	31	23	15	7	0	0	0	0	0
695	705	50	40	32	24	16	8	0	0	0	0	0
705	715	51	42	33	25	17	9	1	0	0	0	0
715	725	52	43	34	26	18	10	2	0	0	0	0
725	735	54	44	35	27	19	11	3	0	0	0	0
735	745	55	45	36	28	20	12	4	0	0	0	0
745	755	56	46	37	29	21	13	5	0	0	0	0
755	765	57	48	38	30	22	14	6	0	0	0	0
765	775	58	49	39	31	23	15	7	0	0	0	0
775	785	60	50	40	32	24	16	8	0	0	0	0
785	795	61	51	42	33	25	17	9	1	0	0	0
795	805	62	52	43	34	26	18	10	2	0	0	0
805	815	63	54	44	35	27	19	11	3	0	0	0
815	825	64	55	45	36	28	20	12	4	0	0	0
825	835	66	56	46	37	29	21	13	5	0	0	0
835	845	67	57	48	38	30	22	14	6	0	0	0
845	855	68	58	49	39	31	23	15	7	0	0	0
855	865	69	60	50	40	32	24	16	8	0	0	0
865	875	70	61	51	42	33	25	17	9	1	0	0
875	885	72	62	52	43	34	26	18	10	2	0	0
885	895	73	63	54	44	35	27	19	11	3	0	0
895	905	74	64	55	45	36	28	20	12	4	0	0
905	915	75	66	56	46	37	29	21	13	5	0	0

Wage Bracket Method Tables for Income Tax Withholding

MARRIED Persons—WEEKLY Payroll Period

(For Wages Paid through December 31, 2018)

And the wages are—		And the number of withholding allowances claimed is—										
At least	But less than	0	1	2	3	4	5	6	7	8	9	10
		The amount of income tax to be withheld is—										
$915	$925	$76	$67	$57	$48	$38	$30	$22	$14	$6	$0	$0
925	935	78	68	58	49	39	31	23	15	7	0	0
935	945	79	69	60	50	41	32	24	16	8	0	0
945	955	80	70	61	51	42	33	25	17	9	1	0
955	965	81	72	62	52	43	34	26	18	10	2	0
965	975	82	73	63	54	44	35	27	19	11	3	0
975	985	84	74	64	55	45	36	28	20	12	4	0
985	995	85	75	66	56	47	37	29	21	13	5	0
995	1,005	86	76	67	57	48	38	30	22	14	6	0
1,005	1,015	87	78	68	58	49	39	31	23	15	7	0
1,015	1,025	88	79	69	60	50	41	32	24	16	8	0
1,025	1,035	90	80	70	61	51	42	33	25	17	9	1
1,035	1,045	91	81	72	62	53	43	34	26	18	10	2
1,045	1,055	92	82	73	63	54	44	35	27	19	11	3
1,055	1,065	93	84	74	64	55	45	36	28	20	12	4
1,065	1,075	94	85	75	66	56	47	37	29	21	13	5
1,075	1,085	96	86	76	67	57	48	38	30	22	14	6
1,085	1,095	97	87	78	68	59	49	39	31	23	15	7
1,095	1,105	98	88	79	69	60	50	41	32	24	16	8
1,105	1,115	99	90	80	70	61	51	42	33	25	17	9
1,115	1,125	100	91	81	72	62	53	43	34	26	18	10
1,125	1,135	102	92	82	73	63	54	44	35	27	19	11
1,135	1,145	103	93	84	74	65	55	45	36	28	20	12
1,145	1,155	104	94	85	75	66	56	47	37	29	21	13
1,155	1,165	105	96	86	76	67	57	48	38	30	22	14
1,165	1,175	106	97	87	78	68	59	49	39	31	23	15
1,175	1,185	108	98	88	79	69	60	50	41	32	24	16
1,185	1,195	109	99	90	80	71	61	51	42	33	25	17
1,195	1,205	110	100	91	81	72	62	53	43	34	26	18
1,205	1,215	111	102	92	82	73	63	54	44	35	27	19
1,215	1,225	112	103	93	84	74	65	55	45	36	28	20
1,225	1,235	114	104	94	85	75	66	56	47	37	29	21
1,235	1,245	115	105	96	86	77	67	57	48	38	30	22
1,245	1,255	116	106	97	87	78	68	59	49	39	31	23
1,255	1,265	117	108	98	88	79	69	60	50	41	32	24
1,265	1,275	118	109	99	90	80	71	61	51	42	33	25
1,275	1,285	120	110	100	91	81	72	62	53	43	34	26
1,285	1,295	121	111	102	92	83	73	63	54	44	35	27
1,295	1,305	122	112	103	93	84	74	65	55	45	36	28
1,305	1,315	123	114	104	94	85	75	66	56	47	37	29
1,315	1,325	124	115	105	96	86	77	67	57	48	38	30
1,325	1,335	126	116	106	97	87	78	68	59	49	39	31
1,335	1,345	127	117	108	98	89	79	69	60	50	41	32
1,345	1,355	128	118	109	99	90	80	71	61	51	42	33
1,355	1,365	129	120	110	100	91	81	72	62	53	43	34
1,365	1,375	130	121	111	102	92	83	73	63	54	44	35
1,375	1,385	132	122	112	103	93	84	74	65	55	45	36
1,385	1,395	133	123	114	104	95	85	75	66	56	47	37
1,395	1,405	134	124	115	105	96	86	77	67	57	48	38
1,405	1,415	135	126	116	106	97	87	78	68	59	49	39
1,415	1,425	136	127	117	108	98	89	79	69	60	50	41
1,425	1,435	138	128	118	109	99	90	80	71	61	51	42
1,435	1,445	139	129	120	110	101	91	81	72	62	53	43
1,445	1,455	140	130	121	111	102	92	83	73	63	54	44
1,455	1,465	141	132	122	112	103	93	84	74	65	55	45
1,465	1,475	142	133	123	114	104	95	85	75	66	56	47
1,475	1,485	144	134	124	115	105	96	86	77	67	57	48
1,485	1,495	145	135	126	116	107	97	87	78	68	59	49
1,495	1,505	146	136	127	117	108	98	89	79	69	60	50
1,505	1,515	147	138	128	118	109	99	90	80	71	61	51
1,515	1,525	148	139	129	120	110	101	91	81	72	62	53
1,525	1,535	150	140	130	121	111	102	92	83	73	63	54
1,535	1,545	151	141	132	122	113	103	93	84	74	65	55
1,545	1,555	152	142	133	123	114	104	95	85	75	66	56
1,555	1,565	153	144	134	124	115	105	96	86	77	67	57
1,565	1,575	154	145	135	126	116	107	97	87	78	68	59

$1,575 and over		Use Table 1(b) for a MARRIED person on page 46. Also see the instructions on page 44.

Wage Bracket Method Tables for Income Tax Withholding

SINGLE Persons—**BIWEEKLY** Payroll Period

(For Wages Paid through December 31, 2018)

And the wages are–		And the number of withholding allowances claimed is—										
At least	But less than	0	1	2	3	4	5	6	7	8	9	10
		The amount of income tax to be withheld is—										
$ 0	$145	$0	$0	$0	$0	$0	$0	$0	$0	$0	$0	$0
145	150	1	0	0	0	0	0	0	0	0	0	0
150	155	1	0	0	0	0	0	0	0	0	0	0
155	160	2	0	0	0	0	0	0	0	0	0	0
160	165	2	0	0	0	0	0	0	0	0	0	0
165	170	3	0	0	0	0	0	0	0	0	0	0
170	175	3	0	0	0	0	0	0	0	0	0	0
175	180	4	0	0	0	0	0	0	0	0	0	0
180	185	4	0	0	0	0	0	0	0	0	0	0
185	190	5	0	0	0	0	0	0	0	0	0	0
190	195	5	0	0	0	0	0	0	0	0	0	0
195	200	6	0	0	0	0	0	0	0	0	0	0
200	205	6	0	0	0	0	0	0	0	0	0	0
205	210	7	0	0	0	0	0	0	0	0	0	0
210	215	7	0	0	0	0	0	0	0	0	0	0
215	220	8	0	0	0	0	0	0	0	0	0	0
220	225	8	0	0	0	0	0	0	0	0	0	0
225	230	9	0	0	0	0	0	0	0	0	0	0
230	235	9	0	0	0	0	0	0	0	0	0	0
235	240	10	0	0	0	0	0	0	0	0	0	0
240	245	10	0	0	0	0	0	0	0	0	0	0
245	250	11	0	0	0	0	0	0	0	0	0	0
250	260	11	0	0	0	0	0	0	0	0	0	0
260	270	12	0	0	0	0	0	0	0	0	0	0
270	280	13	0	0	0	0	0	0	0	0	0	0
280	290	14	0	0	0	0	0	0	0	0	0	0
290	300	15	0	0	0	0	0	0	0	0	0	0
300	310	16	0	0	0	0	0	0	0	0	0	0
310	320	17	1	0	0	0	0	0	0	0	0	0
320	330	18	2	0	0	0	0	0	0	0	0	0
330	340	19	3	0	0	0	0	0	0	0	0	0
340	350	20	4	0	0	0	0	0	0	0	0	0
350	360	21	5	0	0	0	0	0	0	0	0	0
360	370	22	6	0	0	0	0	0	0	0	0	0
370	380	23	7	0	0	0	0	0	0	0	0	0
380	390	24	8	0	0	0	0	0	0	0	0	0
390	400	25	9	0	0	0	0	0	0	0	0	0
400	410	26	10	0	0	0	0	0	0	0	0	0
410	420	27	11	0	0	0	0	0	0	0	0	0
420	430	28	12	0	0	0	0	0	0	0	0	0
430	440	29	13	0	0	0	0	0	0	0	0	0
440	450	30	14	0	0	0	0	0	0	0	0	0
450	460	31	15	0	0	0	0	0	0	0	0	0
460	470	32	16	0	0	0	0	0	0	0	0	0
470	480	33	17	1	0	0	0	0	0	0	0	0
480	490	34	18	2	0	0	0	0	0	0	0	0
490	500	35	19	3	0	0	0	0	0	0	0	0
500	520	37	21	5	0	0	0	0	0	0	0	0
520	540	39	23	7	0	0	0	0	0	0	0	0
540	560	42	25	9	0	0	0	0	0	0	0	0
560	580	44	27	11	0	0	0	0	0	0	0	0
580	600	46	29	13	0	0	0	0	0	0	0	0
600	620	49	31	15	0	0	0	0	0	0	0	0
620	640	51	33	17	1	0	0	0	0	0	0	0
640	660	54	35	19	3	0	0	0	0	0	0	0
660	680	56	37	21	5	0	0	0	0	0	0	0
680	700	58	39	23	7	0	0	0	0	0	0	0
700	720	61	42	25	9	0	0	0	0	0	0	0
720	740	63	44	27	11	0	0	0	0	0	0	0
740	760	66	46	29	13	0	0	0	0	0	0	0
760	780	68	49	31	15	0	0	0	0	0	0	0
780	800	70	51	33	17	1	0	0	0	0	0	0
800	820	73	54	35	19	3	0	0	0	0	0	0
820	840	75	56	37	21	5	0	0	0	0	0	0
840	860	78	58	39	23	7	0	0	0	0	0	0
860	880	80	61	42	25	9	0	0	0	0	0	0
880	900	82	63	44	27	11	0	0	0	0	0	0
900	920	85	66	46	29	13	0	0	0	0	0	0
920	940	87	68	49	31	15	0	0	0	0	0	0
940	960	90	70	51	33	17	1	0	0	0	0	0

Wage Bracket Method Tables for Income Tax Withholding

SINGLE Persons—BIWEEKLY Payroll Period

(For Wages Paid through December 31, 2018)

And the wages are–		And the number of withholding allowances claimed is—										
At least	But less than	0	1	2	3	4	5	6	7	8	9	10
		The amount of income tax to be withheld is—										
$960	$980	$92	$73	$54	$35	$19	$3	$0	$0	$0	$0	$0
980	1,000	94	75	56	37	21	5	0	0	0	0	0
1,000	1,020	97	78	58	39	23	7	0	0	0	0	0
1,020	1,040	99	80	61	42	25	9	0	0	0	0	0
1,040	1,060	102	82	63	44	27	11	0	0	0	0	0
1,060	1,080	104	85	66	47	29	13	0	0	0	0	0
1,080	1,100	106	87	68	49	31	15	0	0	0	0	0
1,100	1,120	109	90	70	51	33	17	1	0	0	0	0
1,120	1,140	111	92	73	54	35	19	3	0	0	0	0
1,140	1,160	114	94	75	56	37	21	5	0	0	0	0
1,160	1,180	116	97	78	59	39	23	7	0	0	0	0
1,180	1,200	118	99	80	61	42	25	9	0	0	0	0
1,200	1,220	121	102	82	63	44	27	11	0	0	0	0
1,220	1,240	123	104	85	66	47	29	13	0	0	0	0
1,240	1,260	126	106	87	68	49	31	15	0	0	0	0
1,260	1,280	128	109	90	71	51	33	17	1	0	0	0
1,280	1,300	130	111	92	73	54	35	19	3	0	0	0
1,300	1,320	133	114	94	75	56	37	21	5	0	0	0
1,320	1,340	135	116	97	78	59	39	23	7	0	0	0
1,340	1,360	138	118	99	80	61	42	25	9	0	0	0
1,360	1,380	140	121	102	83	63	44	27	11	0	0	0
1,380	1,400	142	123	104	85	66	47	29	13	0	0	0
1,400	1,420	145	126	106	87	68	49	31	15	0	0	0
1,420	1,440	147	128	109	90	71	51	33	17	1	0	0
1,440	1,460	150	130	111	92	73	54	35	19	3	0	0
1,460	1,480	152	133	114	95	75	56	37	21	5	0	0
1,480	1,500	154	135	116	97	78	59	39	23	7	0	0
1,500	1,520	157	138	118	99	80	61	42	25	9	0	0
1,520	1,540	159	140	121	102	83	63	44	27	11	0	0
1,540	1,560	162	142	123	104	85	66	47	29	13	0	0
1,560	1,580	164	145	126	107	87	68	49	31	15	0	0
1,580	1,600	166	147	128	109	90	71	51	33	17	1	0
1,600	1,620	169	150	130	111	92	73	54	35	19	3	0
1,620	1,640	171	152	133	114	95	75	56	37	21	5	0
1,640	1,660	176	154	135	116	97	78	59	40	23	7	0
1,660	1,680	180	157	138	119	99	80	61	42	25	9	0
1,680	1,700	184	159	140	121	102	83	63	44	27	11	0
1,700	1,720	189	162	142	123	104	85	66	47	29	13	0
1,720	1,740	193	164	145	126	107	87	68	49	31	15	0
1,740	1,760	198	166	147	128	109	90	71	52	33	17	1
1,760	1,780	202	169	150	131	111	92	73	54	35	19	3
1,780	1,800	206	171	152	133	114	95	75	56	37	21	5
1,800	1,820	211	176	154	135	116	97	78	59	40	23	7
1,820	1,840	215	180	157	138	119	99	80	61	42	25	9
1,840	1,860	220	184	159	140	121	102	83	64	44	27	11
1,860	1,880	224	189	162	143	123	104	85	66	47	29	13
1,880	1,900	228	193	164	145	126	107	87	68	49	31	15
1,900	1,920	233	198	166	147	128	109	90	71	52	33	17
1,920	1,940	237	202	169	150	131	111	92	73	54	35	19
1,940	1,960	242	206	171	152	133	114	95	76	56	37	21
1,960	1,980	246	211	176	155	135	116	97	78	59	40	23
1,980	2,000	250	215	180	157	138	119	99	80	61	42	25
2,000	2,020	255	220	184	159	140	121	102	83	64	44	27
2,020	2,040	259	224	189	162	143	123	104	85	66	47	29
2,040	2,060	264	228	193	164	145	126	107	88	68	49	31
2,060	2,080	268	233	198	167	147	128	109	90	71	52	33
2,080	2,100	272	237	202	169	150	131	111	92	73	54	35
2,100	2,120	277	242	206	171	152	133	114	95	76	56	37
2,120	2,140	281	246	211	176	155	135	116	97	78	59	40
2,140	2,160	286	250	215	180	157	138	119	100	80	61	42
2,160	2,180	290	255	220	185	159	140	121	102	83	64	44
2,180	2,200	294	259	224	189	162	143	123	104	85	66	47
2,200	2,220	299	264	228	193	164	145	126	107	88	68	49
2,220	2,240	303	268	233	198	167	147	128	109	90	71	52
2,240	2,260	308	272	237	202	169	150	131	112	92	73	54

$2,260 and over   Use Table 2(a) for a SINGLE person on page 46. Also see the instructions on page 44.

Wage Bracket Method Tables for Income Tax Withholding

MARRIED Persons—BIWEEKLY Payroll Period

(For Wages Paid through December 31, 2018)

And the wages are—		And the number of withholding allowances claimed is—										
At least	But less than	0	1	2	3	4	5	6	7	8	9	10
		The amount of income tax to be withheld is—										
$ 0	$445	$0	$0	$0	$0	$0	$0	$0	$0	$0	$0	$0
445	455	1	0	0	0	0	0	0	0	0	0	0
455	465	2	0	0	0	0	0	0	0	0	0	0
465	475	3	0	0	0	0	0	0	0	0	0	0
475	485	4	0	0	0	0	0	0	0	0	0	0
485	495	5	0	0	0	0	0	0	0	0	0	0
495	505	6	0	0	0	0	0	0	0	0	0	0
505	525	7	0	0	0	0	0	0	0	0	0	0
525	545	9	0	0	0	0	0	0	0	0	0	0
545	565	11	0	0	0	0	0	0	0	0	0	0
565	585	13	0	0	0	0	0	0	0	0	0	0
585	605	15	0	0	0	0	0	0	0	0	0	0
605	625	17	1	0	0	0	0	0	0	0	0	0
625	645	19	3	0	0	0	0	0	0	0	0	0
645	665	21	5	0	0	0	0	0	0	0	0	0
665	685	23	7	0	0	0	0	0	0	0	0	0
685	705	25	9	0	0	0	0	0	0	0	0	0
705	725	27	11	0	0	0	0	0	0	0	0	0
725	745	29	13	0	0	0	0	0	0	0	0	0
745	765	31	15	0	0	0	0	0	0	0	0	0
765	785	33	17	1	0	0	0	0	0	0	0	0
785	805	35	19	3	0	0	0	0	0	0	0	0
805	825	37	21	5	0	0	0	0	0	0	0	0
825	845	39	23	7	0	0	0	0	0	0	0	0
845	865	41	25	9	0	0	0	0	0	0	0	0
865	885	43	27	11	0	0	0	0	0	0	0	0
885	905	45	29	13	0	0	0	0	0	0	0	0
905	925	47	31	15	0	0	0	0	0	0	0	0
925	945	49	33	17	1	0	0	0	0	0	0	0
945	965	51	35	19	3	0	0	0	0	0	0	0
965	985	53	37	21	5	0	0	0	0	0	0	0
985	1,005	55	39	23	7	0	0	0	0	0	0	0
1,005	1,025	57	41	25	9	0	0	0	0	0	0	0
1,025	1,045	59	43	27	11	0	0	0	0	0	0	0
1,045	1,065	61	45	29	13	0	0	0	0	0	0	0
1,065	1,085	63	47	31	15	0	0	0	0	0	0	0
1,085	1,105	65	49	33	17	1	0	0	0	0	0	0
1,105	1,125	67	51	35	19	3	0	0	0	0	0	0
1,125	1,145	69	53	37	21	5	0	0	0	0	0	0
1,145	1,165	71	55	39	23	7	0	0	0	0	0	0
1,165	1,185	73	57	41	25	9	0	0	0	0	0	0
1,185	1,205	75	59	43	27	11	0	0	0	0	0	0
1,205	1,225	78	61	45	29	13	0	0	0	0	0	0
1,225	1,245	80	63	47	31	15	0	0	0	0	0	0
1,245	1,265	83	65	49	33	17	1	0	0	0	0	0
1,265	1,285	85	67	51	35	19	3	0	0	0	0	0
1,285	1,305	87	69	53	37	21	5	0	0	0	0	0
1,305	1,325	90	71	55	39	23	7	0	0	0	0	0
1,325	1,345	92	73	57	41	25	9	0	0	0	0	0
1,345	1,365	95	75	59	43	27	11	0	0	0	0	0
1,365	1,385	97	78	61	45	29	13	0	0	0	0	0
1,385	1,405	99	80	63	47	31	15	0	0	0	0	0
1,405	1,425	102	83	65	49	33	17	1	0	0	0	0
1,425	1,445	104	85	67	51	35	19	3	0	0	0	0
1,445	1,465	107	87	69	53	37	21	5	0	0	0	0
1,465	1,485	109	90	71	55	39	23	7	0	0	0	0
1,485	1,505	111	92	73	57	41	25	9	0	0	0	0
1,505	1,525	114	95	76	59	43	27	11	0	0	0	0
1,525	1,545	116	97	78	61	45	29	13	0	0	0	0
1,545	1,565	119	99	80	63	47	31	15	0	0	0	0
1,565	1,585	121	102	83	65	49	33	17	1	0	0	0
1,585	1,605	123	104	85	67	51	35	19	3	0	0	0
1,605	1,625	126	107	88	69	53	37	21	5	0	0	0
1,625	1,645	128	109	90	71	55	39	23	7	0	0	0
1,645	1,665	131	111	92	73	57	41	25	9	0	0	0
1,665	1,685	133	114	95	76	59	43	27	11	0	0	0
1,685	1,705	135	116	97	78	61	45	29	13	0	0	0
1,705	1,725	138	119	100	80	63	47	31	15	0	0	0
1,725	1,745	140	121	102	83	65	49	33	17	1	0	0
1,745	1,765	143	123	104	85	67	51	35	19	3	0	0

Wage Bracket Method Tables for Income Tax Withholding

MARRIED Persons—BIWEEKLY Payroll Period

(For Wages Paid through December 31, 2018)

And the wages are–		And the number of withholding allowances claimed is—										
At least	But less than	0	1	2	3	4	5	6	7	8	9	10
		The amount of income tax to be withheld is—										
$1,765	$1,785	$145	$126	$107	$88	$69	$53	$37	$21	$5	$0	$0
1,785	1,805	147	128	109	90	71	55	39	23	7	0	0
1,805	1,825	150	131	112	92	73	57	41	25	9	0	0
1,825	1,845	152	133	114	95	76	59	43	27	11	0	0
1,845	1,865	155	135	116	97	78	61	45	29	13	0	0
1,865	1,885	157	138	119	100	80	63	47	31	15	0	0
1,885	1,905	159	140	121	102	83	65	49	33	17	1	0
1,905	1,925	162	143	124	104	85	67	51	35	19	3	0
1,925	1,945	164	145	126	107	88	69	53	37	21	5	0
1,945	1,965	167	147	128	109	90	71	55	39	23	7	0
1,965	1,985	169	150	131	112	92	73	57	41	25	9	0
1,985	2,005	171	152	133	114	95	76	59	43	27	11	0
2,005	2,025	174	155	136	116	97	78	61	45	29	13	0
2,025	2,045	176	157	138	119	100	80	63	47	31	15	0
2,045	2,065	179	159	140	121	102	83	65	49	33	17	1
2,065	2,085	181	162	143	124	104	85	67	51	35	19	3
2,085	2,105	183	164	145	126	107	88	69	53	37	21	5
2,105	2,125	186	167	148	128	109	90	71	55	39	23	7
2,125	2,145	188	169	150	131	112	92	73	57	41	25	9
2,145	2,165	191	171	152	133	114	95	76	59	43	27	11
2,165	2,185	193	174	155	136	116	97	78	61	45	29	13
2,185	2,205	195	176	157	138	119	100	81	63	47	31	15
2,205	2,225	198	179	160	140	121	102	83	65	49	33	17
2,225	2,245	200	181	162	143	124	104	85	67	51	35	19
2,245	2,265	203	183	164	145	126	107	88	69	53	37	21
2,265	2,285	205	186	167	148	128	109	90	71	55	39	23
2,285	2,305	207	188	169	150	131	112	93	73	57	41	25
2,305	2,325	210	191	172	152	133	114	95	76	59	43	27
2,325	2,345	212	193	174	155	136	116	97	78	61	45	29
2,345	2,365	215	195	176	157	138	119	100	81	63	47	31
2,365	2,385	217	198	179	160	140	121	102	83	65	49	33
2,385	2,405	219	200	181	162	143	124	105	85	67	51	35
2,405	2,425	222	203	184	164	145	126	107	88	69	53	37
2,425	2,445	224	205	186	167	148	128	109	90	71	55	39
2,445	2,465	227	207	188	169	150	131	112	93	73	57	41
2,465	2,485	229	210	191	172	152	133	114	95	76	59	43
2,485	2,505	231	212	193	174	155	136	117	97	78	61	45
2,505	2,525	234	215	196	176	157	138	119	100	81	63	47
2,525	2,545	236	217	198	179	160	140	121	102	83	65	49
2,545	2,565	239	219	200	181	162	143	124	105	85	67	51
2,565	2,585	241	222	203	184	164	145	126	107	88	69	53
2,585	2,605	243	224	205	186	167	148	129	109	90	71	55
2,605	2,625	246	227	208	188	169	150	131	112	93	73	57
2,625	2,645	248	229	210	191	172	152	133	114	95	76	59
2,645	2,665	251	231	212	193	174	155	136	117	97	78	61
2,665	2,685	253	234	215	196	176	157	138	119	100	81	63
2,685	2,705	255	236	217	198	179	160	141	121	102	83	65
2,705	2,725	258	239	220	200	181	162	143	124	105	85	67
2,725	2,745	260	241	222	203	184	164	145	126	107	88	69
2,745	2,765	263	243	224	205	186	167	148	129	109	90	71
2,765	2,785	265	246	227	208	188	169	150	131	112	93	74
2,785	2,805	267	248	229	210	191	172	153	133	114	95	76
2,805	2,825	270	251	232	212	193	174	155	136	117	97	78
2,825	2,845	272	253	234	215	196	176	157	138	119	100	81
2,845	2,865	275	255	236	217	198	179	160	141	121	102	83
2,865	2,885	277	258	239	220	200	181	162	143	124	105	86
2,885	2,905	279	260	241	222	203	184	165	145	126	107	88
2,905	2,925	282	263	244	224	205	186	167	148	129	109	90
2,925	2,945	284	265	246	227	208	188	169	150	131	112	93
2,945	2,965	287	267	248	229	210	191	172	153	133	114	95
2,965	2,985	289	270	251	232	212	193	174	155	136	117	98
2,985	3,005	291	272	253	234	215	196	177	157	138	119	100
3,005	3,025	294	275	256	236	217	198	179	160	141	121	102
3,025	3,045	296	277	258	239	220	200	181	162	143	124	105
3,045	3,065	299	279	260	241	222	203	184	165	145	126	107
3,065	3,085	301	282	263	244	224	205	186	167	148	129	110

$3,085 and over   Use Table 2(b) for a MARRIED person on page 46. Also see the instructions on page 44.

Wage Bracket Method Tables for Income Tax Withholding

SINGLE Persons—SEMIMONTHLY Payroll Period

(For Wages Paid through December 31, 2018)

And the wages are—		And the number of withholding allowances claimed is—										
At least	But less than	0	1	2	3	4	5	6	7	8	9	10
		The amount of income tax to be withheld is—										
$ 0	$160	$0	$0	$0	$0	$0	$0	$0	$0	$0	$0	$0
160	165	1	0	0	0	0	0	0	0	0	0	0
165	170	1	0	0	0	0	0	0	0	0	0	0
170	175	2	0	0	0	0	0	0	0	0	0	0
175	180	2	0	0	0	0	0	0	0	0	0	0
180	185	3	0	0	0	0	0	0	0	0	0	0
185	190	3	0	0	0	0	0	0	0	0	0	0
190	195	4	0	0	0	0	0	0	0	0	0	0
195	200	4	0	0	0	0	0	0	0	0	0	0
200	205	5	0	0	0	0	0	0	0	0	0	0
205	210	5	0	0	0	0	0	0	0	0	0	0
210	215	6	0	0	0	0	0	0	0	0	0	0
215	220	6	0	0	0	0	0	0	0	0	0	0
220	225	7	0	0	0	0	0	0	0	0	0	0
225	230	7	0	0	0	0	0	0	0	0	0	0
230	235	8	0	0	0	0	0	0	0	0	0	0
235	240	8	0	0	0	0	0	0	0	0	0	0
240	245	9	0	0	0	0	0	0	0	0	0	0
245	250	9	0	0	0	0	0	0	0	0	0	0
250	260	10	0	0	0	0	0	0	0	0	0	0
260	270	11	0	0	0	0	0	0	0	0	0	0
270	280	12	0	0	0	0	0	0	0	0	0	0
280	290	13	0	0	0	0	0	0	0	0	0	0
290	300	14	0	0	0	0	0	0	0	0	0	0
300	310	15	0	0	0	0	0	0	0	0	0	0
310	320	16	0	0	0	0	0	0	0	0	0	0
320	330	17	0	0	0	0	0	0	0	0	0	0
330	340	18	1	0	0	0	0	0	0	0	0	0
340	350	19	2	0	0	0	0	0	0	0	0	0
350	360	20	3	0	0	0	0	0	0	0	0	0
360	370	21	4	0	0	0	0	0	0	0	0	0
370	380	22	5	0	0	0	0	0	0	0	0	0
380	390	23	6	0	0	0	0	0	0	0	0	0
390	400	24	7	0	0	0	0	0	0	0	0	0
400	410	25	8	0	0	0	0	0	0	0	0	0
410	420	26	9	0	0	0	0	0	0	0	0	0
420	430	27	10	0	0	0	0	0	0	0	0	0
430	440	28	11	0	0	0	0	0	0	0	0	0
440	450	29	12	0	0	0	0	0	0	0	0	0
450	460	30	13	0	0	0	0	0	0	0	0	0
460	470	31	14	0	0	0	0	0	0	0	0	0
470	480	32	15	0	0	0	0	0	0	0	0	0
480	490	33	16	0	0	0	0	0	0	0	0	0
490	500	34	17	0	0	0	0	0	0	0	0	0
500	520	36	18	1	0	0	0	0	0	0	0	0
520	540	38	20	3	0	0	0	0	0	0	0	0
540	560	40	22	5	0	0	0	0	0	0	0	0
560	580	42	24	7	0	0	0	0	0	0	0	0
580	600	44	26	9	0	0	0	0	0	0	0	0
600	620	47	28	11	0	0	0	0	0	0	0	0
620	640	49	30	13	0	0	0	0	0	0	0	0
640	660	52	32	15	0	0	0	0	0	0	0	0
660	680	54	34	17	0	0	0	0	0	0	0	0
680	700	56	36	19	2	0	0	0	0	0	0	0
700	720	59	38	21	4	0	0	0	0	0	0	0
720	740	61	40	23	6	0	0	0	0	0	0	0
740	760	64	43	25	8	0	0	0	0	0	0	0
760	780	66	45	27	10	0	0	0	0	0	0	0
780	800	68	48	29	12	0	0	0	0	0	0	0
800	820	71	50	31	14	0	0	0	0	0	0	0
820	840	73	52	33	16	0	0	0	0	0	0	0
840	860	76	55	35	18	0	0	0	0	0	0	0
860	880	78	57	37	20	2	0	0	0	0	0	0
880	900	80	60	39	22	4	0	0	0	0	0	0
900	920	83	62	41	24	6	0	0	0	0	0	0
920	940	85	64	44	26	8	0	0	0	0	0	0
940	960	88	67	46	28	10	0	0	0	0	0	0
960	980	90	69	48	30	12	0	0	0	0	0	0
980	1,000	92	72	51	32	14	0	0	0	0	0	0
1,000	1,020	95	74	53	34	16	0	0	0	0	0	0

Wage Bracket Method Tables for Income Tax Withholding

SINGLE Persons—SEMIMONTHLY Payroll Period

(For Wages Paid through December 31, 2018)

And the wages are–		And the number of withholding allowances claimed is—										
At least	But less than	0	1	2	3	4	5	6	7	8	9	10
		The amount of income tax to be withheld is—										
$1,020	$1,040	$97	$76	$56	$36	$18	$1	$0	$0	$0	$0	$0
1,040	1,060	100	79	58	38	20	3	0	0	0	0	0
1,060	1,080	102	81	60	40	22	5	0	0	0	0	0
1,080	1,100	104	84	63	42	24	7	0	0	0	0	0
1,100	1,120	107	86	65	45	26	9	0	0	0	0	0
1,120	1,140	109	88	68	47	28	11	0	0	0	0	0
1,140	1,160	112	91	70	49	30	13	0	0	0	0	0
1,160	1,180	114	93	72	52	32	15	0	0	0	0	0
1,180	1,200	116	96	75	54	34	17	0	0	0	0	0
1,200	1,220	119	98	77	57	36	19	2	0	0	0	0
1,220	1,240	121	100	80	59	38	21	4	0	0	0	0
1,240	1,260	124	103	82	61	41	23	6	0	0	0	0
1,260	1,280	126	105	84	64	43	25	8	0	0	0	0
1,280	1,300	128	108	87	66	45	27	10	0	0	0	0
1,300	1,320	131	110	89	69	48	29	12	0	0	0	0
1,320	1,340	133	112	92	71	50	31	14	0	0	0	0
1,340	1,360	136	115	94	73	53	33	16	0	0	0	0
1,360	1,380	138	117	96	76	55	35	18	1	0	0	0
1,380	1,400	140	120	99	78	57	37	20	3	0	0	0
1,400	1,420	143	122	101	81	60	39	22	5	0	0	0
1,420	1,440	145	124	104	83	62	41	24	7	0	0	0
1,440	1,460	148	127	106	85	65	44	26	9	0	0	0
1,460	1,480	150	129	108	88	67	46	28	11	0	0	0
1,480	1,500	152	132	111	90	69	49	30	13	0	0	0
1,500	1,520	155	134	113	93	72	51	32	15	0	0	0
1,520	1,540	157	136	116	95	74	53	34	17	0	0	0
1,540	1,560	160	139	118	97	77	56	36	19	1	0	0
1,560	1,580	162	141	120	100	79	58	38	21	3	0	0
1,580	1,600	164	144	123	102	81	61	40	23	5	0	0
1,600	1,620	167	146	125	105	84	63	42	25	7	0	0
1,620	1,640	169	148	128	107	86	65	45	27	9	0	0
1,640	1,660	172	151	130	109	89	68	47	29	11	0	0
1,660	1,680	174	153	132	112	91	70	49	31	13	0	0
1,680	1,700	176	156	135	114	93	73	52	33	15	0	0
1,700	1,720	179	158	137	117	96	75	54	35	17	0	0
1,720	1,740	181	160	140	119	98	77	57	37	19	2	0
1,740	1,760	184	163	142	121	101	80	59	39	21	4	0
1,760	1,780	186	165	144	124	103	82	61	41	23	6	0
1,780	1,800	191	168	147	126	105	85	64	43	25	8	0
1,800	1,820	195	170	149	129	108	87	66	46	27	10	0
1,820	1,840	199	172	152	131	110	89	69	48	29	12	0
1,840	1,860	204	175	154	133	113	92	71	50	31	14	0
1,860	1,880	208	177	156	136	115	94	73	53	33	16	0
1,880	1,900	213	180	159	138	117	97	76	55	35	18	1
1,900	1,920	217	182	161	141	120	99	78	58	37	20	3
1,920	1,940	221	184	164	143	122	101	81	60	39	22	5
1,940	1,960	226	188	166	145	125	104	83	62	42	24	7
1,960	1,980	230	192	168	148	127	106	85	65	44	26	9
1,980	2,000	235	197	171	150	129	109	88	67	46	28	11
2,000	2,020	239	201	173	153	132	111	90	70	49	30	13
2,020	2,040	243	205	176	155	134	113	93	72	51	32	15
2,040	2,060	248	210	178	157	137	116	95	74	54	34	17
2,060	2,080	252	214	180	160	139	118	97	77	56	36	19
2,080	2,100	257	219	183	162	141	121	100	79	58	38	21
2,100	2,120	261	223	185	165	144	123	102	82	61	40	23
2,120	2,140	265	227	189	167	146	125	105	84	63	42	25
2,140	2,160	270	232	194	169	149	128	107	86	66	45	27
2,160	2,180	274	236	198	172	151	130	109	89	68	47	29
2,180	2,200	279	241	203	174	153	133	112	91	70	50	31
2,200	2,220	283	245	207	177	156	135	114	94	73	52	33
2,220	2,240	287	249	211	179	158	137	117	96	75	54	35
2,240	2,260	292	254	216	181	161	140	119	98	78	57	37
2,260	2,280	296	258	220	184	163	142	121	101	80	59	39
2,280	2,300	301	263	225	187	165	145	124	103	82	62	41
2,300	2,320	305	267	229	191	168	147	126	106	85	64	43

$2,320 and over	Use Table 3(a) for a SINGLE person on page 46. Also see the instructions on page 44.

Wage Bracket Method Tables for Income Tax Withholding

MARRIED Persons—SEMIMONTHLY Payroll Period

(For Wages Paid through December 31, 2018)

And the wages are–		And the number of withholding allowances claimed is—										
At least	But less than	0	1	2	3	4	5	6	7	8	9	10
		The amount of income tax to be withheld is—										
$ 0	$485	$0	$0	$0	$0	$0	$0	$0	$0	$0	$0	$0
485	495	1	0	0	0	0	0	0	0	0	0	0
495	505	2	0	0	0	0	0	0	0	0	0	0
505	525	3	0	0	0	0	0	0	0	0	0	0
525	545	5	0	0	0	0	0	0	0	0	0	0
545	565	7	0	0	0	0	0	0	0	0	0	0
565	585	9	0	0	0	0	0	0	0	0	0	0
585	605	11	0	0	0	0	0	0	0	0	0	0
605	625	13	0	0	0	0	0	0	0	0	0	0
625	645	15	0	0	0	0	0	0	0	0	0	0
645	665	17	0	0	0	0	0	0	0	0	0	0
665	685	19	2	0	0	0	0	0	0	0	0	0
685	705	21	4	0	0	0	0	0	0	0	0	0
705	725	23	6	0	0	0	0	0	0	0	0	0
725	745	25	8	0	0	0	0	0	0	0	0	0
745	765	27	10	0	0	0	0	0	0	0	0	0
765	785	29	12	0	0	0	0	0	0	0	0	0
785	805	31	14	0	0	0	0	0	0	0	0	0
805	825	33	16	0	0	0	0	0	0	0	0	0
825	845	35	18	1	0	0	0	0	0	0	0	0
845	865	37	20	3	0	0	0	0	0	0	0	0
865	885	39	22	5	0	0	0	0	0	0	0	0
885	905	41	24	7	0	0	0	0	0	0	0	0
905	925	43	26	9	0	0	0	0	0	0	0	0
925	945	45	28	11	0	0	0	0	0	0	0	0
945	965	47	30	13	0	0	0	0	0	0	0	0
965	985	49	32	15	0	0	0	0	0	0	0	0
985	1,005	51	34	17	0	0	0	0	0	0	0	0
1,005	1,025	53	36	19	2	0	0	0	0	0	0	0
1,025	1,045	55	38	21	4	0	0	0	0	0	0	0
1,045	1,065	57	40	23	6	0	0	0	0	0	0	0
1,065	1,085	59	42	25	8	0	0	0	0	0	0	0
1,085	1,105	61	44	27	10	0	0	0	0	0	0	0
1,105	1,125	63	46	29	12	0	0	0	0	0	0	0
1,125	1,145	65	48	31	14	0	0	0	0	0	0	0
1,145	1,165	67	50	33	16	0	0	0	0	0	0	0
1,165	1,185	69	52	35	18	0	0	0	0	0	0	0
1,185	1,205	71	54	37	20	2	0	0	0	0	0	0
1,205	1,225	73	56	39	22	4	0	0	0	0	0	0
1,225	1,245	75	58	41	24	6	0	0	0	0	0	0
1,245	1,265	77	60	43	26	8	0	0	0	0	0	0
1,265	1,285	79	62	45	28	10	0	0	0	0	0	0
1,285	1,305	82	64	47	30	12	0	0	0	0	0	0
1,305	1,325	84	66	49	32	14	0	0	0	0	0	0
1,325	1,345	87	68	51	34	16	0	0	0	0	0	0
1,345	1,365	89	70	53	36	18	1	0	0	0	0	0
1,365	1,385	91	72	55	38	20	3	0	0	0	0	0
1,385	1,405	94	74	57	40	22	5	0	0	0	0	0
1,405	1,425	96	76	59	42	24	7	0	0	0	0	0
1,425	1,445	99	78	61	44	26	9	0	0	0	0	0
1,445	1,465	101	80	63	46	28	11	0	0	0	0	0
1,465	1,485	103	83	65	48	30	13	0	0	0	0	0
1,485	1,505	106	85	67	50	32	15	0	0	0	0	0
1,505	1,525	108	87	69	52	34	17	0	0	0	0	0
1,525	1,545	111	90	71	54	36	19	2	0	0	0	0
1,545	1,565	113	92	73	56	38	21	4	0	0	0	0
1,565	1,585	115	95	75	58	40	23	6	0	0	0	0
1,585	1,605	118	97	77	60	42	25	8	0	0	0	0
1,605	1,625	120	99	79	62	44	27	10	0	0	0	0
1,625	1,645	123	102	81	64	46	29	12	0	0	0	0
1,645	1,665	125	104	83	66	48	31	14	0	0	0	0
1,665	1,685	127	107	86	68	50	33	16	0	0	0	0
1,685	1,705	130	109	88	70	52	35	18	0	0	0	0
1,705	1,725	132	111	91	72	54	37	20	2	0	0	0
1,725	1,745	135	114	93	74	56	39	22	4	0	0	0
1,745	1,765	137	116	95	76	58	41	24	6	0	0	0
1,765	1,785	139	119	98	78	60	43	26	8	0	0	0
1,785	1,805	142	121	100	80	62	45	28	10	0	0	0
1,805	1,825	144	123	103	82	64	47	30	12	0	0	0
1,825	1,845	147	126	105	84	66	49	32	14	0	0	0

Wage Bracket Method Tables for Income Tax Withholding

MARRIED Persons—SEMIMONTHLY Payroll Period

(For Wages Paid through December 31, 2018)

And the wages are–		And the number of withholding allowances claimed is—										
At least	But less than	0	1	2	3	4	5	6	7	8	9	10
		The amount of income tax to be withheld is—										
$1,845	$1,865	$149	$128	$107	$87	$68	$51	$34	$16	$0	$0	$0
1,865	1,885	151	131	110	89	70	53	36	18	1	0	0
1,885	1,905	154	133	112	92	72	55	38	20	3	0	0
1,905	1,925	156	135	115	94	74	57	40	22	5	0	0
1,925	1,945	159	138	117	96	76	59	42	24	7	0	0
1,945	1,965	161	140	119	99	78	61	44	26	9	0	0
1,965	1,985	163	143	122	101	80	63	46	28	11	0	0
1,985	2,005	166	145	124	104	83	65	48	30	13	0	0
2,005	2,025	168	147	127	106	85	67	50	32	15	0	0
2,025	2,045	171	150	129	108	88	69	52	34	17	0	0
2,045	2,065	173	152	131	111	90	71	54	36	19	2	0
2,065	2,085	175	155	134	113	92	73	56	38	21	4	0
2,085	2,105	178	157	136	116	95	75	58	40	23	6	0
2,105	2,125	180	159	139	118	97	77	60	42	25	8	0
2,125	2,145	183	162	141	120	100	79	62	44	27	10	0
2,145	2,165	185	164	143	123	102	81	64	46	29	12	0
2,165	2,185	187	167	146	125	104	84	66	48	31	14	0
2,185	2,205	190	169	148	128	107	86	68	50	33	16	0
2,205	2,225	192	171	151	130	109	88	70	52	35	18	0
2,225	2,245	195	174	153	132	112	91	72	54	37	20	2
2,245	2,265	197	176	155	135	114	93	74	56	39	22	4
2,265	2,285	199	179	158	137	116	96	76	58	41	24	6
2,285	2,305	202	181	160	140	119	98	78	60	43	26	8
2,305	2,325	204	183	163	142	121	100	80	62	45	28	10
2,325	2,345	207	186	165	144	124	103	82	64	47	30	12
2,345	2,365	209	188	167	147	126	105	84	66	49	32	14
2,365	2,385	211	191	170	149	128	108	87	68	51	34	16
2,385	2,405	214	193	172	152	131	110	89	70	53	36	18
2,405	2,425	216	195	175	154	133	112	92	72	55	38	20
2,425	2,445	219	198	177	156	136	115	94	74	57	40	22
2,445	2,465	221	200	179	159	138	117	96	76	59	42	24
2,465	2,485	223	203	182	161	140	120	99	78	61	44	26
2,485	2,505	226	205	184	164	143	122	101	81	63	46	28
2,505	2,525	228	207	187	166	145	124	104	83	65	48	30
2,525	2,545	231	210	189	168	148	127	106	85	67	50	32
2,545	2,565	233	212	191	171	150	129	108	88	69	52	34
2,565	2,585	235	215	194	173	152	132	111	90	71	54	36
2,585	2,605	238	217	196	176	155	134	113	93	73	56	38
2,605	2,625	240	219	199	178	157	136	116	95	75	58	40
2,625	2,645	243	222	201	180	160	139	118	97	77	60	42
2,645	2,665	245	224	203	183	162	141	120	100	79	62	44
2,665	2,685	247	227	206	185	164	144	123	102	81	64	46
2,685	2,705	250	229	208	188	167	146	125	105	84	66	48
2,705	2,725	252	231	211	190	169	148	128	107	86	68	50
2,725	2,745	255	234	213	192	172	151	130	109	89	70	52
2,745	2,765	257	236	215	195	174	153	132	112	91	72	54
2,765	2,785	259	239	218	197	176	156	135	114	93	74	56
2,785	2,805	262	241	220	200	179	158	137	117	96	76	58
2,805	2,825	264	243	223	202	181	160	140	119	98	78	60
2,825	2,845	267	246	225	204	184	163	142	121	101	80	62
2,845	2,865	269	248	227	207	186	165	144	124	103	82	64
2,865	2,885	271	251	230	209	188	168	147	126	105	85	66
2,885	2,905	274	253	232	212	191	170	149	129	108	87	68
2,905	2,925	276	255	235	214	193	172	152	131	110	89	70
2,925	2,945	279	258	237	216	196	175	154	133	113	92	72
2,945	2,965	281	260	239	219	198	177	156	136	115	94	74
2,965	2,985	283	263	242	221	200	180	159	138	117	97	76
2,985	3,005	286	265	244	224	203	182	161	141	120	99	78
3,005	3,025	288	267	247	226	205	184	164	143	122	101	81
3,025	3,045	291	270	249	228	208	187	166	145	125	104	83
3,045	3,065	293	272	251	231	210	189	168	148	127	106	85
3,065	3,085	295	275	254	233	212	192	171	150	129	109	88
3,085	3,105	298	277	256	236	215	194	173	153	132	111	90
3,105	3,125	300	279	259	238	217	196	176	155	134	113	93
3,125	3,145	303	282	261	240	220	199	178	157	137	116	95
3,145	3,165	305	284	263	243	222	201	180	160	139	118	97

| $3,165 and over | Use Table 3(b) for a MARRIED person on page 46. Also see the instructions on page 44. |

Wage Bracket Method Tables for Income Tax Withholding

SINGLE Persons—MONTHLY Payroll Period

(For Wages Paid through December 31, 2018)

And the wages are—		And the number of withholding allowances claimed is—										
At least	But less than	0	1	2	3	4	5	6	7	8	9	10
		The amount of income tax to be withheld is—										
$ 0	$305	$0	$0	$0	$0	$0	$0	$0	$0	$0	$0	$0
305	325	1	0	0	0	0	0	0	0	0	0	0
325	345	3	0	0	0	0	0	0	0	0	0	0
345	365	5	0	0	0	0	0	0	0	0	0	0
365	385	7	0	0	0	0	0	0	0	0	0	0
385	405	9	0	0	0	0	0	0	0	0	0	0
405	425	11	0	0	0	0	0	0	0	0	0	0
425	445	13	0	0	0	0	0	0	0	0	0	0
445	465	15	0	0	0	0	0	0	0	0	0	0
465	485	17	0	0	0	0	0	0	0	0	0	0
485	505	19	0	0	0	0	0	0	0	0	0	0
505	525	21	0	0	0	0	0	0	0	0	0	0
525	545	23	0	0	0	0	0	0	0	0	0	0
545	565	25	0	0	0	0	0	0	0	0	0	0
565	585	27	0	0	0	0	0	0	0	0	0	0
585	605	29	0	0	0	0	0	0	0	0	0	0
605	645	32	0	0	0	0	0	0	0	0	0	0
645	685	36	1	0	0	0	0	0	0	0	0	0
685	725	40	5	0	0	0	0	0	0	0	0	0
725	765	44	9	0	0	0	0	0	0	0	0	0
765	805	48	13	0	0	0	0	0	0	0	0	0
805	845	52	17	0	0	0	0	0	0	0	0	0
845	885	56	21	0	0	0	0	0	0	0	0	0
885	925	60	25	0	0	0	0	0	0	0	0	0
925	965	64	29	0	0	0	0	0	0	0	0	0
965	1,005	68	33	0	0	0	0	0	0	0	0	0
1,005	1,045	72	37	3	0	0	0	0	0	0	0	0
1,045	1,085	76	41	7	0	0	0	0	0	0	0	0
1,085	1,125	80	45	11	0	0	0	0	0	0	0	0
1,125	1,165	85	49	15	0	0	0	0	0	0	0	0
1,165	1,205	89	53	19	0	0	0	0	0	0	0	0
1,205	1,245	94	57	23	0	0	0	0	0	0	0	0
1,245	1,285	99	61	27	0	0	0	0	0	0	0	0
1,285	1,325	104	65	31	0	0	0	0	0	0	0	0
1,325	1,365	109	69	35	0	0	0	0	0	0	0	0
1,365	1,405	113	73	39	4	0	0	0	0	0	0	0
1,405	1,445	118	77	43	8	0	0	0	0	0	0	0
1,445	1,485	123	81	47	12	0	0	0	0	0	0	0
1,485	1,525	128	86	51	16	0	0	0	0	0	0	0
1,525	1,565	133	91	55	20	0	0	0	0	0	0	0
1,565	1,605	137	96	59	24	0	0	0	0	0	0	0
1,605	1,645	142	101	63	28	0	0	0	0	0	0	0
1,645	1,685	147	105	67	32	0	0	0	0	0	0	0
1,685	1,725	152	110	71	36	1	0	0	0	0	0	0
1,725	1,765	157	115	75	40	5	0	0	0	0	0	0
1,765	1,805	161	120	79	44	9	0	0	0	0	0	0
1,805	1,845	166	125	83	48	13	0	0	0	0	0	0
1,845	1,885	171	129	88	52	17	0	0	0	0	0	0
1,885	1,925	176	134	93	56	21	0	0	0	0	0	0
1,925	1,965	181	139	98	60	25	0	0	0	0	0	0
1,965	2,005	185	144	102	64	29	0	0	0	0	0	0
2,005	2,045	190	149	107	68	33	0	0	0	0	0	0
2,045	2,085	195	153	112	72	37	3	0	0	0	0	0
2,085	2,125	200	158	117	76	41	7	0	0	0	0	0
2,125	2,165	205	163	122	80	45	11	0	0	0	0	0
2,165	2,205	209	168	126	85	49	15	0	0	0	0	0
2,205	2,245	214	173	131	90	53	19	0	0	0	0	0
2,245	2,285	219	177	136	94	57	23	0	0	0	0	0
2,285	2,325	224	182	141	99	61	27	0	0	0	0	0
2,325	2,365	229	187	146	104	65	31	0	0	0	0	0
2,365	2,405	233	192	150	109	69	35	0	0	0	0	0
2,405	2,445	238	197	155	114	73	39	4	0	0	0	0
2,445	2,485	243	201	160	118	77	43	8	0	0	0	0
2,485	2,525	248	206	165	123	82	47	12	0	0	0	0
2,525	2,565	253	211	170	128	87	51	16	0	0	0	0
2,565	2,605	257	216	174	133	91	55	20	0	0	0	0
2,605	2,645	262	221	179	138	96	59	24	0	0	0	0
2,645	2,685	267	225	184	142	101	63	28	0	0	0	0
2,685	2,725	272	230	189	147	106	67	32	0	0	0	0
2,725	2,765	277	235	194	152	111	71	36	2	0	0	0

Wage Bracket Method Tables for Income Tax Withholding

SINGLE Persons—MONTHLY Payroll Period

(For Wages Paid through December 31, 2018)

And the wages are—		And the number of withholding allowances claimed is—										
At least	But less than	0	1	2	3	4	5	6	7	8	9	10
		The amount of income tax to be withheld is—										
$2,765	$2,805	$281	$240	$198	$157	$115	$75	$40	$6	$0	$0	$0
2,805	2,845	286	245	203	162	120	79	44	10	0	0	0
2,845	2,885	291	249	208	166	125	83	48	14	0	0	0
2,885	2,925	296	254	213	171	130	88	52	18	0	0	0
2,925	2,965	301	259	218	176	135	93	56	22	0	0	0
2,965	3,005	305	264	222	181	139	98	60	26	0	0	0
3,005	3,045	310	269	227	186	144	103	64	30	0	0	0
3,045	3,085	315	273	232	190	149	107	68	34	0	0	0
3,085	3,125	320	278	237	195	154	112	72	38	3	0	0
3,125	3,165	325	283	242	200	159	117	76	42	7	0	0
3,165	3,205	329	288	246	205	163	122	80	46	11	0	0
3,205	3,245	334	293	251	210	168	127	85	50	15	0	0
3,245	3,285	339	297	256	214	173	131	90	54	19	0	0
3,285	3,325	344	302	261	219	178	136	95	58	23	0	0
3,325	3,365	349	307	266	224	183	141	100	62	27	0	0
3,365	3,405	353	312	270	229	187	146	104	66	31	0	0
3,405	3,445	358	317	275	234	192	151	109	70	35	0	0
3,445	3,485	363	321	280	238	197	155	114	74	39	4	0
3,485	3,525	368	326	285	243	202	160	119	78	43	8	0
3,525	3,565	374	331	290	248	207	165	124	82	47	12	0
3,565	3,605	382	336	294	253	211	170	128	87	51	16	0
3,605	3,645	391	341	299	258	216	175	133	92	55	20	0
3,645	3,685	400	345	304	262	221	179	138	96	59	24	0
3,685	3,725	409	350	309	267	226	184	143	101	63	28	0
3,725	3,765	418	355	314	272	231	189	148	106	67	32	0
3,765	3,805	426	360	318	277	235	194	152	111	71	36	2
3,805	3,845	435	365	323	282	240	199	157	116	75	40	6
3,845	3,885	444	369	328	286	245	203	162	120	79	44	10
3,885	3,925	453	377	333	291	250	208	167	125	84	48	14
3,925	3,965	462	386	338	296	255	213	172	130	89	52	18
3,965	4,005	470	394	342	301	259	218	176	135	93	56	22
4,005	4,045	479	403	347	306	264	223	181	140	98	60	26
4,045	4,085	488	412	352	310	269	227	186	144	103	64	30
4,085	4,125	497	421	357	315	274	232	191	149	108	68	34
4,125	4,165	506	430	362	320	279	237	196	154	113	72	38
4,165	4,205	514	438	366	325	283	242	200	159	117	76	42
4,205	4,245	523	447	371	330	288	247	205	164	122	81	46
4,245	4,285	532	456	380	334	293	251	210	168	127	85	50
4,285	4,325	541	465	389	339	298	256	215	173	132	90	54
4,325	4,365	550	474	398	344	303	261	220	178	137	95	58
4,365	4,405	558	482	406	349	307	266	224	183	141	100	62
4,405	4,445	567	491	415	354	312	271	229	188	146	105	66
4,445	4,485	576	500	424	358	317	275	234	192	151	109	70
4,485	4,525	585	509	433	363	322	280	239	197	156	114	74
4,525	4,565	594	518	442	368	327	285	244	202	161	119	78
4,565	4,605	602	526	450	374	331	290	248	207	165	124	82
4,605	4,645	611	535	459	383	336	295	253	212	170	129	87
4,645	4,685	620	544	468	392	341	299	258	216	175	133	92
4,685	4,725	629	553	477	401	346	304	263	221	180	138	97
4,725	4,765	638	562	486	409	351	309	268	226	185	143	102
4,765	4,805	646	570	494	418	355	314	272	231	189	148	106
4,805	4,845	655	579	503	427	360	319	277	236	194	153	111
4,845	4,885	664	588	512	436	365	323	282	240	199	157	116
4,885	4,925	673	597	521	445	370	328	287	245	204	162	121
4,925	4,965	682	606	530	453	377	333	292	250	209	167	126
4,965	5,005	690	614	538	462	386	338	296	255	213	172	130
5,005	5,045	699	623	547	471	395	343	301	260	218	177	135
5,045	5,085	708	632	556	480	404	347	306	264	223	181	140
5,085	5,125	717	641	565	489	413	352	311	269	228	186	145
5,125	5,165	726	650	574	497	421	357	316	274	233	191	150
5,165	5,205	734	658	582	506	430	362	320	279	237	196	154
5,205	5,245	743	667	591	515	439	367	325	284	242	201	159
5,245	5,285	752	676	600	524	448	372	330	288	247	205	164
5,285	5,325	761	685	609	533	457	380	335	293	252	210	169
5,325	5,365	770	694	618	541	465	389	340	298	257	215	174
5,365	5,405	778	702	626	550	474	398	344	303	261	220	178

| $5,405 and over | | Use Table 4(a) for a SINGLE person on page 46. Also see the instructions on page 44. |

Wage Bracket Method Tables for Income Tax Withholding

MARRIED Persons—**MONTHLY** Payroll Period

(For Wages Paid through December 31, 2018)

At least	But less than	0	1	2	3	4	5	6	7	8	9	10
						The amount of income tax to be withheld is—						
$ 0	$950	$0	$0	$0	$0	$0	$0	$0	$0	$0	$0	$0
950	990	1	0	0	0	0	0	0	0	0	0	0
990	1,030	5	0	0	0	0	0	0	0	0	0	0
1,030	1,070	9	0	0	0	0	0	0	0	0	0	0
1,070	1,110	13	0	0	0	0	0	0	0	0	0	0
1,110	1,150	17	0	0	0	0	0	0	0	0	0	0
1,150	1,190	21	0	0	0	0	0	0	0	0	0	0
1,190	1,230	25	0	0	0	0	0	0	0	0	0	0
1,230	1,270	29	0	0	0	0	0	0	0	0	0	0
1,270	1,310	33	0	0	0	0	0	0	0	0	0	0
1,310	1,350	37	2	0	0	0	0	0	0	0	0	0
1,350	1,390	41	6	0	0	0	0	0	0	0	0	0
1,390	1,430	45	10	0	0	0	0	0	0	0	0	0
1,430	1,470	49	14	0	0	0	0	0	0	0	0	0
1,470	1,510	53	18	0	0	0	0	0	0	0	0	0
1,510	1,550	57	22	0	0	0	0	0	0	0	0	0
1,550	1,590	61	26	0	0	0	0	0	0	0	0	0
1,590	1,630	65	30	0	0	0	0	0	0	0	0	0
1,630	1,670	69	34	0	0	0	0	0	0	0	0	0
1,670	1,710	73	38	4	0	0	0	0	0	0	0	0
1,710	1,750	77	42	8	0	0	0	0	0	0	0	0
1,750	1,790	81	46	12	0	0	0	0	0	0	0	0
1,790	1,830	85	50	16	0	0	0	0	0	0	0	0
1,830	1,870	89	54	20	0	0	0	0	0	0	0	0
1,870	1,910	93	58	24	0	0	0	0	0	0	0	0
1,910	1,950	97	62	28	0	0	0	0	0	0	0	0
1,950	1,990	101	66	32	0	0	0	0	0	0	0	0
1,990	2,030	105	70	36	1	0	0	0	0	0	0	0
2,030	2,070	109	74	40	5	0	0	0	0	0	0	0
2,070	2,110	113	78	44	9	0	0	0	0	0	0	0
2,110	2,150	117	82	48	13	0	0	0	0	0	0	0
2,150	2,190	121	86	52	17	0	0	0	0	0	0	0
2,190	2,230	125	90	56	21	0	0	0	0	0	0	0
2,230	2,270	129	94	60	25	0	0	0	0	0	0	0
2,270	2,310	133	98	64	29	0	0	0	0	0	0	0
2,310	2,350	137	102	68	33	0	0	0	0	0	0	0
2,350	2,390	141	106	72	37	2	0	0	0	0	0	0
2,390	2,430	145	110	76	41	6	0	0	0	0	0	0
2,430	2,470	149	114	80	45	10	0	0	0	0	0	0
2,470	2,510	153	118	84	49	14	0	0	0	0	0	0
2,510	2,550	157	122	88	53	18	0	0	0	0	0	0
2,550	2,590	161	126	92	57	22	0	0	0	0	0	0
2,590	2,630	166	130	96	61	26	0	0	0	0	0	0
2,630	2,670	171	134	100	65	30	0	0	0	0	0	0
2,670	2,710	176	138	104	69	34	0	0	0	0	0	0
2,710	2,750	180	142	108	73	38	4	0	0	0	0	0
2,750	2,790	185	146	112	77	42	8	0	0	0	0	0
2,790	2,830	190	150	116	81	46	12	0	0	0	0	0
2,830	2,870	195	154	120	85	50	16	0	0	0	0	0
2,870	2,910	200	158	124	89	54	20	0	0	0	0	0
2,910	2,950	204	163	128	93	58	24	0	0	0	0	0
2,950	2,990	209	168	132	97	62	28	0	0	0	0	0
2,990	3,030	214	172	136	101	66	32	0	0	0	0	0
3,030	3,070	219	177	140	105	70	36	1	0	0	0	0
3,070	3,110	224	182	144	109	74	40	5	0	0	0	0
3,110	3,150	228	187	148	113	78	44	9	0	0	0	0
3,150	3,190	233	192	152	117	82	48	13	0	0	0	0
3,190	3,230	238	196	156	121	86	52	17	0	0	0	0
3,230	3,270	243	201	160	125	90	56	21	0	0	0	0
3,270	3,310	248	206	165	129	94	60	25	0	0	0	0
3,310	3,350	252	211	169	133	98	64	29	0	0	0	0
3,350	3,390	257	216	174	137	102	68	33	0	0	0	0
3,390	3,430	262	220	179	141	106	72	37	3	0	0	0
3,430	3,470	267	225	184	145	110	76	41	7	0	0	0
3,470	3,510	272	230	189	149	114	80	45	11	0	0	0
3,510	3,550	276	235	193	153	118	84	49	15	0	0	0
3,550	3,590	281	240	198	157	122	88	53	19	0	0	0
3,590	3,630	286	244	203	161	126	92	57	23	0	0	0
3,630	3,670	291	249	208	166	130	96	61	27	0	0	0
3,670	3,710	296	254	213	171	134	100	65	31	0	0	0

Wage Bracket Method Tables for Income Tax Withholding

MARRIED Persons—MONTHLY Payroll Period

(For Wages Paid through December 31, 2018)

And the wages are–		And the number of withholding allowances claimed is—										
At least	But less than	0	1	2	3	4	5	6	7	8	9	10
		The amount of income tax to be withheld is—										
$3,710	$3,750	$300	$259	$217	$176	$138	$104	$69	$35	$0	$0	$0
3,750	3,790	305	264	222	181	142	108	73	39	4	0	0
3,790	3,830	310	268	227	185	146	112	77	43	8	0	0
3,830	3,870	315	273	232	190	150	116	81	47	12	0	0
3,870	3,910	320	278	237	195	154	120	85	51	16	0	0
3,910	3,950	324	283	241	200	158	124	89	55	20	0	0
3,950	3,990	329	288	246	205	163	128	93	59	24	0	0
3,990	4,030	334	292	251	209	168	132	97	63	28	0	0
4,030	4,070	339	297	256	214	173	136	101	67	32	0	0
4,070	4,110	344	302	261	219	178	140	105	71	36	2	0
4,110	4,150	348	307	265	224	182	144	109	75	40	6	0
4,150	4,190	353	312	270	229	187	148	113	79	44	10	0
4,190	4,230	358	316	275	233	192	152	117	83	48	14	0
4,230	4,270	363	321	280	238	197	156	121	87	52	18	0
4,270	4,310	368	326	285	243	202	160	125	91	56	22	0
4,310	4,350	372	331	289	248	206	165	129	95	60	26	0
4,350	4,390	377	336	294	253	211	170	133	99	64	30	0
4,390	4,430	382	340	299	257	216	174	137	103	68	34	0
4,430	4,470	387	345	304	262	221	179	141	107	72	38	3
4,470	4,510	392	350	309	267	226	184	145	111	76	42	7
4,510	4,550	396	355	313	272	230	189	149	115	80	46	11
4,550	4,590	401	360	318	277	235	194	153	119	84	50	15
4,590	4,630	406	364	323	281	240	198	157	123	88	54	19
4,630	4,670	411	369	328	286	245	203	162	127	92	58	23
4,670	4,710	416	374	333	291	250	208	167	131	96	62	27
4,710	4,750	420	379	337	296	254	213	171	135	100	66	31
4,750	4,790	425	384	342	301	259	218	176	139	104	70	35
4,790	4,830	430	388	347	305	264	222	181	143	108	74	39
4,830	4,870	435	393	352	310	269	227	186	147	112	78	43
4,870	4,910	440	398	357	315	274	232	191	151	116	82	47
4,910	4,950	444	403	361	320	278	237	195	155	120	86	51
4,950	4,990	449	408	366	325	283	242	200	159	124	90	55
4,990	5,030	454	412	371	329	288	246	205	163	128	94	59
5,030	5,070	459	417	376	334	293	251	210	168	132	98	63
5,070	5,110	464	422	381	339	298	256	215	173	136	102	67
5,110	5,150	468	427	385	344	302	261	219	178	140	106	71
5,150	5,190	473	432	390	349	307	266	224	183	144	110	75
5,190	5,230	478	436	395	353	312	270	229	187	148	114	79
5,230	5,270	483	441	400	358	317	275	234	192	152	118	83
5,270	5,310	488	446	405	363	322	280	239	197	156	122	87
5,310	5,350	492	451	409	368	326	285	243	202	160	126	91
5,350	5,390	497	456	414	373	331	290	248	207	165	130	95
5,390	5,430	502	460	419	377	336	294	253	211	170	134	99
5,430	5,470	507	465	424	382	341	299	258	216	175	138	103
5,470	5,510	512	470	429	387	346	304	263	221	180	142	107
5,510	5,550	516	475	433	392	350	309	267	226	184	146	111
5,550	5,590	521	480	438	397	355	314	272	231	189	150	115
5,590	5,630	526	484	443	401	360	318	277	235	194	154	119
5,630	5,670	531	489	448	406	365	323	282	240	199	158	123
5,670	5,710	536	494	453	411	370	328	287	245	204	162	127
5,710	5,750	540	499	457	416	374	333	291	250	208	167	131
5,750	5,790	545	504	462	421	379	338	296	255	213	172	135
5,790	5,830	550	508	467	425	384	342	301	259	218	176	139
5,830	5,870	555	513	472	430	389	347	306	264	223	181	143
5,870	5,910	560	518	477	435	394	352	311	269	228	186	147
5,910	5,950	564	523	481	440	398	357	315	274	232	191	151
5,950	5,990	569	528	486	445	403	362	320	279	237	196	155
5,990	6,030	574	532	491	449	408	366	325	283	242	200	159
6,030	6,070	579	537	496	454	413	371	330	288	247	205	164
6,070	6,110	584	542	501	459	418	376	335	293	252	210	169
6,110	6,150	588	547	505	464	422	381	339	298	256	215	173
6,150	6,190	593	552	510	469	427	386	344	303	261	220	178
6,190	6,230	598	556	515	473	432	390	349	307	266	224	183
6,230	6,270	603	561	520	478	437	395	354	312	271	229	188
6,270	6,310	608	566	525	483	442	400	359	317	276	234	193
6,310	6,350	612	571	529	488	446	405	363	322	280	239	197

$6,350 and over	Use Table 4(b) for a MARRIED person on page 46. Also see the instructions on page 44.

Wage Bracket Method Tables for Income Tax Withholding

SINGLE Persons—**DAILY** Payroll Period

(For Wages Paid through December 31, 2018)

And the wages are–		And the number of withholding allowances claimed is—										
At least	But less than	0	1	2	3	4	5	6	7	8	9	10
		The amount of income tax to be withheld is—										
$ 0	$18	$0	$0	$0	$0	$0	$0	$0	$0	$0	$0	$0
18	21	1	0	0	0	0	0	0	0	0	0	0
21	24	1	0	0	0	0	0	0	0	0	0	0
24	27	1	0	0	0	0	0	0	0	0	0	0
27	30	1	0	0	0	0	0	0	0	0	0	0
30	33	2	0	0	0	0	0	0	0	0	0	0
33	36	2	0	0	0	0	0	0	0	0	0	0
36	39	2	1	0	0	0	0	0	0	0	0	0
39	42	3	1	0	0	0	0	0	0	0	0	0
42	45	3	1	0	0	0	0	0	0	0	0	0
45	48	3	2	0	0	0	0	0	0	0	0	0
48	51	4	2	0	0	0	0	0	0	0	0	0
51	54	4	2	1	0	0	0	0	0	0	0	0
54	57	4	3	1	0	0	0	0	0	0	0	0
57	60	5	3	1	0	0	0	0	0	0	0	0
60	63	5	3	2	0	0	0	0	0	0	0	0
63	66	5	3	2	0	0	0	0	0	0	0	0
66	69	6	4	2	1	0	0	0	0	0	0	0
69	72	6	4	2	1	0	0	0	0	0	0	0
72	75	6	4	3	1	0	0	0	0	0	0	0
75	78	7	5	3	1	0	0	0	0	0	0	0
78	81	7	5	3	2	0	0	0	0	0	0	0
81	84	7	6	4	2	0	0	0	0	0	0	0
84	87	8	6	4	2	1	0	0	0	0	0	0
87	90	8	6	4	3	1	0	0	0	0	0	0
90	93	9	7	5	3	1	0	0	0	0	0	0
93	96	9	7	5	3	2	0	0	0	0	0	0
96	99	9	7	5	4	2	0	0	0	0	0	0
99	102	10	8	6	4	2	1	0	0	0	0	0
102	105	10	8	6	4	3	1	0	0	0	0	0
105	108	10	8	7	5	3	1	0	0	0	0	0
108	111	11	9	7	5	3	2	0	0	0	0	0
111	114	11	9	7	5	3	2	0	0	0	0	0
114	117	11	10	8	6	4	2	1	0	0	0	0
117	120	12	10	8	6	4	2	1	0	0	0	0
120	123	12	10	8	6	4	3	1	0	0	0	0
123	126	12	11	9	7	5	3	1	0	0	0	0
126	129	13	11	9	7	5	3	2	0	0	0	0
129	132	13	11	9	7	6	4	2	0	0	0	0
132	135	14	12	10	8	6	4	2	1	0	0	0
135	138	14	12	10	8	6	4	3	1	0	0	0
138	141	14	12	10	9	7	5	3	1	0	0	0
141	144	15	13	11	9	7	5	3	2	0	0	0
144	147	15	13	11	9	7	5	4	2	0	0	0
147	150	15	13	12	10	8	6	4	2	1	0	0
150	153	16	14	12	10	8	6	4	3	1	0	0
153	156	16	14	12	10	8	7	5	3	1	0	0
156	159	16	15	13	11	9	7	5	3	2	0	0
159	162	17	15	13	11	9	7	5	3	2	0	0
162	165	17	15	13	11	10	8	6	4	2	1	0
165	168	18	16	14	12	10	8	6	4	2	1	0
168	171	19	16	14	12	10	8	6	4	3	1	0
171	174	19	16	14	13	11	9	7	5	3	1	0
174	177	20	17	15	13	11	9	7	5	3	2	0
177	180	21	17	15	13	11	9	7	6	4	2	0
180	183	21	18	16	14	12	10	8	6	4	2	1
183	186	22	18	16	14	12	10	8	6	4	3	1
186	189	23	19	16	14	12	10	9	7	5	3	1
189	192	23	20	17	15	13	11	9	7	5	3	2
192	195	24	20	17	15	13	11	9	7	5	4	2
195	198	24	21	17	15	13	12	10	8	6	4	2
198	201	25	22	18	16	14	12	10	8	6	4	3
201	204	26	22	19	16	14	12	10	8	7	5	3
204	207	26	23	19	16	15	13	11	9	7	5	3
207	210	27	24	20	17	15	13	11	9	7	5	3
210	213	28	24	21	17	15	13	11	10	8	6	4
213	216	28	25	21	18	16	14	12	10	8	6	4
216	219	29	26	22	19	16	14	12	10	8	6	5
219	222	30	26	23	19	16	14	13	11	9	7	5
222	225	30	27	23	20	17	15	13	11	9	7	5

Wage Bracket Method Tables for Income Tax Withholding

SINGLE Persons—**DAILY** Payroll Period

(For Wages Paid through December 31, 2018)

And the wages are—		And the number of withholding allowances claimed is—										
At least	But less than	0	1	2	3	4	5	6	7	8	9	10
		The amount of income tax to be withheld is—										
$225	$228	$31	$28	$24	$21	$17	$15	$13	$11	$9	$8	$6
228	231	32	28	25	21	18	16	14	12	10	8	6
231	234	32	29	25	22	18	16	14	12	10	8	6
234	237	33	30	26	23	19	16	14	12	10	9	7
237	240	34	30	27	23	20	17	15	13	11	9	7
240	243	34	31	27	24	20	17	15	13	11	9	7
243	246	35	32	28	25	21	17	15	13	12	10	8
246	249	36	32	29	25	22	18	16	14	12	10	8
249	252	36	33	29	26	22	19	16	14	12	10	8
252	255	37	34	30	26	23	19	16	15	13	11	9
255	258	38	34	31	27	24	20	17	15	13	11	9
258	261	38	35	31	28	24	21	17	15	13	11	10
261	264	39	35	32	28	25	21	18	16	14	12	10
264	267	40	36	33	29	26	22	19	16	14	12	10
267	270	40	37	33	30	26	23	19	16	14	13	11
270	273	41	37	34	30	27	23	20	17	15	13	11
273	276	42	38	35	31	28	24	21	17	15	13	11
276	279	42	39	35	32	28	25	21	18	16	14	12
279	282	43	39	36	32	29	25	22	18	16	14	12
282	285	44	40	37	33	30	26	23	19	16	14	12
285	288	44	41	37	34	30	27	23	20	17	15	13
288	291	45	41	38	34	31	27	24	20	17	15	13
291	294	46	42	39	35	32	28	25	21	18	15	14
294	297	46	43	39	36	32	29	25	22	18	16	14
297	300	47	43	40	36	33	29	26	22	19	16	14
300	303	48	44	41	37	34	30	27	23	19	17	15
303	306	48	45	41	38	34	31	27	24	20	17	15
306	309	49	45	42	38	35	31	28	24	21	17	15
309	312	50	46	43	39	36	32	28	25	21	18	16
312	315	50	47	43	40	36	33	29	26	22	19	16
315	318	51	47	44	40	37	33	30	26	23	19	16
318	321	52	48	45	41	37	34	30	27	23	20	17
321	324	52	49	45	42	38	35	31	28	24	21	17
324	327	53	49	46	42	39	35	32	28	25	21	18
327	330	54	50	46	43	39	36	32	29	25	22	18
330	333	54	51	47	44	40	37	33	30	26	23	19
333	336	55	51	48	44	41	37	34	30	27	23	20
336	339	56	52	48	45	41	38	34	31	27	24	20
339	341	56	53	49	46	42	38	35	31	28	24	21
341	343	57	53	49	46	42	39	35	32	28	25	21
343	345	57	53	50	46	43	39	36	32	29	25	22
345	347	58	54	50	47	43	40	36	33	29	26	22
347	349	58	54	51	47	44	40	37	33	30	26	23
349	351	59	55	51	48	44	41	37	34	30	27	23
351	353	59	55	52	48	45	41	38	34	31	27	24
353	355	60	56	52	49	45	42	38	35	31	28	24
355	357	60	56	53	49	46	42	39	35	31	28	24
357	359	61	57	53	49	46	42	39	35	32	28	25
359	361	61	57	53	50	46	43	39	36	32	29	25
361	363	62	58	54	50	47	43	40	36	33	29	26
363	365	62	58	54	51	47	44	40	37	33	30	26
365	367	62	59	55	51	48	44	41	37	34	30	27
367	369	63	59	55	52	48	45	41	38	34	31	27
369	371	63	60	56	52	49	45	42	38	35	31	28
371	373	64	60	56	53	49	46	42	39	35	31	28
373	375	64	61	57	53	49	46	42	39	35	32	28
375	377	65	61	57	53	50	46	43	39	36	32	29
377	379	65	62	58	54	50	47	43	40	36	33	29
379	381	66	62	58	54	51	47	44	40	37	33	30
381	383	66	62	59	55	51	48	44	41	37	34	30
383	385	67	63	59	55	52	48	45	41	38	34	31
385	387	67	63	60	56	52	49	45	42	38	35	31
387	389	68	64	60	56	53	49	46	42	39	35	31
389	391	68	64	61	57	53	49	46	42	39	35	32
391	393	69	65	61	57	53	50	46	43	39	36	32
393	395	69	65	62	58	54	50	47	43	40	36	33

$ 395 and over Use Table 8(a) for a SINGLE person on page 47. Also see the instructions on page 44.

Wage Bracket Method Tables for Income Tax Withholding

MARRIED Persons—DAILY Payroll Period

(For Wages Paid through December 31, 2018)

And the wages are—		And the number of withholding allowances claimed is—										
At least	But less than	0	1	2	3	4	5	6	7	8	9	10
		The amount of income tax to be withheld is—										
$0	$50	$0	$0	$0	$0	$0	$0	$0	$0	$0	$0	$0
50	53	1	0	0	0	0	0	0	0	0	0	0
53	56	1	0	0	0	0	0	0	0	0	0	0
56	59	1	0	0	0	0	0	0	0	0	0	0
59	62	2	0	0	0	0	0	0	0	0	0	0
62	65	2	0	0	0	0	0	0	0	0	0	0
65	68	2	1	0	0	0	0	0	0	0	0	0
68	71	3	1	0	0	0	0	0	0	0	0	0
71	74	3	1	0	0	0	0	0	0	0	0	0
74	77	3	2	0	0	0	0	0	0	0	0	0
77	80	3	2	0	0	0	0	0	0	0	0	0
80	83	4	2	1	0	0	0	0	0	0	0	0
83	86	4	2	1	0	0	0	0	0	0	0	0
86	89	4	3	1	0	0	0	0	0	0	0	0
89	92	5	3	1	0	0	0	0	0	0	0	0
92	95	5	3	2	0	0	0	0	0	0	0	0
95	98	5	4	2	0	0	0	0	0	0	0	0
98	101	6	4	2	1	0	0	0	0	0	0	0
101	104	6	4	3	1	0	0	0	0	0	0	0
104	107	6	5	3	1	0	0	0	0	0	0	0
107	110	6	5	3	2	0	0	0	0	0	0	0
110	113	7	5	4	2	0	0	0	0	0	0	0
113	116	7	5	4	2	1	0	0	0	0	0	0
116	119	7	6	4	3	1	0	0	0	0	0	0
119	122	8	6	4	3	1	0	0	0	0	0	0
122	125	8	6	5	3	2	0	0	0	0	0	0
125	128	8	7	5	3	2	0	0	0	0	0	0
128	131	9	7	5	4	2	1	0	0	0	0	0
131	134	9	7	6	4	2	1	0	0	0	0	0
134	137	9	8	6	4	3	1	0	0	0	0	0
137	140	10	8	6	5	3	1	0	0	0	0	0
140	143	10	8	7	5	3	2	0	0	0	0	0
143	146	11	9	7	5	4	2	0	0	0	0	0
146	149	11	9	7	6	4	2	1	0	0	0	0
149	152	11	9	7	6	4	3	1	0	0	0	0
152	155	12	10	8	6	5	3	1	0	0	0	0
155	158	12	10	8	6	5	3	2	0	0	0	0
158	161	12	10	9	7	5	4	2	0	0	0	0
161	164	13	11	9	7	5	4	2	1	0	0	0
164	167	13	11	9	7	6	4	3	1	0	0	0
167	170	13	12	10	8	6	4	3	1	0	0	0
170	173	14	12	10	8	6	5	3	2	0	0	0
173	176	14	12	10	8	7	5	3	2	0	0	0
176	179	15	13	11	9	7	5	4	2	1	0	0
179	182	15	13	11	9	7	6	4	2	1	0	0
182	185	15	13	11	9	8	6	4	3	1	0	0
185	188	16	14	12	10	8	6	5	3	1	0	0
188	191	16	14	12	10	8	7	5	3	2	0	0
191	194	16	14	12	11	9	7	5	4	2	0	0
194	197	17	15	13	11	9	7	6	4	2	1	0
197	200	17	15	13	11	9	7	6	4	3	1	0
200	203	17	15	14	12	10	8	6	5	3	1	0
203	206	18	16	14	12	10	8	6	5	3	2	0
206	209	18	16	14	12	10	9	7	5	4	2	0
209	212	18	17	15	13	11	9	7	5	4	2	1
212	215	19	17	15	13	11	9	7	6	4	3	1
215	218	19	17	15	13	12	10	8	6	4	3	1
218	221	20	18	16	14	12	10	8	6	5	3	2
221	224	20	18	16	14	12	10	8	7	5	3	2
224	227	20	18	16	15	13	11	9	7	5	4	2
227	230	21	19	17	15	13	11	9	7	6	4	2
230	233	21	19	17	15	13	11	9	8	6	4	3
233	236	21	19	18	16	14	12	10	8	6	5	3
236	239	22	20	18	16	14	12	10	8	7	5	3
239	242	22	20	18	16	14	12	11	9	7	5	4
242	245	22	21	19	17	15	13	11	9	7	6	4
245	248	23	21	19	17	15	13	11	9	7	6	4
248	251	23	21	19	17	15	14	12	10	8	6	5
251	254	24	22	20	18	16	14	12	10	8	6	5
254	257	24	22	20	18	16	14	12	10	9	7	5

Wage Bracket Method Tables for Income Tax Withholding

MARRIED Persons—**DAILY** Payroll Period

(For Wages Paid through December 31, 2018)

And the wages are—		And the number of withholding allowances claimed is—										
At least	But less than	0	1	2	3	4	5	6	7	8	9	10
		The amount of income tax to be withheld is—										
$257	$260	$24	$22	$20	$18	$17	$15	$13	$11	$9	$7	$5
260	263	25	23	21	19	17	15	13	11	9	7	6
263	266	25	23	21	19	17	15	13	12	10	8	6
266	269	25	23	21	20	18	16	14	12	10	8	6
269	272	26	24	22	20	18	16	14	12	10	8	7
272	275	26	24	22	20	18	16	15	13	11	9	7
275	278	26	24	23	21	19	17	15	13	11	9	7
278	281	27	25	23	21	19	17	15	13	11	10	8
281	284	27	25	23	21	19	18	16	14	12	10	8
284	287	27	26	24	22	20	18	16	14	12	10	8
287	290	28	26	24	22	20	18	16	14	13	11	9
290	293	28	26	24	22	21	19	17	15	13	11	9
293	296	29	27	25	23	21	19	17	15	13	11	9
296	299	29	27	25	23	21	19	17	15	14	12	10
299	302	29	27	25	24	22	20	18	16	14	12	10
302	305	30	28	26	24	22	20	18	16	14	12	10
305	308	30	28	26	24	22	20	18	17	15	13	11
308	311	30	28	27	25	23	21	19	17	15	13	11
311	314	31	29	27	25	23	21	19	17	15	13	12
314	317	31	29	27	25	23	21	20	18	16	14	12
317	320	31	30	28	26	24	22	20	18	16	14	12
320	323	32	30	28	26	24	22	20	18	16	15	13
323	326	32	30	28	26	24	23	21	19	17	15	13
326	329	33	31	29	27	25	23	21	19	17	15	13
329	332	33	31	29	27	25	23	21	19	18	16	14
332	335	33	31	29	27	26	24	22	20	18	16	14
335	338	34	32	30	28	26	24	22	20	18	16	14
338	341	34	32	30	28	26	24	22	21	19	17	15
341	343	34	32	30	28	27	25	23	21	19	17	15
343	345	35	33	31	29	27	25	23	21	19	17	15
345	347	35	33	31	29	27	25	23	21	19	17	16
347	349	36	33	31	29	27	25	23	22	20	18	16
349	351	36	33	31	29	28	26	24	22	20	18	16
351	353	36	34	32	30	28	26	24	22	20	18	16
353	355	37	34	32	30	28	26	24	22	20	18	17
355	357	37	34	32	30	28	26	24	23	21	19	17
357	359	38	34	32	30	29	27	25	23	21	19	17
359	361	38	35	33	31	29	27	25	23	21	19	17
361	363	39	35	33	31	29	27	25	23	21	19	17
363	365	39	36	33	31	29	27	25	23	22	20	18
365	367	40	36	33	31	29	28	26	24	22	20	18
367	369	40	36	34	32	30	28	26	24	22	20	18
369	371	40	37	34	32	30	28	26	24	22	20	18
371	373	41	37	34	32	30	28	26	24	23	21	19
373	375	41	38	34	32	30	29	27	25	23	21	19
375	377	42	38	35	33	31	29	27	25	23	21	19
377	379	42	39	35	33	31	29	27	25	23	21	19
379	381	43	39	36	33	31	29	27	25	23	22	20
381	383	43	40	36	33	31	29	28	26	24	22	20
383	385	43	40	36	34	32	30	28	26	24	22	20
385	387	44	40	37	34	32	30	28	26	24	22	20
387	389	44	41	37	34	32	30	28	26	24	23	21
389	391	45	41	38	34	32	30	29	27	25	23	21
391	393	45	42	38	35	33	31	29	27	25	23	21
393	395	46	42	39	35	33	31	29	27	25	23	21
395	397	46	43	39	36	33	31	29	27	25	23	22
397	399	47	43	40	36	33	31	29	28	26	24	22
399	401	47	43	40	36	34	32	30	28	26	24	22
401	403	47	44	40	37	34	32	30	28	26	24	22
403	405	48	44	41	37	34	32	30	28	26	24	23
405	407	48	45	41	38	34	32	30	29	27	25	23
407	409	49	45	42	38	35	33	31	29	27	25	23
409	411	49	46	42	39	35	33	31	29	27	25	23
411	413	50	46	43	39	36	33	31	29	27	25	23
413	415	50	47	43	40	36	33	31	29	28	26	24
415	417	51	47	43	40	36	34	32	30	28	26	24

$417 and over   Use Table 8(b) for a MARRIED person on page 47. Also see the instructions on page 44.

Appendix IV

Federal and State Benefits Summary for Employees

Overview

Earlier in this book, we referred to employee benefits several times. In all of these cases, the employee benefits resulted from either employer payments or an employer adopting qualified benefit plans. The common element in both cases was that some action was required by an employer in order for employees to receive the benefits. However, other employee benefits are available that do not require employer decisions. These are benefits that originate with federal and state governments. Except for qualified employer benefit and retirement plans, this appendix summarizes these benefits.

Social Security: Old Age, Survivor, and Disability Insurance (OASDI) Benefits

Overview

As previously discussed, the term "Social Security" encompasses two major elements: OASDI and Medicare, although sometimes "Social Security" is used to refer to only the OASDI element. Most American workers are covered by OASDI when they reach full retirement age. The only employees who are not covered under OASDI are:

- Non-military federal employees hired before January 1, 1984
- Railroad workers (They are covered under the Railroad Retirement Act)
- State and local government employees covered under state and local retirement systems (Based on a formula, there is also a partial offset to OASDI pension income for employees previously covered under OASDI who change jobs and become employees of employers who do not withhold social security, such as state and local goverments. This is called "windfall elimination".)
- Farm workers and domestic workers who do not meet certain earnings requirements
- Self-employed persons with a history of very low earnings

The following discussion refers to the Old Age, Survivor, and Disability Insurance benefits.

Social Security: Old Age, Survivor, and Disability Insurance (OASDI) Benefits, *continued*

Basic Coverage Elements

- Current maximum monthly pension benefit: $2,788
- Current Cost of living adjustment: 2%
- Full retirement age: 66 and 2 months (Gradually increasing to 67)
- The income is determined by quarters of employment, income level, and retirement age (discussed below).

Quarters of Employment

To become elegible for pension income, a person must accumulate at least 40 quarters of full-time work in the "covered employment" discussed above, and were born after after 1928. A "quarter" means a three-month calendar quarter.

Income Level

The income level required required to earn one quarter of credit is determined by formula; the amount of income that must be earned in 2018 to earn one quarter of coverage is $1,320. The table below shows prior year requirements.

Amount of earnings needed to earn one quarter of coverage

Year	Earnings	Year	Earnings	Year	Earnings
1978	$250	1993	$590	2008	$1,050
1979	260	1994	620	2009	1,090
1980	290	1995	630	2010	1,120
1981	310	1996	640	2011	1,120
1982	340	1997	670	2012	1,130
1983	370	1998	700	2013	1,160
1984	390	1999	740	2014	1,200
1985	410	2000	780	2015	1,220
1986	440	2001	830	2016	1,260
1987	460	2002	870	2017	1,300
1988	470	2003	890	2018	1,320
1989	500	2004	900		
1990	520	2005	920		
1991	540	2006	970		
1992	570	2007	1,000		

Source: Social Security

Retirement Age

Pension income is also determined by retirement age. In general, pension benefits begin at age 62 retirement, but are reduced for each month before full retirement age. As well, income benefits increase for each month deferred after full retirement age until age 70. Continuing to work when receiving benefits before full retirement age reduces the monthly income benefit. For 2018, generally

$1 of benefit is deducted for every $2 earned above $17,040. The year of retirement age has a slightly different calculation.

Survivor Beneifts   If a covered worker who has paid Social Security taxes dies, some members of the family may be elegible for benefits. The amount depends on years worked, income, and age at death. Survivor benefits can be paid to a widow or widower (full benefits at full retirement age or reduced benefits as early as 60), a disabled widow or widower (as early as 50), a widow or widower of any age who takes care of the deceased's child who is younger than 16, unmarried children younger than 18 or up to 19 if in school, children who were disabled before 22, dependent parents age 62 or older, and some other special categories.

Disability Insurance (SSDI)   Social security provides for disability insurance; the amount of insurance depends on how many credits were earned when disabled. Credits are like quarters of credit; for example, in 2018, $1,320 of earnings earns one credit. The older the worker when disabled, the greater the number of credits required. There are also two additional tests required: The recent work test, which determines years of recent work, and the duration of work test, that measures the number of years worked. Application can be completed online; call the Social Security Administration number at 800-772-1213 for information. For workers who do not meet these requirements, they can still be elegible under the Supplemental Social Security Income (SSI) program, by demonstrating financial need.

More Information   Not all important details can be covered in this summary. For further information that applies to any particular case, contact the Social Security Administration. Online: www.ssa.gov/, telephone: 800-772-1213, or search online for the Social Security office locator to find a local office.

Medicare and Medicaid

Overview   Medicare, established in 1965 as an amendment to Social Security, is federal health care insurance for people 65 and older, certain younger people with disabilities, and people with severe kidney disease. Medicare consists of the following parts: 1) hospital insurance (Part A), 2) medical insurance for doctors, outpatient, and supplies at generally 80% coverage, which requires premium payments (Part B), 3) optional private company health insurance (Part C), and 4) prescription drugs (Part D), which requires premium payments. Medicaid was established at the same time as Medicare as coverage for low-income Americans, according to income, family size, and other guidelines.

Medicare and Medicaid

Medicare
Eligibility

People are elibile for no-cost Part A coverage when they are 65 or older and are receiving retirement benefits from Social Security, when they are eligible for Social Security but have not yet applied, or had Medicare-covered government employment. Citizenship is not required, provided an indivual is eligible for Social Security retirement benefits. Those not qualifying (i.e. did not qualify for retirement benefits) and are a U.S. citizen or permanent resident, may purchase Part A benefits. If under 65, Medicare is available for those who have collected Medicare disability payments for at least 24 months. Kidney dialysis and transplant patients are automatically covered.

Unemployment Benefits

Overview

Unemployment benefits are paid by individual state unemployment programs, funded by SUTA and FUTA, as discussed in Section II. In all states these benefits are available to workers who are temporarily unemployed through no fault of their own and who are actively seeking work. Specific eligibility rules and benefits vary with each individual state. A common requirement is the verification of recent employment and earnings during a base period (typically, a year), and verification that unemployment was not the result of worker's misconduct or quitting work. In order to receive benefits the recipient must demonstrate that he or she is actively looking for work.

State Disability Insurance

Overview

Currently the states of California, Hawaii, New Jersey, New York, and Rhode Island provide disability insurance, as well as the territory of Puerto Rico. These are temporary wage-replacement programs generally for non-work related disabilities. These are funded either by employers or by employee withholding, depending on the state. Specific eligibility and benefits vary by state. An online search for "disability insurance" referencing one of the six providers above should give more detailed information.

Index